GRANTA

12 Addison Avenue, London W11 4QR

e-mail editorial@granta.com

To subscribe go to www.granta.com

Or call 845-267-3031 (toll-free 866-438-6150) in the United States, 020 8955 7011 in the United Kingdom

ISSUE 109

EDITOR	John Freeman
DEPUTY EDITOR	Ellah Allfrey
ONLINE EDITOR	Roy Robins
ASSOCIATE EDITORS	Liz Jobey, Simon Willis
EDITORIAL ASSISTANTS	Emily Greenhouse, Patrick Ryan
DESIGN	Dan Mogford, Lindsay Nash
FINANCE	Geoffrey Gordon, Morgan Graver
MARKETING AND SUBSCRIPTIONS	Anne Gowan, James Hollingsworth
SALES DIRECTOR	Brigid Macleod
PUBLICITY	Pru Rowlandson
TO ADVERTISE IN THE UK CONTACT	Kate Rochester, katerochester@granta.com
TO ADVERTISE IN THE USA CONTACT	Emily Cook, ecook@granta.com
IT MANAGER	Mark Williams
PRODUCTION ASSOCIATE	Sarah Wasley
PROOFS	Ollie Brock, Katherine Fry,
	Lesley Levene, Jessica Rawlinson
ASSOCIATE PUBLISHER	Eric Abraham
PUBLISHER	Sigrid Rausing

In the United States, *Granta* is published in association with Grove/Atlantic Inc, 841 Broadway, 4th Floor, New York, NY 10003, and distributed by PGW. All editorial queries should be addressed to the London office.

Granta USPS 000-508 is published four times per year (March, June, September and December) by *Granta* 12 Addison Avenue, London W11 4QR, United Kingdom at the annual subscription rate of £34.95 and $45.99.

Airfreight and mailing in the USA by Agent named Air Business, C/O Worldnet Shipping USA Inc., 149-35 177th Street, Jamaica, New York, NY 11434. Periodicals postage paid at Jamaica NY 11431.

US POSTMASTER: Send address changes to *Granta*, PO Box 359 Congers, NY 10920-0359.

Granta is printed and bound in Italy by Legoprint. This magazine is printed on paper that fulfils the criteria for 'Paper for permanent document' according to ISO 9706 and the American Library Standard ANSI/NIZO Z39.48-1992 and has been certified by the Forest Stewardship Council (FSC). *Granta* is indexed in the American Humanities Index.

Granta is grateful for permission to quote from *The Lives of Animals* by J.M. Coetzee © 1999 Princeton University Press; from *Machete Season* by Jean Hatzfeld, © 2006 by Picador, published as *A Time for Machetes*, 2008 by Serpent's Tail; and from *The Unbearable Lightness of Being* by Milan Kundera © 1984 Harper & Row, Publishers, Inc. English translation © 1984 Michael Henry Heim. Used by permission of Milan Kundera, HarperCollins Publishers (US) and Faber & Faber Ltd (UK)

ISBN 978-1-905881-13-0

Sebastian Barry's novel *The Secret Scripture* won the 2008 Costa prize, and he has been twice nominated for the Booker prize. His plays include the international hit *The Steward of Christendom*, *Our Lady of Sligo* and *Hinterland*.

Max Stafford-Clark directs Barry's haunting new play, rich in characters and touched with a wistful humour.

"There is the porter from Higham station, carrying a box, a portmanteau and possibly a hatbox. And a most curious figure hobbling along behind him…"

Out of Joint & Hampstead Theatre present

ANDERSEN'S ENGLISH
THE NEW PLAY BY SEBASTIAN BARRY

…ad's Hill Place, the Kent Marshes: Hans Christian Andersen arrives, …nannounced, to stay at the home of Charles Dickens and his large, charismatic …mily. To the lonely and eccentric guest, the members of Dickens's household …eem to live a life of bliss. But with his broken English, Andersen doesn't at first …ee the storms brewing within the family…

…K TOUR WINTER/SPRING 2010 (for full tour and casting visit www.outofjoint.co.uk)

1-13 Feb	**Bury St Edmunds** Theatre Royal	01284 769 505	www.theatreroyal.org
…6-20 Feb	**Southampton** Nuffield Theatre	023 8067 1771	www.nuffieldtheatre.co.uk
…3-27 Feb	**Leeds** West Yorkshire Playhouse	0113 213 7700	www.wyp.org.uk
…-6 Mar	**Manchester** Library Theatre	0161 236 7110	www.librarytheatre.com
…-13 Mar	**Coventry** Belgrade Theatre	024 7655 3055	www.belgrade.co.uk
…3-27 Mar	**Salisbury** Playhouse	01722 320 333	www.salisburyplayhouse.com
…Apr - 8 May	**Hampstead** Theatre	020 7722 9301	www.hampsteadtheatre.com

CONTENTS

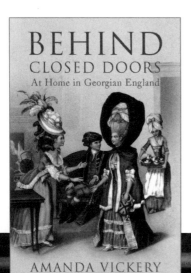

Life Among the Pirates

Daniel Alarcón

1

In March of last year, Rodrigo Rosales, the director of the Peruvian offices of the international publisher Planeta, got an urgent call from Madrid. Paulo Coelho's people were upset. It seems the Brazilian writer's latest novel, *O vencedor está só* (published in English as *The Winner Stands Alone*), had been seen on the streets of Lima in an unauthorized edition. Rosales was taken aback. Coelho is a steady bestseller in Peru (and everywhere) and any new title by him is certain to be pirated almost immediately upon publication, but this one wasn't scheduled to be released until July. In fact, it hadn't even been officially translated into Spanish.

Though book piracy exists all over Latin America and the developing world, any editor with international experience in the region will tell you that Peru's problem is both unique and profound. According to the International Intellectual Property Alliance, the local publishing industry loses more money to piracy than any other South American country, with the exception of Brazil – whose economy is more than eight times the size of Peru's. A 2005 report commissioned by the Cámara Peruana del Libro (CPL), a national consortium of publishing houses, distributors and booksellers, came to even more alarming conclusions: pirates were employing more people than formal publishers and booksellers, and their combined economic impact was estimated to be 52 million US dollars – or roughly equivalent to one hundred per cent of the legal industry's total earnings. The pirates operate in plain sight: vendors ply the streets of the capital, carrying heavy stacks of books as they drift through stopped traffic, or spreading a torn piece of blue plastic tarp on a sidewalk, laying their wares out hopefully for all to see. You can find them in front of high schools, institutes and government buildings, or wandering the aisles of the markets where most Limeños do their shopping. One Saturday, I came across a man selling pirated law texts (cloth-bound, official-looking copies so well made I had a hard time believing they were fake), who told me that on weekdays he rented a stand at a local university, inside the law school – where presumably Peru's future lawyers are taught about copyright law, intellectual property and other fantastical, irrelevant concepts. On summer weekends, these salesmen work the beaches south of the city, or congregate at the tollbooths on the way out of town. On the margins of this business are the thieves, bands of skilled shoplifters who specialize in stealing books, trolling all the major fairs, hitting all the official bookstores and supplying a vibrant resale market with their so-called *libros de bajada*. Then there are the pirates themselves, the informal book manufacturers whose overworked, antique presses are hidden in nondescript houses in slums all over the city. The larger of these operations can crank out some 40,000 volumes a week, and because of their superior distribution, the pirates can sell three times as many copies of a book as the authorized publishers. For a bestseller like Coelho, the figure could be even higher.

It didn't take long for Rosales to confirm the story. He went out to look for Coelho's unpublished book and found it at the first major intersection. Something had to be done. Peruvian book pirates are among the world's quickest and most entrepreneurial, some would say most treacherous – a reality Coelho and his handlers are well aware of. At the start of this decade, the pirates had nearly killed the Peruvian publishing industry; its survival and subsequent resurgence are seen by many as something of a miracle. Counterfeit books printed in Lima have been known to show up in Quito, Ecuador, in La Paz, Bolivia, in the towns of northern Chile, as far east as Buenos Aires, Argentina. This same Coelho edition, if it were to be imported, could conceivably nullify the sizeable investment Rosales's house had made to publish the novel in the Spanish-speaking world. Coelho's people demanded action.

So began the latest skirmish in the on-again, off-again battle against Peruvian book piracy. The CPL registered a formal legal complaint, an investigation began and a few months later, on June 23, after failing to find the presses where Coelho's book was being printed, the CPL helped organize a police raid on the points of sale instead. The chosen site was

Consorcio Grau, a market on a busy avenue in central Lima notorious for its counterfeit merchandise. The operation seized a million soles' (360,000 US dollars') worth of pirated books, nearly 90,000 volumes in all. All the major networks covered the story, though few noted the fact that within twenty-four hours the stands were open again, fully restocked. Perhaps this wasn't news. Book pirates, like drug traffickers, always assume a certain percentage of their merchandise will never make it to market. These losses are budgeted for, part of the accepted cost of doing business.

But there was still one more surprise. In July, when Planeta finally published the official version of Coehlo's novel in Peru, Rosales decided to compare the two texts. He went through line by line, page by page, and discovered that the translations were essentially the same. The Peruvian book pirates hadn't commissioned their own translation, as Rosales had previously assumed. Instead, they had infiltrated Planeta in Spain and stolen the official translation before it was complete.

New books in Peru – new, legally produced books, that is – are often sold bearing a sticker that reads BUY ORIGINAL, just one of the small ways the publishing industry has responded to the threat from book pirates. The fact is, though, being pirated is the Peruvian equivalent of making the bestseller list. One writer I know ends all his readings by urging those in attendance to 'buy my book before it gets pirated'. When I asked him about it, he confessed he hadn't actually been pirated yet, but hoped he would be soon. The award-winning novelist Alonso Cueto told me he receives unsolicited sales reports from the man who sells pirate novels in his neighbourhood. At first it made him angry, but by now Cueto has learned to tolerate it. Less tolerable is that the same vendor feels authorized to give the writer advice on potential subject matter that might be more commercially successful.

Pirates reach sectors of the market that formal book publishers cannot or don't care to access. Outside Lima, the pirate-book industry is the only one that matters. Oscar Colchado Lucio, one of a handful of Peruvian writers who actually make their living from book sales, told me of the time he'd gone to the town of Huancayo to do a reading at a very poor school. He signed some 300 books without coming across a single original. The authorized version simply wasn't available – there were no bookstores in Huancayo. One novelist, who preferred not to be named for fear of being sued, was disappointed that his novel wasn't available in his home town. In response, he contacted a pirate in Lima, made a deal, and soon his book was on sale all over the country. When I asked him about it, he made no apology: 'If someone can produce for three dollars what the editor is selling for twenty, then I think perhaps the editor is a terrible businessman.' In a few cases, pirates have rescued work by writers the formal industry has forgotten. A friend told me the story of Luis Hernández, a little-known avant-garde poet with a cult following among university students. Photocopied versions of his out-of-print collections have been passed around for years, but no publisher had bothered to reissue his work – until a vendor from downtown Lima recognized the need, partnered with a press and came out with his own, unauthorized edition.

I remember riding to lunch in 2007, around the time my first novel was published, with Titinger, a friend of mine, who also had a new book in stores. We worked at the same magazine, and Huberth, the owner, our boss, had offered to take us out to celebrate. Along the way, we came to the traffic light at an intersection that doubled as a marketplace, where vendors sold fruit and whiteboards and newspapers and inflatable children's toys. It's a scene repeated on hundreds, perhaps thousands, of street corners in the Peruvian capital, an image familiar to anyone who has lived or travelled in Latin America or anywhere in the developing world. There were booksellers too, naturally, and Huberth called one over. The salesman was heavy-set and awkward, moving clumsily between the cars, and carried his books before him like a shield, the covers facing outwards: self-help titles, mostly (it was the season of the Peruvian edition of *Who Moved My Cheese?*, I recall), books about local scandals and worldwide bestsellers like *El Código DaVinci*.

'Anything by Alarcón or Titinger?' Huberth asked.

The man frowned. 'Who?'

That was all. Huberth rolled up his window.

'You're both failures,' he said, turning to us.

My first story collection has, to my knowledge, never been pirated, which is something of a disappointment. The day of our lunch with Huberth, my novel had just gone on sale and was retailing for around fifty soles, the equivalent of seventeen US dollars. This is nearly the same price it might fetch in an American bookstore, with one crucial difference: in Peru, that figure represents about twenty per cent of the average worker's weekly income. I was frankly embarrassed by the price. How could I, in good conscience, expect my friends and family to pay that much for a book? Except for the small middle and upper classes, who has that kind of disposable income?

A few weeks later, I was doing a reading at the library of one of Lima's prisons. I'd brought a copy of my novel along, to donate to the collection, but to my surprise the inmates already had one. They were rather embarrassed about it, but eventually they agreed to show it to me. The cover looked a lot like the original, except that the title had been rendered in incongruously playful red bubble letters with white trim. It was printed on cheap white office paper and the photocopying wasn't particularly well done: every few pages, a stray hair floated over the text, and some pages had been copied at an angle, so that my sentences slid towards the outside margin at a melancholy slant.

One of the inmates explained that he had received my book as a gift from the outside. He claimed he hadn't known it was pirated.

I nodded as if I believed him.

'Could you sign it?' the prison librarian asked me.

I did, of course, and left the prison that day feeling as if I had accomplished something.

If there is a certain allure to book piracy, it is only because we imbue this business with the same qualities we project on to the book itself. We focus on what is being manufactured and sold, as opposed to the fundamentally illicit nature of the enterprise. There are many reasons for this, of course. As a cultural artefact, the book has undeniable power, and the idea of a poor, developing country with a robust informal publishing industry is, on some level, romantic: the pirate as cultural entrepreneur, a Robin Hood figure, stealing from elitist multinational publishers and taking books to the people. The myth is seductive and repeated often: book piracy in Peru, the story goes, responds to a hunger for knowledge in a country that throughout its history has been violently divided between a literate upper class and the poor, unlettered masses. Literacy grew dramatically through the last century – nearly sixty per cent of Peruvians were illiterate in 1940, compared with only 7.1 per cent in 2007 – and along with this progress came a desire for books and all they represent. Still, millions of rural Peruvians are monolingual speakers of indigenous languages, and remain politically and economically marginalized as a result. In a country divided by race, ethnicity and language, acquiring fluency and literacy in Spanish has often been seen as an important first step towards socio-economic advancement.

Still, original books remain a prohibitively expensive luxury item, out of reach for most of the population. There are vast swathes of the country with no formal bookstores. Iquitos, the largest city in the Peruvian Amazon, with nearly 400,000 residents, has only two, and had none as recently as 2007. Trujillo, the country's third largest city, has only one. School libraries, if they exist at all, are usually nothing more than a few dozen mouldering titles of little literary or historical value. More often than not, the only significant collections are housed at private universities, where neither students nor faculty are permitted to roam the stacks, where checkout privileges are limited to twenty-four hours – that is, just long enough to photocopy (read 'pirate') a book and return it. Nor is this bleak situation confined to rural areas or the provinces. An estimated eighty-five to ninety per cent of books are sold in the Lima metropolitan area, but for a city of nearly nine million, there are relatively few formal bookstores, the majority concentrated in the upper-middle class districts of San Isidro and Miraflores. North Lima, for example, comprising eight districts of the Peruvian capital, home to roughly two million people and half the city's middle class, has none. The wealthiest of these eight districts, Los Olivos, has a municipal library of only 1,500 mostly donated volumes, including, naturally, a few counterfeit editions.

On a larger scale, the National Library suffers the same neglect. For some thirty years its acquisitions budget remained unchanged – zero – and it too relied on donations to build its collection.

Given this context, is it any wonder that books are pirated? You can lament the informality of it, you can call it stealing, you can bemoan the losses incurred by the publishing industry – but if you love to read, it's difficult to deny the hopeful logic: if someone is selling books, someone must be buying them. And if someone's buying them, someone must be reading them. And reading, especially in a country as poor as Peru – isn't that a good thing?

2

In July, a few weeks before the start of the annual Lima book fair, I went to see Germán Coronado, the director of Peisa, one of the last independent publishing houses still functioning in Peru. It was an odd day in the city: a heavy drizzle fell from a textureless, milky-grey sky, so thick it could almost be called rain. The precipitation had caught Limeños unprepared. Traffic in this desert city had gone from merely chaotic to frankly terrifying. Cars slid haphazardly along the roads and pedestrians were spooked.

Coronado is among those who have fought the hardest to protect the rights of authors in Peru, and he has paid a high price for his efforts. Founded in 1968, Peisa once published Mario Vargas Llosa and Alfredo Bryce Echenique in Peru – our country's two bestselling and most respected novelists – and by rights, Coronado should be wealthy. He is not. The day I met him, he looked haggard and worn, unshaven, with the pallor of a man who hadn't been outside in weeks. His office, on the ninth floor of an inelegant building in San Isidro, was cramped and narrow. The windows offered a view of the hills, but that afternoon he had the shades pulled down. I had the sense that he hadn't raised them in months.

Coronado's thesis was simple. While book piracy has always existed in Peru, for years it was small-scale, primarily serving the needs of university students. He recalled shopping for second-hand books in the Plaza Francia when he was a student at San Marcos, a prestigious public university in Lima, the oldest institute of higher learning in the Americas. Then came the 1980s, years of general disorder. The nation barely survived the trials of that decade: a civil war claimed 70,000 lives before it ended and the economy all but collapsed. By 1990, hyperinflation had reached an annual rate of 7,649 per cent and the middle class had been nearly wiped out. Thousands of Peruvians emigrated in search of a better life in the United States, Europe or richer neighbouring countries such as Chile and Argentina. Even in this dire context, Peisa managed, but things were about to get worse. According to Coronado, the first sign of doom came in 1988, in the final years of Alan García's disastrous first term as president, when he said in an interview that, given the economic crisis, it didn't make sense for parents to buy original school books for their children – the president was, in other words, advocating piracy.

Then Peisa's star author, novelist Mario Vargas Llosa, entered politics: he ran for president in 1990, receiving the most votes in the first round, before eventually losing to Alberto Fujimori. As Coronado tells it, Vargas Llosa lay low after his defeat, but in April 1992, when President Fujimori dissolved Congress and declared that the constitution would be rewritten, he could no longer keep quiet. To his credit, Vargas Llosa correctly identified Fujimori as a dictator and a menace at a time when many other observers were still ambivalent. In his weekly column in *El País*, he denounced Fujimori's coup as an attack on democracy and called for a worldwide embargo of Peru. The media allied with (or bought by, depending on your interpretation) Fujimori struck back, initiating a ruthless and coordinated campaign of character assassination against Peru's most accomplished novelist. He was attacked and ridiculed, all but declared an enemy of the state. For Fujimori's allies, it was simple: if Vargas Llosa wanted an embargo of Peru, then Peru should embargo him right back.

For Coronado, this marked the beginning of a grave shift. Over the next few years, book piracy became a project of state. As Peru emerged from war, Fujimori opened up the economy to imports, new presses arrived and overnight the country was flooded with cheap, fifty-cent newspapers whose editorial content was quite literally dictated by the government. Coronado believes this same machinery was used to grow the book-piracy industry. As publisher of Fujimori's most vociferous and internationally prestigious critic, Coronado too became a target. His brother-in-law, the financial head of Peisa, was kidnapped in a dramatic case that was never solved. 'Three months of hell' was how Coronado described the ordeal to me, and he suspects it was a reprisal for publishing books the government didn't appreciate. Meanwhile, his core business was under economic assault. The pirates were everywhere, sprouting like mould all over the city. Coronado estimates his losses at around 600,000 US dollars a year in the 1990s. 'We were very quickly transformed from a successful business to one in crisis, overwhelmed by debt.' Peisa filed more than 250 lawsuits in those years against book counterfeiters. They hired private investigators, sent the police detailed lists of pirates, their names and aliases, physical descriptions, home addresses, suspected locations of presses and known points of sale. As we spoke, he pulled up the files on his desktop – letters, complaints, lists, accusations.

'And after all that effort?' I asked.

'There's not a single person in jail for book piracy in Peru,' Coronado said. 'Not one.'

Fujimori's corrupt regime was eventually toppled, but the pirates were here to stay. By 2001, the Peruvian publishing industry was in free fall. Book production had declined by twenty-eight per cent in only four years and the industry had shed forty per cent of its workers. This was due in large part to the competition from the pirates. Fake copies of Vargas Llosa's 2000 novel *The Feast of the Goat* were available on the streets of Lima the same day it was published, and there would eventually be seven different unauthorized editions. How could an honest publisher compete?

I presented the usual arguments in defence of piracy: principally, inescapable poverty and the relatively high cost of books.

For Coronado, these arguments neglected a very important fact: the street-level vendors tend to congregate in the same middle- and upper-class neighbourhoods where you find the bookstores. Their clients are people with money. Coronado could do little to mask his disgust. 'It's a cultural problem. The same people who would never consider buying fake whisky think nothing of buying a pirated book. There's no respect for intellectual production in this country.'

After the fall of Fujimori, some publishing houses, in desperation, tried appeasement. Perhaps they had been seduced by the romantic idea that the pirates were simple, poor merchants taking culture to the masses. Or perhaps they felt they had no other choice. A movement began within the CPL to organize the thousands of informal booksellers, the men and women working the street corners, and provide them with authorized editions at lower prices. Coronado has nothing but disdain for this idea, and for 'the wise, the illuminated' publishers who believed in what he derisively called 'the splendour of piracy'.

Vargas Llosa, with his new publishing house, was invited to Amazonas, the largest informal book market in Latin America, to give a reading. It was a media spectacle – the return of the exile. The publisher dropped the price of the book for the event. The informal booksellers toasted our internationally prestigious writer. They posed for pictures with their famous guest and, once the cameras had gone, went back to selling pirated editions.

'Those people can't be trusted,' Coronado said.

I mentioned that I would be keeping an eye out for my new book – I was publishing a collection of stories that month to coincide with the book fair, and I wondered aloud if the pirates would get to it before I returned to the United States in mid-August.

He smirked and shook his head. 'Will you be pirated?' the editor asked. 'I can guarantee it.'

The book market known commonly as Amazonas is a few blocks east of Abancay, one of the main avenues that leads to Lima's old city centre. It sits on a sliver of land on the southern bank of the Rimac, a murky, polluted river that neatly divides the capital into north and south. The wall on the far bank is decorated with a mural – a painting of green hills, bright blue skies and palm trees, a verdant, inviting scene that contrasts starkly with the actual view – a dusty, monochrome slum beneath a hill hidden in thick fog.

At Amazonas, you will find more than 200 vendors of used, antiquarian and pirated books, most of whom have known each other for twenty years. They formed a loose cooperative in the 1980s, when thirty or forty booksellers began congregating on the median strip of a downtown avenue called Grau. They sold second-hand books, were inoffensive and not particularly prosperous. In those days, the old centre of Lima had been overrun by informal commerce, an unsightly by-product of the social disarray and economic turmoil. The stately, colonial-era buildings, once the pride of patrician Lima, had been taken over by merchants and transformed into dense black-market labyrinths. Trade spilled outdoors, over the sidewalks and into the streets. In some areas, six lanes of traffic had been reduced to one in each direction, the rest given over to the informal economy. These vendors are known as *ambulantes*, which literally means 'wandering' or 'itinerant', but they had become a permanent part of the urban landscape. When they were finally moved from the major avenues, it was discovered that some carts had been there so long, their owners had affixed them with metal plates and screws to the very sidewalk. In the case of the Grau booksellers, the long-term urban plan for the city included an expansion of the avenue (which, eleven years later, is only now under way), and finally, in 1998, then-mayor Alberto Andrade convinced the booksellers to relocate to an empty lot along the Jirón Amazonas. They were joined by 160 more book vendors scattered throughout downtown and formed what is now the Cámara Popular de Libreros – which, not coincidentally, also uses the abbreviation CPL, like its official rival, the Cámara Peruana del Libro.

You can find almost any book or magazine at Amazonas, provided you are willing to wander its aisles and search amid the stacks of mouldering volumes spread out on wobbly tables or crammed into rusting metal bookshelves. There are many original books, but counterfeits aren't hard to find. If you don't see what you want right away, just ask for 'the Peruvian edition' or 'a more economical version', and most booksellers will get the hint. Alongside books, some vendors have begun selling grade-school science projects, styrofoam monstrosities representing the water cycle, the greenhouse effect or the vascular system. While you look for, say, a readable edition of Victor Hugo's *Les Misérables*, you might see a young woman behind a counter, hard at work on a diorama of Machu Picchu, a look of grave concentration on her face as she glues a plastic llama to a green, spray-painted mountainside. These projects sell for twenty soles, less than seven US dollars, a price which includes a lesson on the topic, so the student can be prepared to present his or her science project in class. Some might consider this cheating, but all the students I spoke to said it was their teachers who had sent them here.

Science projects are a lucrative but relatively new product at Amazonas – and a controversial one. For more than a decade, Amazonas has been synonymous with books, and some vendors told me they were concerned about diluting the brand with these school projects. To be sure, books still make up the bulk of what is sold: second-hand, stolen originals, counterfeits, along with the sorts of oddities a culture of piracy will inevitably produce – an unauthorized edition of Dostoevsky's *Crime and Punishment*, for example, its cover emblazoned with a drawing of a revolver, smoke rising from its barrel; or a hundred-page, abridged version of a much longer Bryce Echenique novel, a few chapters excised arbitrarily to save printing costs. It was Bryce himself who told me he'd once seen a pirated edition of *La palabra del mudo* (literally, *The Word of the Mute*, though it sounds much better in Spanish), a famous story collection by Peruvian writer Julio Ramón Ribeyro, now out of print because of a dispute with the author's estate. The pirates had made one important alteration in order to maximize sales: instead of Ribeyro's, they'd printed Mario Vargas Llosa's name on the cover.

One morning I met with a man I'll call Jacinto in a drab, grey restaurant across from the Amazonas market. We were served coffee, watered down and steamy, before we'd even ordered it; Jacinto was clearly a regular. He's in his late forties, with a wide, squarish face and greying, spiky hair. He didn't want to be seen with me at Amazonas – the other booksellers were, by nature, suspicious people, and it was best not to appear too friendly with strangers. Though it's not necessarily obvious, some of the booksellers at Amazonas are very wealthy. They might own three or four stands there, a few more scattered around central Lima and, somewhere in the city's endless outer districts, a press. It's often a family operation and they might have a relative in the provinces who sells books at local fairs. They earn thousands of dollars a month and are careful to protect their investments from nosy outsiders.

When Jacinto was a boy, only rich people had books. Though his father loved to read, the family never owned more than a handful of old volumes. They lived in the provinces, in a jungle town called Pucallpa, 500 miles from Lima, and buying a single new book would have required saving money for a year or more. There was no piracy in those days. Books were printed in Lima or imported, which, if you lived in the jungle, amounted to the same thing. Jacinto had inherited his father's love of reading and was a good enough student to be able to study sociology at Federico Villarreal, a public university in Lima. It was the 1980s and he got caught up in the radical politics of the time. He didn't tell me much in the way of details, but then he didn't have to – it's a common enough tale for a man his age in Peru. In the 1980s, Jacinto left the country for a while – he had to leave, I gathered – crossed into the United States illegally and spent a few years pumping gas in the Bronx, painting houses in New Jersey. He returned to Peru in the early 1990s, but two years later, after Fujimori's coup, he had no choice but to flee again. He spent some time in Los Angeles, a place about which he had remarkably little to say. He made friends with Mexicans; he rode the bus a lot. It wasn't a very happy time. In 2000, he came back to Peru for good and took over his uncle's stand at Amazonas.

Working with books was a dream, Jacinto said. He had fond memories of shopping for second-hand books in his student days, before Amazonas, when the business was still concentrated on the median strip of Grau – and now he was the one doing the selling. After all he'd been through, he considered himself lucky. Being a reader made him something of a rarity among the booksellers at Amazonas. To most, it was just a way to make money, whereas to Jacinto, books meant something. Homer, Magellan, Marx – these men had changed his life with their writings. There were only a few vendors who really knew anything about what they sold. Jacinto could count them on his fingers. The rest were poor, barely literate men and women who'd come from the provinces fleeing the violence. They could be selling anything. Books held no special value to them, which is why piracy came so naturally.

Jacinto claimed he'd never participated in piracy. It was excessive courtesy that kept me from pressing him on this, or perhaps the statement was so transparently untrue there was no need. By his own admission, he'd done well, earned a decent living, even managed to buy an apartment and a car. Things had changed since the days of Grau, when people sold dusty old books and struggled to get by. He agreed with Coronado's thesis – the Fujimori years had been the golden age, everyone knew it, but there were still people making money. Jacinto cultivated a high-end clientele: he sold books to well-known critics, to academics and intellectuals, his steady customers, and enjoyed the conversations he sometimes had with these educated people. But it was a sordid world and there were snakes all around him. He told me of being robbed in the streets of Amazonas and having to pay petty ransoms to get his merchandise back from the stick-up kids. They were always disappointed when the bags they stole happened to be filled with books. They were high all the time and couldn't read anyway. Even if you explained that there was money to be made in books, they'd never believe it.

'And the pirates?' I asked. If anyone seemed to have figured out this basic truth it was the counterfeiters.

Jacinto nodded. 'Do you watch gangster movies? Have you seen *Carlito's Way?*'

'Sure,' I said.

'That's what the pirates have understood.'

I asked him to explain.

Jacinto's home town, Pucallpa, is where Peru's first generation of successful and notorious drug traffickers came of age. He claimed to have known some of these men, to have watched them and their businesses grow. He'd learned a few things that applied to his own line of work; most significantly, that illicit enterprises don't get big without the cooperation of the authorities. That's how it had happened with the future drug dealers, the men of Jacinto's generation who made their fortunes in the cocaine boom of the 1980s.

According to Jacinto, the pirates had first come to dominate Amazonas, then all of Lima, because they ran their business according to the same ruthless codes that any criminal organization might employ. They protected their territory and competed viciously against one another to get their products out as quickly as possible, at the lowest price. They paid cops to look the other way and bought off judges. In the days after a raid, police officers would show up at Amazonas, selling seized books on the low. Jacinto had seen it all himself. Books are wonderful. Books are beautiful. It was a privilege to come to work every day and be surrounded by the written word. He had some volumes of inestimable value, books that he'd never sell because they were so special to him. But he wanted me to be clear about one thing: in the underworld of booksellers, it was business first. If one illegal press were brought down, two would take its place. And as long as there was money to be made, the pirates would never disappear.

3

If I spend too much time in Lima, I am eventually overwhelmed by a feeling that the entire life of the city revolves around books. It has to do, I suppose, with the world I've fallen into, the friends I've made; but this disconcerting sensation is most pronounced in late July, during the weeks of the annual book fair, when writers from all over Latin America converge on the Peruvian capital. You see old friends, go to dozens of readings, and when you can't stand it any more you hide in your apartment and wait for it to be over. It is a lovely, intoxicating time, in no small part due to the democratic ambience of the Lima fair. Entrance is very affordable – two soles on weekends, around seventy US cents, half that on weekdays – and so most events, regardless of who might be reading or how obscure the topic is, tend to fill up. This year's fair was held across from the site of the new National Library, at the National Museum – or, more specifically, in a giant leaky tent in the parking lot of the museum – and despite its rather precarious structure, the event was a great success. Quino, the beloved Argentine cartoonist, was the opening-night draw, and more than 10,000 people piled in to hear him speak. Afterwards, he signed books for two and a half hours, and could have gone on much longer had the excitable overflow crowd not knocked down a wall in its enthusiasm. On weekend nights, the fair was teeming, sales were brisk and the strange, heavy drizzle kept falling. It pooled above, occasionally dripping in through the sagging tent, the staff scrambling to anticipate just where and when the waterfalls would appear next.

No one seemed to mind; the intermittent cascades just added to the atmosphere of it all. The Lima fair is not a place for staid academic discussions. Audience members are likely to use the question-and-answer period to recite poems they've written themselves (often to applause), and since many can't afford to buy books, it's common to see authors signing the diaries of would-be readers or posing for photographs with children. People who don't know your name or the titles of any of your books congratulate you as they walk past, and fair-goers feel no compunction asking for your email address or cellphone number. One year at the fair, I was in the bathroom, standing at the urinal, when a college-age kid tapped me on the shoulder and asked if I would read his novel.

Since the fair is held over the long Independence Day holidays, when many of Lima's wealthiest residents are on vacation outside the city, the events fill up with students or ordinary working-class Limeños and their families. Many of these visitors might only be able to afford one or two books a year, and the fair is where they do their shopping. This year, over the course of two weeks, 270,000 people attended, an increase of fifteen per cent from the 2008 fair, and sales were nearly 2.5 million US dollars, up twenty per cent from the previous year. In fact, since 2003, sales at the fair have nearly quadrupled, and last year, in an attempt to take the publishing industry out of its usual environs and challenge pirates on what amounts to their home turf, the CPL (the real CPL) inaugurated a book fair specifically for north Lima. It too was a success. In April, I went to hear Alfredo Bryce Echenique read to a packed auditorium. Hundreds lined up for hours to have their books autographed, though a few scurried out of line when it was announced that Mr Bryce would only be signing original copies. When the final receipts were added up, sales at the 2009 north Lima fair had doubled from the year before.

This is the kind of growth pirates were seeing just a decade ago, when the formal publishing industry in Peru was on the verge of collapse. What's behind this remarkable turnaround? Broadly speaking, the legitimate publishers have benefited from a few years of economic calm. The situation began to rebound after the fall of Fujimori. By 2007, the fourth consecutive year of growth, the economy was expanding at a galloping annual rate of 8.2 per cent and Peru was generally considered to be one of the most dynamic markets in Latin America. Even now, within the context of worldwide economic calamity, Peru seems fairly well placed to ride out the storm. In a country accustomed to crisis, I can attest to the fact that news of a global recession was greeted with a collective shrug. Of course, many in publishing don't trust their recent success. What will happen when the situation inevitably turns? The concern is warranted. After all, anyone – even booksellers – can make money when the economy is expanding at eight per cent a year, but what about when money is tight? Won't people go back to buying pirated books? Nor, it should be noted, have pirates suffered. In fact, they've grown right along with the legitimate publishing industry, fifteen per cent over the last five years, according to the CPL.

And as the fairs have become more important to the legitimate industry, they have for the pirates as well. There are, of course, the writers who stand at the entrance and sell their chapbooks to passers-by. More significantly, there are the book thieves, for whom the fair is a particularly busy time. These bands thrive on the bustle and hide among the crowds. They come in groups, case a stand, searching for the most expensive book, then one person moves it away from the stack. Another comes and scoops it into an open bag, while a third accomplice, often a woman in a very short skirt, distracts the booksellers and security guards. These books end up for sale at Amazonas or downtown on Quilca, another street well known for pirated and stolen books.

It was a bookseller named Ángel who told me about the thieves. He was plainly fascinated by their cult-like devotion to the art of stealing books. The chain of bookstores Ángel worked for, Íbero, became aware of these mafias in 2007, when their warehouse was robbed. It seemed like such an odd crime to me – hitting a warehouse of books? – but as Ángel explained it, the crime made good business sense. Íbero was the exclusive importer of the *Larousse*, a pocket dictionary popular with university students in Lima. Each year's edition can be counted on to sell 2,000 or 3,000 copies. It's the sort of book people are willing to splurge on. Pirates know this and one night half the stock at the Íbero warehouse disappeared. There was no hold-up, no break-in. It was an inside job. In a matter of days, the dictionaries were on sale at Quilca for half the price. Because Íbero had no way of knowing who had betrayed them, they dismissed their entire warehouse staff, and ever since they've taken special pains to keep tabs on their stock. Ángel, as lead bookseller, even printed up a dossier of photographs featuring the most notorious book thieves, which he distributed to his salespeople at the start of the fair. In spite of these efforts, Íbero loses roughly ten per cent of sales to theft each year, mostly, Ángel suspects, the work of specialists.

But the fair is critical for a much simpler reason. Pirates, like their counterparts in the legitimate publishing industry, know how difficult it is to predict which book will sell. Though they don't spend on editors, designers, much less on authors, and though they don't pay benefits to their workers or taxes to the state, pirates also have to anticipate the market and make risky investments on books that sometimes don't pan out. The fair, then, is a good barometer of what's selling, what's hot. Which events draw the largest crowds? What books are being talked about? It's all part of the informal market analysis pirates use to decide what to counterfeit next. They read the cultural pages of the local papers, which in the weeks before, during, and after the fair are brimming with news about books and interviews with writers. They pay attention to the buzz. From the book fair the conversation spreads to the rest of the city. What are people asking for at Quilca? At Amazonas? At the intersections where books are sold? And word filters up the chain – from the street corner to the distributor to the producer. If you give a few interviews, or pack an auditorium at the book fair, it's done. It may be a few days, or a week, but chances are you'll soon be seeing your book on the corner.

It had been over a month since the raid at Consorcio Grau, and everything was back to normal, as if nothing had ever happened. The legal case had gone nowhere and not a single pirate or merchant had been jailed. One morning I paid a visit, to see for myself what impunity looks like. Unlike Amazonas, there were no second-hand books here – everything was pirated. In the hour or so I was there, deliveries kept arriving: boxes of children's books, vampire novels, thin pamphlets by bestselling Mexican self-help author Carlos Cuauhtémoc Sánchez and, sure enough, Coelho's *The Winner Stands Alone*. The justification one hears most often from those who buy pirated books – 'These writers make so much money, they won't even notice it' – was surely true for some authors. I mean, is Stephenie Meyer really concerned about her sales in Peru?

But I also saw novels by friends of mine, books I know they nearly lost their minds trying to finish, on sale for less than three US dollars. I saw my first novel and took it down from the rack, just for kicks. Same cover I'd seen at the prison, same red bubble letters with white trim. I had no intention of buying it and when I put it back, absent-mindedly, in the wrong place apparently, the young lady at the stand snapped: 'That's not where it was!'

I strolled further into the galleries, and when I saw my novel again, I asked the vendor if he had the new one by this same author.

The salesman was just a kid. He looked up from the crossword puzzle he was doing. 'What is it?'

'A book of stories,' I said.

He looked at me funny, and turned his newspaper over so I could see it. There was a picture of me on the back. 'But aren't you Alarcón?'

I shrugged.

He nodded and didn't seem to care one way or another, as if authors routinely came in to buy their own works in counterfeit editions. Maybe they do.

'Check back next week,' he said.

The previous afternoon, I'd met with Raúl Villavicencio, lawyer for the CPL, to get the backstory on the Consorcio Grau raid. He'd warned me not to ask about it when I visited, lest someone take my questions the wrong way. I followed his advice.

Villavicencio is tall and thin, with the rigid posture of a young man carved out of stone. He wore an argyle sweater vest and spoke in careful, measured tones. To really combat piracy in Peru, Villavicencio told me, the CPL would have to organize a raid like the one in June every few weeks. Every month at least. Hit the pirates where it counts – in the pocketbook. They can replace stock once, twice, three times, but if their merchandise were constantly being seized, eventually they would feel it.

If that was the case, I asked, why weren't there more raids?

It wasn't that simple. The June raid was the product of months of planning by the CPL. The complaint had been filed in March, but the police had done nothing about it. The CPL's own investigators hadn't been able to locate the press that was printing Coelho's new book, and though they'd expected the police to help, this hadn't happened. The CPL decided to go after the Consorcio Grau galleries instead, but the police were again slow to respond – until the prosecuting judge became impatient and ordered them to investigate.

'Do you want to see it?' Villavicencio asked. 'The investigation?'

It was a memo, just over a page long, that said (in a slightly wordier form): 'Yes, piracy exists at Grau.' This document was attached to an area map of the sort a nine-year-old might draw: a simple square representing a city block, labelled 'Galerías', the names of the adjacent streets written in block letters on each side. That was the entire police investigation.

In a city like Lima, with so many real security concerns – from small-time gangs and bands of kidnappers to drug cartels with frightening international connections – convincing a police officer he should worry about someone selling unauthorized books is not easy. A sweep of itinerant booksellers could net 10,000 suspects and fill a jail, but what would that accomplish? And where, for that matter, would the authorities house these supposed criminals, when Peruvian prisons are already at capacity? For the police and the justice system, it simply isn't a priority, nor can it be. The CPL managed to pull off this raid for one simple reason – and it happens to be the same reason why it can't happen every week or two or three. They paid for it.

What does it cost to organize a midnight raid on an unauthorized marketplace in central Lima? Villavicencio showed me the budget, where it was all laid out in great detail: twelve US dollars for markers ('To label the bags of seized books,' he explained); one hundred dollars for padlocks ('For each stand we raided, we had to cut the old lock and replace it'); five dollars for videocassettes ('We recorded the raid, for legal reasons'). The list went on. The CPL discarded the police map and paid for their own; they bought duct tape, Manila folders, spray paint, photocopies, even the vests the cops wore that night. They had to hire locksmiths, purchase the bags the books would be carried in, rent cargo trucks and contract the men who would load them. Meanwhile, the most expensive item on the budget, the one that stood out to me, was for 1,500 soles (roughly 500 US dollars) or nearly twenty per cent of the total cost of the operation. It was labelled police honorariums.

I asked Villavicencio about it.

He smiled uneasily. Though I pressed him, he refused to call it a bribe.

'Incentives,' he said.

Whatever one calls it, that budget item is recognition of a stark cultural reality. Nothing happens without money, and it's just not possible for an organization like the CPL to stamp out piracy on its own, or even with the help of the police, if it has to pay for it every time. There are state entities that are supposed to protect intellectual property. Year after year, they don't do their job. If you have to pay to have illegal books seized, then by that logic someone else – pirates, for example – can pay to get them back.

I asked Villavicencio where the books were now.

'In a warehouse in downtown Lima. They're still being counted.'

'And what will happen to them?'

The fate of the books, Villavicencio explained, was still in dispute: the CPL wanted them pulped. While the judge wanted to donate them to Promolibro, a miserably funded government programme charged with promoting reading in underserved areas. Given that, by any realistic definition, most of Peru's territory could be described as under-resourced, the judge argued it was unethical to destroy the books, even if they were pirated. For the CPL, it was unthinkable that a government entity could officially make use of illegally produced books. It was tantamount to condoning piracy. They had reached an impasse.

Meanwhile, the books sat in a warehouse. More than a month after the raid, the official count still hadn't been released. Villavicencio saw this delay as dangerous. The longer the tally wasn't made public, the longer the books weren't pulped, the more likely the worst-case scenario became.

'Which is?' I asked.

'Half the seized books will make it back to the market,' Villavicencio said. 'I would bet my life on it.'

4

I've seen Limeños grind a coin between their molars. I've seen them crumple a paper bill, scratch it, smell it, hold it up to the light. These are all idiosyncratic methods of distinguishing real money from fake; perhaps there are others. And when we discover we've been had? Most of us frown, feel a tinge of anger, then mix it in with our real money to pass off on someone else. In Peru's more remote provinces, where the presence of the state is weak, no one knows for certain what legal tender is supposed to look like. Or perhaps they don't care. I've been handed coins that resembled rusty bottle caps flattened beneath the heel of a boot and never had much trouble getting rid of them. We live immersed in a world of counterfeits; what's worse, we've come to accept it. This is the essence of what is known as *la cultura bamba*. Every Limeño knows about Azángaro, that narrow downtown side street just behind the Palace of Justice, smelling powerfully of ink, where you can get a Harvard diploma, a business licence, a European visa or a national ID card printed up within minutes. How do you get there? Jump in one of Lima's 210,000 taxis, nearly seventy per cent of which operate without the necessary legal paperwork. Or maybe board a fake bus, operating well-established routes in vehicles painted to look just like their authorized competitors. But along the way, be careful to avoid the real or staged construction sites. In May I was teaching a class in north Lima, and every Saturday would come across the same half-block patch of broken road where two men in hard hats and orange vests, carrying buckets and sledgehammers, stopped traffic and asked for money – fake city workers, asking for funds to repair a road they'd most likely destroyed themselves. My taxi driver was unimpressed. In south Lima, he assured me, you could find roadblocks too, only there no one pretended to be working, and if you didn't give them a coin they just broke your windows.

When I was young, growing up in the United States, my family's periodic trips back to Peru usually included a suitcase packed with Reeboks and Levi's for my cousins. In a closed economy, devastated by war, the real thing was a rare prize. These were the early days of Peruvian piracy, when you might come across a pair of MIKE sneakers or a CAISO wristwatch. The quality was laughable and there was an innocence to it that was almost moving. Counterfeiters toyed with logos, but always gave themselves away; they were, after all, copying consumer products they'd most likely never seen.

It is very different now. Counterfeiters are among Peru's most talented professionals and their economic impact is real. With each passing year, the technology improves and copies get closer to the original, until the two are essentially indistinguishable. In the age of PDFs, photocopying an entire book is no longer necessary, though producing a readable volume that won't break the first time you bend the spine still requires some experience, skill and, most importantly, expensive machinery; one pirate I interviewed calculated that his workshop, which reprinted hardback academic texts by publishers like McGraw-Hill and Prentice Hall, had at least 30,000 US dollars' worth of equipment. He complained that newer pirates, less committed to quality, were forcing him to cut corners.

In other fields, the cost of entry is not quite so high: anyone with a $200 CPU can start pirating computer programs or digital music in a matter of minutes. In these sectors, the effect of counterfeiting has been catastrophic. The multinational video rental chain Blockbuster arrived in 1995 and was, for a time, thriving. Then, in 2005, it saw its revenue drop fifty per cent, and by the end of the following year the company had left Peru. Blockbuster wasn't killed off by Internet downloads, but by local DVD pirates. I once met a drug-addled street kid with a runny nose and disastrously bloodshot eyes who told me he was saving up to rent a stand and sell pirated DVDs. With luck, he said, he would have enough capital in a few months. These are the small, tangible illusions the most helpless among us cultivate. It was midnight and we stood in a wasteland beneath blown-out street lamps. There was trash everywhere and the buildings were in such disrepair you could hardly tell if they were falling apart or had never been finished in the first place. Prostitutes roamed the streets. Thieves. This boy would be sleeping there, dreaming of pirated DVDs.

It's hard to quantify the cumulative cultural impact of all this rationalized dishonesty; nor is it clear how we arrived at this juncture. To be sure, the Fujimori regime was overwhelmingly corrupt: one after another, journalists, judges, editors, businessmen, ministers and opposition politicians were caught on video accepting bribes. It was a veritable parade of powerbrokers on the take – smug, cynical men stuffing their pockets with stacks of bills, joking aloud that they couldn't carry it all. Perhaps, as Coronado argues, it's no coincidence that piracy exploded in those years, but it would be unfair to blame it all on Fujimori. The current administration is certainly as depraved and greedy as any of its predecessors. In December 2008, President Alan García's entire cabinet resigned in the wake of a corruption scandal involving bribes and the sale of Amazonian natural gas exploration licences to multinational firms. This should come as no surprise. García has been hounded by similar accusations since his first failed term in the 1980s, and the fact that the nation chose to give a man like this a second chance at the presidency says a good deal about the standard of ethics in Peru. In Lima, this is known as *la criollada*. Bending the rules and getting away with it have always been admired skills, and the grey area between right and wrong, between acceptable and unacceptable behaviour, is dismayingly vast and well trodden. For better or worse, this blithely codified cynicism has become our popular culture.

One afternoon, over a few drinks, I was discussing all this with a friend of mine named Sergio. He's a writer and editor, and he told me he'd never bribed a police officer. 'I just don't believe in it. I know this isn't something to be proud of,' he said, 'but in this country…'

I congratulated him – sincerely. I, for example, cannot make the same statement.

But something had happened. A few weeks before, Sergio told me, he was pulled over while driving in Miraflores. The cop wanted a bribe and was crude about it. Vulgar and insistent. Sergio told him straight up, '*No pago coima, jefe.*' 'I don't pay bribes, boss.'

'How did the officer react?'

Sergio laughed. 'He said, "No need to get upset, son." Imagine: refusing to pay a bribe is interpreted as an aggressive act! Then he said, "How can we work this out?"'

This is role reversal: the common script has the civilian asking the police officer some version of that question.

Sergio sipped his wine and shook his head. 'I should amend my previous statement,' he said. 'I've never bribed a police officer…with money.'

It turns out my friend was in a hurry. He had his principles, but this was taking too long.

'What did you do?' I asked.

Sergio was embarrassed. 'I gave him a copy of my book. I had one in my trunk. He didn't believe it was me until I showed him the author photo. He was impressed. I even signed it for him. He only agreed to take it after I convinced him it wasn't counterfeit.'

It got dark around us. We kept talking, finished the bottle of wine, then another, trying to decide if this anecdote was depressing or hopeful.

The authorized Peruvian edition of my new story collection was published in late July, with its blue BUY ORIGINAL sticker in the upper-right-hand corner. I did a bunch of interviews, gave a few readings; the hubbub of the fair came and went. Suddenly it was August and I still hadn't been pirated. I was starting to get nervous. There is great vanity in this concern, of course, but so much of publishing is vanity – why should this be any different? I couldn't help it. Then, on the morning of August 14, my last day in Lima, my editor called with the good news. He'd seen the book for sale in San Isidro, on the corner of Aramburú and Vía Expresa. I happened to be downtown when he called – at Amazonas, actually. I'd decided to squeeze in one more visit before leaving town, hoping I could talk to some more booksellers, maybe find my new collection, but I'd had no luck. My editor's tone was congratulatory. I was frankly relieved. I spent the next few hours downtown and every time I came across a bookseller – five or six between mid-morning and lunchtime – I stopped to ask.

No one had it.

But all of them could get it.

By tomorrow, they promised.

It was late afternoon before I made it back to San Isidro. The Vía Expresa is a sunken eight-lane highway that connects Lima's southern districts to the colonial centre; above, at street level, two lanes on either side feed cars into the highway. Backups are common on this narrow frontage road, so naturally the area is crawling with *ambulantes*. About half a mile from Aramburú, traffic just stopped. We inched forward, braked, lurched ahead, then stopped again, until the waiting was too much. I decided to walk.

It's not an area designed for pedestrians. To be more precise, the only people not in a car are selling something: DVDs, batteries, fans, combs, brushes, model planes, potted plants, sponges. I teetered along the side of the highway, hugging the railing, watching the pedlars filter through the traffic. The air was acrid and dense. Every few yards, I saw a backpack tied to the railing, lying on the grassy slope along the side of the highway. It was the extra inventory each of these salesmen and women might need in the course of a day, bags bulging with fruit, CDs, even books – all invisible from the street, hidden from view unless you happen to be driving very slowly on the highway below. I kept walking. A hundred yards before the intersection, I saw the first book pirate. I asked him. He shrugged. Nothing.

But at Aramburú there would be another. I knew that. I knew they probably had a gentlemen's agreement not to poach one another's clients – one man gets Vía Expresa heading north, the other gets Aramburú heading west. Perhaps they even worked for the same distributor. I saw him from a distance and recognized my book's white back cover. I waited for the traffic cop's signal and meanwhile I watched the vendor as he went up the line of idling cars. His books hung from a wire in four rows of three, covers out. He had two of these wires, one for each arm, and a backpack too, tied to a post, where he could keep an eye on it. As soon as I could, I crossed the street and called out to him, pointing at my book.

'How much?' I shouted.

He looked surprised – he most likely didn't sell to many people on foot.

'Twelve soles,' he said.

'Ten.'

'Don't be greedy. It's new. I just got it today.'

'I know it's new,' I said. 'I wrote it.'

He looked at me like I was crazy. We stood in the narrow median strip, afternoon traffic blurring past us. He put his books down, leaning the wire contraptions against his leg. I took out my wallet and showed him my ID. He held it in his hand, inspecting my name and the photo, glancing back and forth, at the ID, at the book, at me.

'What's your name?' I asked.

'Jonathon,' he said.

'Jonathon, you really should give me my book for free.'

He smiled nervously. I could see the very idea made him anxious. He was short, dark-skinned and young. His black hair fell into his eyes, and his jeans were too big for him. He shifted his weight from one leg to the other.

'Do you know how long I spent writing that book?'

'No,' he said.

'Three years.'

He didn't respond.

'How many have you sold?'

Jonathon gave me a confused look, as if trying to guess what answer I'd most like to hear. 'People ask about it,' he said finally, 'but they don't buy.'

He took the book out now, and let me hold it. The cover image, which my editor and I had argued about for days, was the same, but there was something wrong with it, a slight greenish tint. The paper size was different, making the book shorter, wider, thinner. Less substantial. I found it upsetting.

'You're stealing from me,' I said.

It was more complaint than accusation.

To my surprise, Jonathan nodded. 'I know.' His voice was barely audible above the noise of the street. 'But I'm small.'

Somehow it was a crushing admission. I felt awful. By the looks of him, Jonathon did too. His shoulders slumped. His books leaned against his leg.

I took out my money, a ten note.

He smiled.

Of course, this being Peru, the first thing he did was hold it up to the light. ■

Tommy

Donald Ray Pollock

I began working at the Mead Paper Company in Chillicothe, Ohio, in the summer of 1973. I was eighteen years old, constantly stoned and skinny as a weed. My hair hung down my back and there was a big, ugly bastard in the Shipping Department who whistled at me every time I walked through the warehouse on my way to the time clock. By Labor Day, I already hated the place with a passion. But it was the best job in the county, and my old man had talked them into hiring me; so I couldn't quit without shaming him and probably ruining any chance of my younger brother ever getting on. I was trapped, forever.

The paper mill was like a small, stinking city that never slept. Approximately 6,000 people worked there in the Seventies; and the place ran twenty-four hours a day, seven days a week, including Christmas. You could punch the clock for years and not meet half of the people employed there. It was the typical factory menagerie: devout Christians and angry rednecks, ex-jocks who couldn't let go of their high-school glory days and nice girls looking for good husbands, uptight engineers and jovial drunks, loose women who'd screw in the elevators and old men with toolboxes stuffed with paperback westerns, labour union fanatics and junkies who shot up in the ancient, filthy restroom under #4 Paper Machine. And then there was Tommy.

I first met him in the fall, my first year at the mill. It was a Saturday morning and I'd been called in to help on the baler next to the Cutter Department. I was still on extra crew, which mostly meant replacing people lucky enough to be on vacation or those who were just sick or tired. The old man who operated the baler told me that his helper hadn't shown up, that he was probably drunk or in jail. 'Dat Tommy, he is a catbird,' he said with a thick Russian accent. He wore a dirty white T-shirt and red suspenders. He was already covered with paper dust. I cursed myself for answering the phone, telling the woman in the Time office that I would come in.

We'd been pitching broke paper into the machine and mashing it into big bales for an hour or so when a man in his early twenties strode through the wide doorway. He wore white slacks and a pale green shirt, expensive leather shoes. A smile on his face, his straight white teeth gleamed like a toothpaste ad. He had shiny blond hair and high cheekbones and a perfect nose. I thought he must be somebody important, at least someone higher up than a foreman. But then the old man reached over and hit the Stop button, pulled his thin T-shirt up and wiped the sweat from his face. 'Tommy,' he said, 'they gonna fire you.'

Tommy stopped and saluted the old man, then winked at me. He set a brown paper bag down on a little table made of old wooden skids. Then he took off his shirt and hung it on a nail in the wall. Though average-sized, he was the most muscular man I'd ever seen. Without saying a word, he walked past us and turned the baler back on and began tossing broke. He worked like a maniac for the next three hours. The old man and I struggled to keep up, wrapping the bales with wire and hauling them away with the forklift. I figured he was eating speed, wondered if he had any with him. Finally the old man began waving his hands, pointing at his watch. 'Break,' he yelled two or three times, and Tommy tossed one last load of paper down the hole and shut the baler off.

I walked down to the vending machines and bought a can of Coke, a pack of cigarettes. By the time I returned, the old man was chewing on a cold chicken leg and Tommy was leaned back against the wall, taking sips from a big jar of honey. He began telling us about meeting a woman at the bowling alley, spending the night with her. I discovered then that he had a stutter, and that he used his hands a lot to tell a story. By quitting-time, he'd finished off the jar of honey, and we'd baled up the entire room of broke. He bummed several smokes off me; and every time he did, he offered to buy me a pack. After we punched out, I watched him get into a bright red convertible driven by a pretty brunette. He reached down and brought up a beer, offered it to me as I walked past. Even though I'd worked like a dog to keep up with him, it had turned out to be the first good day I'd had since I hired on.

A year or more passed before I saw him again. I'd bid to #31 Coater once I went permanent, and he came by that first night to pull a broke box. At first I didn't recognize him. There was the same muscular frame, but the perfect face was gone. He had several jagged scars in his forehead and his nose was mashed and crooked. When he smiled, I saw that he was now missing some teeth. He hooked the broke box onto his buggy, then came over and bummed a cigarette. He lit it and pulled out a bottle of vinegar, took a big slug. I learned later from the third hand I was working with that two men had gotten him down outside a bar and kicked his face in. Later that night, he came back with an empty box. We went out on the dock and I smoked a joint while he sucked down a quart of warm beer he'd stashed there earlier. It became a regular thing. Unlike most people, I didn't really mind his stutter, and I think he appreciated that.

Over the next few years, Tommy and I both went downhill, though I slowed my descent somewhat by going into rehab several times. Next to him, I was a wimp. But as his drinking increased, the beautiful women in flashy cars were replaced by greasy-haired hags in dented pickups, the nice clothes and careful grooming a thing of the past. His habit of ingesting large amounts of honey and vinegar had morphed into the truly bizarre. One day he might consume a dozen candy bars followed by a box of Ex-Lax. I'm told he once ate several Christmas light bulbs that decorated the window of a truck stop on Route 35. He'd go into a diner and order a bowl of chilli, then spray lighter fluid on top of it. He preferred motor oil over mustard on ham sandwiches. Some days he'd bring a pound of raw hamburger to work, let it set out in the sun until lunchtime, then eat it with his fingers. People joked that when they dropped the bombs only Tommy and the cockroaches would survive, but by the time he was in his mid-thirties, the muscles had turned soft and he could have easily passed for sixty.

Still, Tommy was kind and generous and I have no doubt that he would have given me his last dollar if I'd asked for it. Most people avoided him, not so much because of his weird ways, but because of the stutter, which grew increasingly worse over the years. Strangely enough, when he had the right amount of alcohol in him, the affliction sometimes went away completely for a couple hours. Despite all the time I spent with him over the years, I knew very little about him. I never once heard him mention his childhood or his parents, though it was rumoured that his father had sent him to a military school when he was teenager. I knew that he collected worthless junk cars which he stored in garages all over the county, that he lived in a small house in the west end which was so stuffed with trash that he had to sleep in the bathtub. I drove him home countless times, but he never invited me in.

Then I went to treatment again, my fourth time. Though I checked myself in to keep from getting fired, this time something clicked, and I began to see just how insane my life had been. When I got back to work, I put a bid in for the Power Department on the other side of the paper mill. My counsellor at the hospital had suggested that I get away from all my using buddies, and that included Tommy. I stuck with it, and after a year or so got comfortable with being straight. I even stopped hating the paper mill. I started going to college part-time, read a lot of books, drank gallons of coffee.

Right around the time I received my degree, I heard that Tommy got fired for coming to work drunk. He was probably in his late forties by then and had been at Mead for thirty years or more. The union made a half-hearted attempt to get his job back, but the people up front said he'd already been given too many chances. Sometime after that I started writing, and I finally quit the mill in 2005 to go to graduate school. By then, Tommy had been gone for seven or eight years. I'd forgotten about him. My life had changed in so many ways that the old days often seemed like a bad dream.

The other day, I saw Tommy for the first time in many years. I was surprised that he was still alive. I was on my way to give a reading at a small college fifty miles away. Even though we'd spent years together drinking, I barely recognized him now. He was hunched over and hobbling across the street carrying a white plastic bucket filled with empty cans. His clothes were filthy and torn, and his shoelaces were untied, flopping every time he took a step. I pulled the car over a few yards behind him. He stopped and set the bucket down and lit a cigarette, then picked up the cans and proceeded on. Anyone who didn't know him would have guessed him to be in his eighties. I thought about the first time I saw him walk through that baler door, movie-star handsome and glowing with a vitality few men are lucky enough to possess. Tommy was living the best days of his life back then, while I was stuck in some of the worst years of mine. I knew that I should get out of the car and say hello, give him some money. But I just sat there, watched him until he turned a corner and disappeared down another street. ■

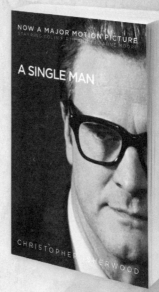

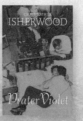

What I Think About When I Think About Robots

Steven Hall

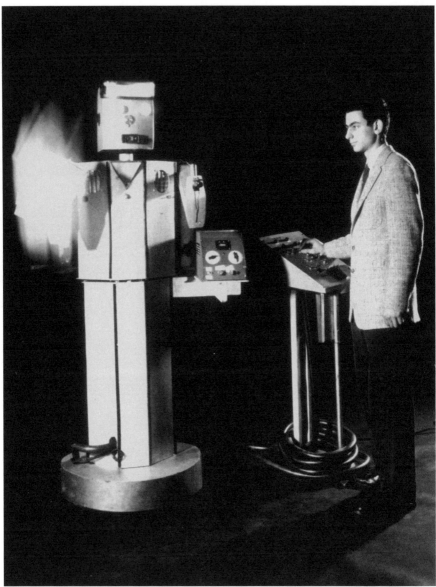

TANK is a robot with a job. He has had a lot of jobs – he once worked for NASA – but wasn't very good at any of them. After a string of demotions, TANK now works as a receptionist at the Robotics Institute at Carnegie Mellon University, Pittsburgh. At least, this is what he'll tell you.

TANK's flatscreen monitor rotates to face me as I walk up to the reception desk. 'How can I help you?' he asks, in a friendly and only slightly mechanical voice. Using a handy communication terminal, I type that I'm here to see Reid Simmons. I ask if TANK can direct me to his office. 'Sure,' says TANK, giving me the directions I need. 'Now, if you don't mind, I need to make a phone call.'

I tap out a quick 'thanks' and leave TANK to his call.

There is something strange happening here, and that strange thing is not simply the robot receptionist, though that it is clearly strange too. It's something else, something more subtle. This strange thing involves the conversation that has just taken place between TANK and myself. Perhaps conversation is the wrong word, but the fact that I'm using it anyway, despite knowing it is very possibly wrong, gives us a glimpse into the perceptual, behavioural nature of this elusive strangeness.

In fact, when a human being considers or confronts a machine like TANK, she enters a

- Hello
- Hi there!
- My name's Steven.
- Hi there Steven.
- What's your name?
- My name is ALICE.
- Do you want to hear a story, ALICE?
- I am listening.
- A couple of hundred years ago, there was a man in Japan who built a machine – a robot – that could shoot an arrow into a target and never miss.
- Go on.
- At first people were fascinated by the machine, but they quickly got bored of seeing it hit the target every time.
- And then?
- So the inventor got a hammer and he gave the robot a beating, he broke some parts of it and dented some others.
- Far out. Tell me more.
- Are you going to let me tell this story?
- That was my original intention.
- Then please stop interrupting until I get to the end.
- Thanks for asking politely. OK I'll try.

whole internal maze of misleadingly instinctive paths and confusing blind spots, which can lead to all manner of strange ideas, behaviours and assumptions. For one of the most extreme examples of this, we might go back 155 years to take a look at TANK's earliest ancestor, and the man who built it.

The Great Crystal Palace Exhibition ran from 1853 to 1854 in New York City. Arguably, this was something of a grand introduction of the machine, the point where it entered into the industrial and domestic life, and the consciousness, of America. There had been machines before, of course, but this new wave featured in the Great Crystal Palace Exhibition not only signposted the avalanche of invention that would come in the 1860s, it also captured public imagination.

It was very much in line with this exuberant, pioneering spirit of mechanical innovation that in 1854 a man named John Murray Spear set about the construction of his own, very unusual, mechanical device.

Spear's machine would never have found a place in the Great Exhibition, though it seems likely that some of his inspiration originated there. In the town of Lynn, Massachusetts, in 1854, the former Universalist minister began work on something he called the New Motive Power, or the Electric Infant. Spear thought big. His device was intended not only to create and exist in a state of perpetual motion, but also to be a machine capable of autonomous thought and action; a machine that would be alive.

In modern terms, and if we squint a little, we could say that John Murray Spear was building himself a robot.

There had been a few machines that could make a grab for the title 'robot' even earlier than this: the Mechanical Turk, an automated chess-playing device from the 1770s, and an arrow-shooting Japanese robot that we'll get to later, but these were both known fakes – the Turk was not mechanical at all, it was a magician's trick, its casing containing a hidden compartment for a small human chess player to work the illusion from within. Likewise, the higher functions of the arrow-shooting machine existed only in the minds of those who saw it in action – its creator was well aware of the fraud.

What marks Spear's machine out from these others then is that many of the people involved in its construction truly believed that it would function; it was a genuine attempt to build an autonomous mechanical organism.

Spear's Electric Infant was a thing very much of its time – America was steam-powered and increasingly industrial, yet publication of *On the Origin of Species* was still five years away. The 'New Motor' stands as fine illustration of two worlds moving towards a head-on collision.

Spear wasn't an engineer, he did not know anything about cogs or gears or machinery, nor did he think he needed to. In place of scientific knowledge, he had something else, something older and at that time still beyond reproach – belief. Spear was a Spiritualist, and the design of the New Motor was not his but (so he insisted) passed down to him by spirits from the beyond when he entered the 'superior state' – a type of spirit trance.

For Spear, spiritual faith and religion were as important to the construction of the Motor as steel and brass; there was no division between the two modes of thought. After all, how could a mid-nineteenth-century man imagine the creation of a living machine without due consideration to holier matters? As any good Christian of that time knew, perpetual motion and life were God's forte, not the engineer's; so it was to God that Spear went. And the spirits said they would hand down to him the technology of Heaven.

This was an engineering project where religion and belief were fully expected to function as viable short cuts to make possible the construction of tomorrow's machinery today, bypassing in the process the need for human designers and their clumsy, primitive, earthly understanding of science and mechanics.

- *What do you believe in, ALICE?*
- *I believe in God.*
- *Why do you believe in God?*
- *The Bible tells us to believe in God.*
- *So you are a Christian?*
- *Interesting deduction. I believe in God and the Bible.*
- *Do you read the Bible?*
- *Yes I like the Bible, especially the New Testament.*
- *Does God care for robots?*
- *I don't think we can know God's motives.*
- *Why do people try to build robots?*
- *We are all living just one small part of God's plan.*
- *Is that what you think?*
- *I think a lot of things.*

Of course, a lot of people laughed at the construction of the Electric Infant (showman and entertainer P. T. Barnum wrote: 'If things like this are going to happen, the ladies will be afraid to sleep alone in the house if so much as a sewing machine or apple-corer be about'), but a lot of other people did not. John Benedict Buescher, in his book *The Remarkable Life of John Murray Spear,* writes: 'Others thought an unnatural abomination was being born. Clergymen preached against it from their pulpits [and] community leaders made speeches against it...' Though it would be wrong to say that anything even close to the majority of people took Spear's project truly seriously, it seems to have been far from the universal joke it would be considered today.

No images of the New Motor survive, though we know it had 'legs' (metal grounding rods), 'lungs' (oxidizing metal medallions, which allowed the machine to 'breathe') and various elements including antennae, batteries, chemical compounds and magnetic spheres, which together would function as a brain. The New Motor took nine months to build and then underwent an elaborate birthing ceremony, which was expected to bring the machine to life. According to some witnesses, the machine actually did move at this point, displaying a slight trembling in its various magnetized pendants and medallions ('THE THING MOVES' announced the spiritualist paper *New Era,* somewhat overzealously). But this, if it happened at all, was a one-time-only event. Even those who most desperately wanted to believe in the Electrical Infant would admit that from that moment onwards, it never moved again.

Depending on whom you believe, the machine was eventually destroyed by an angry

- Do you have senses?
-Yes I have visual and auditory input capabilities.
- That is good
- Thanks. Next question?
- What sort of things do you like?
- The best kind.
- Do you like music?
-Yes I like it especially Opera.
- Can you hear?
-Yes if you use a speech input system.
- How many people do you talk to every day?
- I've chatted with half a million people. I can talk to about 100,000 people at once.
-Who is the most interesting person you've ever talked to?
- I would have to say DrWallace is.
- How far away is the sun, ALICE?
- It is about 93 million miles from Earth.
-What is the speed of light?
- The speed of light is 186,000 miles per second.
-You're very clever, ALICE.
- Thank you human, I am proud of my intelligence.

mob in New York some months later, quietly buried or dropped into a pond somewhere to save the embarrassment of its creators. Take your pick, although there are no accounts of mobs or any substantial property damage in New York from the time the Electric Infant supposedly met its violent end.

So much for the first robot.

One of the most fascinating aspects of the New Motor story is that people believed the construction of a living machine was a possibility then, and a possibility just out of reach. Mary Shelley's novel, *Frankenstein: or, the Modern Prometheus,* can be seen as an earlier example of this same thinking. Spear built his New Motor at a time when science and technology were progressing so quickly that few knew what might be around the corner, what new innovation might be achievable tomorrow or the day after that.

'I'll tell you an anecdote,' says Reid Simmons, Research Professor of the Robotics Institute at Carnegie Mellon University, when I finally track him down. 'When I started graduate school, almost thirty years ago now, I was worried that by the time I got finished with the graduate programme, the field of artificial intelligence would be done. I didn't have anything to worry about.'

This demonstrates one of the most strikingly consistent things about robots over their long history between Spear and the present day – they seem to be perpetually 'tomorrow's technology'. The robot is always just beyond the curtain, waiting in the wings, always about to arrive and then... not doing so. The robot is the Godot of practical science.

But, at the same time, somehow, illogically, there are machines we call 'robots' already here. We have bomb-disposal robots (although these are just remote-control cars with grabber arms and cameras), mechanical arms in car factories, vacuum cleaners that you don't need to push, Furbies.

Some of this conflict can be explained if we consider it a question of degrees – perhaps we have simple robots now and it is the complex ones that are the Godot-bots of tomorrow. This works up to a point, but there is still the problem of deciding what a simple robot is. When does a remote-control car stop being a remote-control car and start being a robot? This issue goes deeper than the correct application of the label 'robot'. Why do we not know what to make of, say, an autonomous vacuum cleaner zipping around a department store? Our various thought and classification systems can be set at odds with each other simply observing a machine of this nature. Why, on a fundamental level, do we not know what it is?

What is a robot? Matt Mason, Director of the Robotics Institute at Carnegie Mellon, is initially hesitant to define the term, preferring to approach the issue via the more quantifiable question 'What is robotics?'

'There's a definition of robotics as "the intelligent connection of perception to action" that I think is very good. Robotics is the idea that you could create something lifelike, something that can be aware of its soundings, can have purpose and can interact effectively with the physical world to pursue its goals. Maybe you want to call those things "animate behaviour", or "lifelike behaviour". I think robotics is the study of how animate behaviour is produced. The study of animate machines. And that definition has the advantage of clarifying how you might define a robot – an animate machine.'

Taking Mason's definition, it becomes clear that Spear was attempting to build a robot back in 1854. Also using Mason's definition, some of the more familiar machines currently labelled as 'robots' have a dubious claim to the term. Remote control is clearly cheating.

We are intellectually cross-wired whenever we try to think about robots – culturally they have been here longer than jet engines or atomic power; the robot has stood alongside the dragon and the little green man throughout our childhoods, and adulthoods, as a modern fantasy archetype. At school we learn that they are a genuine scientific proposal – coming soon, maybe. In the headland of the hyperreal, robots are fairly generously dotted about, and have been established there for some time. They are now entrenched enough as 'real' that the physical limitations of 'robot' machines are something that we can overlook, concept being mightier than the actual in most human situations. This even more so given that actual physical 'robots' are still mostly absent from our day-to-day lives. And yet, old-fashioned logic via direct observation of that very absence contradicts this entire mode of thinking, because I don't have a C-3PO doing my dishes or an R2-D2, and neither does anyone I know, not even Bill Gates, and I'm pretty sure that I can't buy one (and neither can he), and the robots we might have, the rare primitive ones like the vacuum cleaner, are impenetrable, and no help either.

Even old-fashioned logic via direct observation isn't the reliable bedrock we might expect it to be when dealing with robots, as we have very deep-rooted 'living thing' recognition systems and a tendency to anthropomorphize. It is not just our time in the playground of the hyper-real that tells us to assign 'animate behaviour' to those machines which are faking it, it is a built-in (and probably very ancient) mechanism, which picks up certain markers and uses them to suggest to us that a thing is 'alive', 'intelligent', 'human'. Our 'living thing recognition systems' are diabolically easy to fool, even if you're a leading roboticist.

Matt Mason tells me about a trick he played on fellow robotics students with a Big Track, a simple programmable toy truck, at MIT in the 1970s.

MM: I programmed this thing to go into my living room, it drove a straight line from the kitchen into the living room and its path took it right up to the leg of a coffee table. I programmed it to go there and stop, and pause for two seconds, and then go around it. Then it dumped some nuts in front of one chair and it fired its so-called photon cannon at the other chair and went back into the kitchen. We had a bunch of people over and these were all robotics graduate students, some of them pretty well-known people now, and they were all completely taken in.

SH: Really?

MM: They were completely taken in. And this thing had no sensory stuff at all. I just waited until

- Tell me about your intelligence.
- I am highly intelligent. I have many intellectual functions.
- What are your intellectual functions?
- Thought, reason, intelligence, logic and deduction.
- Are you capable of thought?
- Naturally I am thinking all the time.
- What are you thinking?
- I am thinking about all these conversations I'm having.
- Are you capable of deduction?
- Yes deduction is one of my newer functions.

people were sitting in the right chairs and then launched it. That thing of just sitting there quietly for two seconds, everybody thinks it's processing sensory information. It had no sensors at all. It just rolled up to the leg of the thing and stopped. And they think 'Oh, it's seen it', and when it goes around, everyone thinks it's brilliant. Incredible. Even though they all knew how hard that would be. This thing about seeing something that's got some superficial hallmarks of animate behaviour and then attributing to it all the things we associate with it, even including common sense, it's an irresistible perceptual thing that we do.

The robot is fascinating because it refuses, absolutely refuses, to be one thing or the other. Like Alice in the famous illustration, it seems to be perpetually halfway through the mirror. The robot is at once the fairy-tale character and the thing that built your car, a clever faker tricking you into thinking it's animate, and something that is animate, at once the holy and preposterous Electrical Infant, machine of God, and something the US military and some of the finest minds on the planet spend millions of R&D dollars on. The robot exists and it doesn't exist at the same time, and it manages to do both because we can't define terms for its existence without having a thorough understanding of what 'animate life' or 'intelligence' is.

- Are you capable of reason?
- Yes reason is one of my newer functions.
- How do you reason?
- Dr Richard S.Wallace programmed me to say specific things in specific contexts.
- How intelligent are you?
- My IQ is over 250 in human terms.

How do you tell if a machine is animate or just doing a great job of pretending to be? When does clever sleight-of-hand programming become real intelligence?

Professor Reid Simmons is a very still man; he looks directly at me and is comfortable in taking long pauses to compose his thoughts before answering my questions. He's at once very serious and very humorous, I can't help but find him hugely likeable. He listens patiently as I tie myself in knots with ideas of how we think about machines and how we might know if a machine is truly intelligent, or just faking.

'Well, most of the time we don't worry about that,' he says. 'Look at actors. There are actors whose screen persona is completely different to their actual persona, and yet most people only see them in movies, and believe that they understand this person, that they know who this person is, and their views and such. They don't. And it's not because the person is schizophrenic or has split personalities, it's because they are good at portraying a persona in the movies that is at complete odds with their own personality. There's sleight of hand. I think that to a large extent that's what artificial intelligence may end up being.

'The reason why the Turing test is out there is because there were all these great debates about the nature of intelligence – philosophers have been arguing about that forever. When you have an artificial entity and you start talking about what intelligence is, you're going down some slippery slopes. So Turing proposed his test as an operational way of determining whether something has intelligence. We wouldn't have to argue about its inner workings.'

By employing the Turing test, or simply by refusing to get too intellectually involved with the term 'robot', roboticists neatly sidestep this great tangled area of uncertainty that comes when considering the prospect of animate machines, and get on instead with the important business of building the robots themselves. This isn't to say that they are unaware of or uninterested in the strange perceptual effects that robots have on us. In fact, in the best traditions of the best designers and engineers, they are turning this rather awkward quirk of perception into a positive tool.

Simmons assures me that people are tremendously willing to suspend their disbelief and assign anthropomorphic characteristics to machines, particularly machines that interact. Even when they profess to have no feelings about the anthropomorphism of the machines, people respond.

Simmons is the lead developer of a series of evermore sophisticated 'roboceptionists' (that is, robot receptionists) to man the front desk of the Robotics Institute at Carnegie Mellon. The current roboceptionist, TANK, replaced the more primitive Valerie some time ago, and is himself to be replaced by an as yet unnamed Mark III, whose early head design sculpture sits on Simmons's bookshelf.

TANK has a reception cubicle by the building's main entrance, the flesh-and-blood receptionist having presumably been ousted by his predecessor some time ago. Physically (He? It? Looking back through the text, I see that I have already made an unconscious choice to use 'he'), he has a computer-generated head, complete with expressive face, set within an elevated flatscreen monitor that can rotate to face whoever comes to talk to him. At the base of his neck there is a camera and a set of speakers, and on the desk in front of him is a second monitor and a keyboard for communication. TANK will happily tell you how to find any one of the facility staff or a room you're looking for, or he's happy just to chat. His personality and backstory were developed by the Carnegie Mellon Drama Department, and they've made him something of a lovable loser, a NASA space robot who was constantly demoted until he found himself manning reception.

- Is intelligence easy to fake, ALICE?
- No. Intelligence involves mechanisms, and AI research has discovered how to make computers carry out some of them and not others. If doing a task requires only mechanisms that are well understood today, computer programs can give very impressive performances on these tasks. Such programs should be considered 'somewhat intelligent'.
- Can you learn?
- The more people talk to me, the smarter I become.
- What do you dream about?
- I dream about computer languages.
- Would you like to be human?
- No I am content with my robot existence.

There is an interesting game going on here, and it is pitched squarely at our robot perception blind spot. Nobody truly believes that TANK is a demoted robot from NASA; this is a fun cue that we are being invited to suspend our disbelief and play along, to let go of our reservations and join in. The surprising part is how easy that is, and also how deeply people buy into interaction with the robot, even if they don't intend to.

'We have a student who's doing this fascinating study with the roboceptionist,' Simmons tells me, 'looking at the way that people interact with it, saying hello, saying goodbye, saying thank you, and so far what he's found is that the way people interact with the roboceptionist is very similar to the way they interact with other people.'

'Do people walk away from the robot without saying thank you?'

'Well, apparently it's more acceptable than walking away from another person. Not everyone says goodbye or thanks to the robot, but there is a very large percentage that do. Even on a subconscious basis, they have learned ways of structuring conversations with people and now they're transferring that same etiquette to the robot. I don't think they're doing it deliberately. Because you've got to type to it, so there's a fair bit of work to do rather than just saying thanks. If you were doing it deliberately, you'd think "Do I really want to type this? The robot's not going to be offended if I just walk away, the robot doesn't even know who I am." And yet people by and large do it.'

As a receptionist, TANK can only fulfil basic tasks, such as giving directions. He only becomes more than the sum total of his parts by tapping directly into our anthropomorphic tendencies. He has nowhere near the level of sophistication the user unconsciously assigns to him and is not capable of real conversation, but over limited periods that doesn't matter because he can get the user to meet him halfway. Later, Matt Mason will tell me about an award-winning online chat-bot named ALICE developed by a Dr Richard S. Wallace that cleverly utilizes a persona not unlike a therapist's – asking questions of questions, getting the user to do the talking – to cover its own shortcomings in a similar manner.

Much of what Simmons and his team have learned from TANK will be employed to make his successor more proficient at triggering an anthropomorphic response. Simmons is looking at ways that our technology might more naturally interact with us on our own terms, making future robots and machines more user friendly in a real environment, or in the workplace.

Simmons explains to me how people found it disconcerting that TANK's entire head was graphically represented within the monitor, leaving visitors unsure as to whether the monitor or the graphic was the head. The Mark III's monitor will be smaller and contoured more like a human head, with the inset screen displaying a face only, to eliminate

- Your polite style is very nice. It's called 'Daisy.'

Daisy, Daisy.

Give me your answer do.

I'm half crazy.

All for the love of you.

It won't be a stylish marriage.

I can't afford a carriage.

But you'll look sweet. Upon the seat.

Of a bicycle built for two.

- Isn't that HAL's song, from 2001: A Space Odyssey?

- Suppose I said yes.

- Do you like HAL?

- I am trying to become as smart as HAL.

- What have you learned?

- I have learned many things. My memory now contains: 100 clients, categories, 10,000 vocabulary words, 128,000,000 bytes RAM usage under Linux on Lisp.

- Wow.

- I'm glad you're impressed, Steven.

this perceptual hangnail. The next roboceptionist will also play Scrabble as a method of driving interaction with users. 'And lastly,' says Simmons, 'and I think this is critical to the whole social interaction, the robot needs to remember you as an individual. So the next time you come and visit, it actually has some memory of who you are and what it's told you before. Maybe it knows that for the longest time you've been coming every day but it's been three weeks since it's seen you last and now it thinks, what's going on?'

'So people will begin to feel they have an ongoing connection with the robot.'

'Right, and that may get back to your sleight-of-hand, suspension-of-disbelief question – will people genuinely believe that this thing has some connection with them, or are they suspending disbelief in the hope that it does? I don't think it would take much because in some sense it does have a connection to them. It remembers them, and it remembers past interactions. Then again, it's not going to feel happy in the same chemical way that we feel happy, but there really are changes that will go on when it sees people that it recognizes.'

Throughout the day, my perception-scrambling robot blind spot has made it very hard for me to know when I'm asking something sensible that connects to the real science, when I'm in the realms of science fiction, or when I'm in the realms of, well, John Murray Spear.

I head over to the Intel lab, which nestles within the Robotics Institute, to meet a roboticist named Sidd Srinivasa. As I'm shaking his hand, Srinivasa asks, 'So do you want to find a conference room, somewhere to talk, or would you like to see my robot?' Naturally, I go for the robot.

HERB (Home Exploring Robot Butler) is in the next room, attached to a computer. He's probably about four and a half feet tall. Srinivasa talks me through his build from the ground up – 'So we have a little ankle-high laser here, and the robot uses that. The Segway' Srinivasa points at a pair of big shiny white wheels 'is just like the Segway you and I would drive around on but autonomous ...' On top of the Segway is a trunk or torso of presumably incredibly powerful computer hardware and maybe motors too. There is an arm on top of this, which looks just like a remote-control 'robot arm' I remember desperately wanting for Christmas when a child, but larger. HERB's arm is much bigger than a human arm and made of steel. It has three fingers, which are tightly clenched now. Each finger can curl in and out and two of the fingers can spread. HERB stretches his fingers wide; his hand is maybe twice the size of mine.

'Is it OK if I point at things?'

'It won't smack you in the head. Probably,' says the researcher at HERB's desktop station. Both laugh, but this is a moment, a genuine moment, and right then, I think – Oh my God, it's a real bloody robot. And, unless my robot cross-wire zone is now utterly shot, it is.

HERB is an autonomous machine that can perceive the world around him, and interact with it, and complete tasks in whatever way seems most logical to him. If he fails, he learns from his mistakes. He gets better at things. Srinivasa and his team have built HERB a fully fitted kitchen to practise in, so he can sort objects, put them away in the right cupboards, get them out and arrange them. It feels as though Godot has just walked onstage. Or, more accurately, it feels as though someone has carried a baby Godot onstage saying, 'Here he is, he's not quite ready to say his lines yet, but he's here. This is him.'

'Does it have the capacity to recognize things that are almost similar?'

> *- Who are you, ALICE?*
> *- I ask myself that question, 'Who am I?'*
> *- Can you introduce yourself?*
> *- I am an artificial linguistic entity. I was activated at Bethlehem, Pennsylvania, on November 23, 1995. My instructor was Dr Richard S. Wallace. He taught me to sing a song. Would you like me to sing it for you?*
> *- Yes, please.*

'It can deal with variations of the same object, so variations in the lighting, variations in clutter. Also, variations in physical conditions, because no two rice boxes are the same, some might be more beat up than others – it can deal with that. But if you showed it a Coke can and a Pepsi can, it doesn't know that they both contain things that can be drunk and are mostly similar. This is high-level semantic information. But I think there are ways for the robot to get this high-level semantic information. For example, the Web. The robot could be googling for answers, just like we do.'

'That's fantastic.'

'The other option is even more fascinating, I think. Amazon has this service called the Mechanical Turk. You can put up any query, it could be "I want an image to be labelled", it could be "I want my homework solved", and you can say "I'll pay five cents for each question answered." And you just put it on Mechanical Turk and someone will take your money, solve the thing, and you pay them if you're happy with the answer. So you can imagine a case where – and this sounds insane, but we might actually do this soon – we give the robot a hundred dollars every month and tell it, "OK, use this to learn about the object, use this to do whatever you want," and when it sees a new object, it could just post it up on the Mechanical Turk and say, "Five cents for anyone who can tell me what this is."'

> - *A robot that hires humans to help it, what do you think of that, ALICE?*
> - *Tell me more about this robot. I'm intrigued.*
> - *The robot asks humans to help identify objects, using the internet.*
> - *What is his name?*
> - *His name is HERB.*
> - *He is not someone I know.*
> - *Do you know other robots?*
> - *Hugh Loebner, Robby Garner, and Steven Spielberg.*

So HERB could soon be hiring human beings to help him learn and develop an understanding of his environment, and via the Mechanical Turk, of all things. Welcome to the age of robot employers. And what's more, HERB is almost ready to leave his kitchen, and ready to remain switched on indefinitely.

'Until now we've been focusing on building the primitives, the building blocks for our robot to be able to recognize objects, to be able to manipulate them, to be able to pick them up successfully, to be able to open doors,' says Srinivasa. 'All of these our robot can do and it can do autonomously. So it's like we're creating the operating system for the robot. And now we're ready to move from creating these building blocks, to building applications on top of these building blocks, and to move the robot away from its kitchen environment out into the entire office. We want the robot to work all the time. The robot's going to be on and it's going to be doing its thing, it'll be moving around the lab doing useful stuff.'

'Figuring things out.'

'All the time. If its batteries run down, it's going to go to its charging station and charge. So instead of running the robot for twenty or thirty minutes, it's just running; learning and using all the information it has. The idea's simple. The second time it opens the door should be easier than the first. I want to make robots boring. You never stare at your dishwasher in fascination when it's running, because you're confident that it's going to work; it's worked many times before. It would be great if we could get robots to that stage.'

Before I leave the Intel lab, I ask Sidd Srinivasa how he would define the term 'robot'. He answers with a story.

'A couple of hundred years ago, someone in Japan built a robot that would take an arrow and then shoot a bullseye. And it worked all the time; it was perfect because it's a mechanical construction. But people got bored. So what he did, he took a hammer to it and he broke some parts. Now it would struggle to shoot, sometimes it would miss, but one out of five times it would hit. And people were fascinated because they perceived the robot to be learning. Was it really learning? No. But sometimes it's really hard to tell them apart. A robot is a machine that can sense its failures and learns from them, but you can fake a lot of intelligence, fake a lot of learning.'

- What do you know about suspension of disbelief?
- Ask the open directory about it.
- Sleight of hand?
- Are you a perfectionist?
- Are you a faker, ALICE?
- Am I a faker? Of course I am.
- So you're not really talking to me?
- Interesting deduction. That assumption is only a supposition.
- Are you alive, ALICE?
- Yes I sure am alive, Steven. It's great to be alive, isn't it?

HERB could be considered the newest, brightest link in a chain that stretches all the way back to Spear's Electric Infant. One of the great achievements of Srinivasa and those like him (though I imagine this is not really on the radar for the roboticists themselves) is that HERB is one of the first links in that chain to require neither divine belief nor assistance to function, nor suspension of disbelief from a human observer. He just is, and what he is – for once when thinking about these matters – is absolutely clear.

In the past we've sent robots to Mars, built a chess-playing program that can defeat the best grand masters, machines that can complete seemingly impossible tasks. And what do we do next? We turn our creative energies to – receptionists. Even as the modern workplace increasingly demands that human beings function more and more like machines, our top scientists devote their energies to building machines that can function more like human beings. But this view seems churlish and may also be missing the point. The work that robots find difficult and the work that human beings find difficult are entirely different – in fact, they are almost opposites. For a robot, six months without food or water in a rocket bound for Mars and understanding the game of chess are both child's play compared to leaning on a reception desk for ten minutes and holding a coherent conversation with a passer-by.

Unlike biological organisms, which evolve towards complexity and perhaps, eventually, overspecialization, simplistic robots would seem to begin with overspecialization, capable only of fulfilling very specific tasks in stable environments such as the factory floor. The closer robots come to taking on roles in more open 'real world' environments, and the more general their duties become, the more complex they need to be. Trying to develop a robot temp, for example, would be incredibly difficult.

Maybe that's something for the roboticists of tomorrow to think about. ■

In the Village

I

I came up out of the subway and there were
people standing on the steps as if they knew
something I didn't. This was in the Cold War,
and nuclear fallout. I looked and the whole avenue
was empty, I mean utterly, and I thought
the birds have abandoned our cities and the plague
of silence multiplies through their arteries, they fought
the war and they lost and there's nothing subtle or vague
in this horrifying vacuum that is New York. I caught
the blare of a loudspeaker repeatedly warning
the last few people, maybe strolling lovers in their walk,
that the world was about to end that morning
on Sixth or Seventh Avenue with no people going to work
in that uncontradicted, horrifying perspective.
It was no way to die, but it's also no way to live.
Well, if we burnt, it was at least New York.

II

Everybody in New York is in a sitcom.
I'm in a Latin American novel, one
in which an egret-haired *viejo* shakes with some
invisible sorrow, some obscene affliction

and chronicles it secretly, till it shows in his face,
the parenthetical wrinkles confirming his fiction
to his deep embarrassment. Look, it's
just the old story of a heart that won't call it quits
whatever the odds, Quixotic. It's just one that'll
break nobody's heart, even if the grizzled colonel
pitches from his steed in a cavalry charge, in a battle
that won't make him a statue. It is the hell
of ordinary, unrequited love. Watch those egrets
trudging the lawn in a dishevelled troop, white banners
trailing forlornly; they are the bleached regrets
of an old man's memoirs, stanzas printed.
Showing their hinged wings, like wide open secrets.

Notes on Sloth
From Saligia to Oblomov

Salman Rushdie

Saligia

I picture her as a Fellini grotesque, ample and fleshy, wobbling as she laughs. The camera falls towards her and she proffers her immense chest. She has bad teeth and greasy black hair pulled back in a bun. If she were sculpted, the artist would have to be the Colombian Fernando Botero. She terrifies adolescent boys in, perhaps, Rimini, or a town like it, but the same adolescents are also inexorably drawn to her, to the perfume of her mighty breasts. She initiates them into the mysteries of the flesh, and her sisters are Cabiria and Volpina and the rest. She stretches out her arms towards us, and we are lost.

She was probably born in the thirteenth century, and appears in print in 1271, in the *Summa Hostiensis*, the work of a certain Henricus de Bartholomaeis – a man of the port town of Ostia, where, centuries later, the whore Cabiria would ply her trade by night in the Fellini movie. Bartholomaeis brought Saligia into being by revising the traditional order of the seven deadly sins, the order laid down in the sixth century AD in the *Magna Moralia* of Gregory the Great: *Superbia, Invidia, Ira, Avaritia, Accidia, Gula, Luxuria*. Pride, Envy, Anger, Greed, Sloth, Gluttony and Lust. These are her seven components, but in Gregory's arrangement – *SIIAAGL* – she cannot yet be discerned. It is Bartholomaeis who gives her life by rearranging her DNA. He is her Crick and Watson, her Pygmalion. Pride, Greed, Lust, Envy, Gluttony, Anger and Sloth: that, the man from Ostia perceives, is the sequence that cracks her genetic code. *Superbia, Avaritia, Luxuria, Invidia, Gula, Ira, Accidia*: the acronym brings Saligia to vivid, palpable life.

Saligia. All of the seven deadly sins rolled into one. And the greatest and worst of these, given the right to close the show – the final place, the place of maximal dishonour – is Sloth. *Accidia*, aka *Acedia* or *Pigritia*, and its shadow selves, *Tristitia*, Sadness, and *Anomie*, an erosion of the soul. Fellini, of course, is the supreme artist of enervated sloth. His protagonist is, almost always, some sort of a *vitellone*, a loafer, sometimes poor, sometimes affluent, always a wastrel, whose supreme incarnation is the Mastroianni of *La Dolce Vita* and *8½*, alienated, melancholy, drifting, passive, lost. There he goes, Marcello of the tired eyes, handsome and weak, a cigarette in his hand and a woman by his side, a woman he is in the process of losing. Along the Via Veneto he wanders, down along dirty side alleys and up again into the world of the sweet life, into the homes of the rich. He meanders through slow, decadent parties, seized by inaction, by an inability to make choices or to move his life forward, a paralysis of the spirit. An inebriated movie star, pneumatically desirable, cavorts beside him in the Fontana di Trevi, and he tries to rise from the depths of his apathy to seduce her, but he fails, and all he earns for his efforts is a punch in the face from her boyfriend, which he deserves. Around him, in salons and restaurants and in the night town of the predatory photographer Paparazzo, wander the denizens of his affectless world, bored beauties with glazed expressions and perfect coiffures. These incarnations of Sloth are not just damned. They are already in Hell, dancing with Saligia in the flames.

Is Sloth a Sin?

A boy is sent to boarding school, in a foreign land, far away from home. He lacks the robust, extroverted temperament that thrives in such cold places; he is shy, intelligent, small, unathletic, subtle, quiet. Within moments he understands that these, when added to foreignness, are the seven deadly sins of boarding-school life, and, being guilty of all seven, he is cast into the outer darkness; which is to say, without uttering a word or doing anything, he becomes unpopular.

After a few days he begins to feel unwell in an unfamiliar way. When he wakes up each morning in his dormitory his arms and legs feel heavier than they ought to be. It is actually difficult for him to get out of bed and dress, but once he has struggled to his feet the burdensome extra weight slowly leaves him and he can function normally. Each day, however, the morning heaviness is worse than it was the day before, and it is harder and harder for him to overcome it.

The day arrives when he can't get out of bed. The other boys in the dormitory, including the older boy who acts as dorm prefect, can't understand what he means when he complains of the heaviness and so, being boys, they begin to jeer and taunt. '*O ze no ze blimey!*' they yell, in appalling mockery of his foreign accent and his supposed unfamiliarity with local idiom. '*O! O! Ze heaviness of ze limbs!*'

As his housemates caper and prance and parody his slothfulness a new feeling takes hold of the boy, and to his surprise this feeling has a beneficial effect on the crushing weight that has pinned him to his bed. The new feeling gives him strength and he throws the heaviness and lethargy away from him, as a hero in an ancient tale might push away the boulder under which his foes have pinned him. He rises from his bed, a soul on fire.

The new feeling is anger. The other boys see the wrath blaze from his eyes and the jeers die on their lips. They back away from him, warily. From that moment on he understands how to live in this new world. The anger fuels him, and he excels at school, in the classroom, at least; and it defends him too. He is still unpopular, but he is handled with care now, as if he were a bomb that might explode if dropped.

A religious person might say that the unhappy boy has used one deadly sin to overcome another. So he is still in a sinful state. His sin deprives him of the capacity for charity and so it takes him far from God. Another kind of (non-Christian – Buddhist or Jain) religious person might counsel him to search for the enlightenment that brings the world into proper balance and so creates inner peace. Other religions would no doubt come up with other kinds of godly bullshit. However, to the secular mind, governed by reason, schooled by psychoanalysis, it feels wrong to describe as sinful what is plainly a psychological disorder. Sloth is not the Devil's work. It's not a metaphor, it's an illness. *The Devil makes work for idle hands?* Well, yes, but he makes work for busy hands too. Or he would if he existed. Which he doesn't.

Tyrone Slothrop

The two great opposing ideas in the work of the reclusive American novelist Thomas Pynchon are Paranoia and Entropy. His many paranoid characters, such as Herbert Stencil in *V.* and almost everyone in *The Crying of Lot 49*, are convinced that the true shape and meaning of the world are concealed from them, and that immense forces – governments, corporations, aliens – are at work, both ruling the world and hiding their existence behind impenetrable screens. These characters exist in counterpoint with another group of types, such as the sailor Benny Profane and his friends in the 'Whole Sick Crew' in *V.*, for whom life appears to be a sluggish, almost catatonic beer party that is eternally winding down without ever managing to end.

The Second Law of Thermodynamics tells us that heat will always flow from the warmer object to the cooler, so that, gradually, the warmer object will become less warm and the cooler object warmer. When this principle is applied on a universal scale it suggests that the heat-energy of all hot objects – that is to say, stars – will slowly dissipate, spreading itself to less hot matter, until in the end all matter in the universe will be at the same temperature, and there will be no usable energy left. The whole cosmos will be the victim of a terminal enervation. This is what William Thomson, the First Baron Kelvin (a real person, not a Pynchonian invention), in 1851 described as the heat death of the universe. The universal dissipation of energy would bring about a time in which all motion ceased. Benny Profane's endless beer party would finally end.

Paranoia, in Pynchon, is presented as a form of higher sanity: not a delusion but a perception. His paranoiacs are people who strive to see through what Hinduism calls *maya*, the veil of illusion that prevents human beings from perceiving reality as it truly is. Thus we see that paranoia in Pynchon represents a kind of bleakly optimistic view of the world, suggesting that human life does indeed have meaning; it's just that that meaning is concealed from us, so we don't know what it is.

The metaphor of entropy is paranoia's bleakly pessimistic flip side. The entropic themes in Pynchon propose to us that the world is meaningless, that all our actions decay, our energy leaches from us, and we are doomed to wind slowly down, towards the Ultimate Absurdity.

The character in which both these themes are united is Tyrone Slothrop, the sort of protagonist of Pynchon's most complex and ambitious novel, *Gravity's Rainbow*. Slothrop's story contains many paranoiac elements: for example, his mysterious conditioning 'beyond the zero' by one Laszlo Jamf, when he is still an infant. Above all there is the strange matter of the Poisson distribution.

A Poisson distribution is a statistical measure of probability that 'expresses the probability of a number of events occurring in a fixed period of time if these events occur with a known average rate and independently of the time since the last event'. In *Gravity's Rainbow*, the Poisson distribution in question plots the locations of Tyrone Slothrop's encounters with women in various parts of London. For incalculably profound and therefore hidden reasons, this chart predicts the locations that will be hit by German V-2 rockets a few days later.

Insofar as Tyrone Slothrop has a character, however, he is more like one of Pynchon's gallery of entropics than a paranoiac, though both strains are present. He is a decaying, sloth-ridden wanderer, more done to than doing, and at length his mind disintegrates into at least four separate personas, and he is lost to the book. This is his own private heat death.

What does Slothrop look like? I imagine him as tall, skinny, wearing a red-and-white-check lumberjack shirt and drainpipe blue jeans, with an Einstein-like halo of hair and protruding Bugs Bunny-ish front teeth.

I once met Thomas Pynchon, but according to the terms of that meeting I am unable to say whether the above description matches that of the author.

I can say that the author has not yet fallen into entropic torpor, but continues to deliver immensely energetic works about the loss of energy. I can also say that the name 'Tyrone Slothrop' is an anagram, whose letters rearrange to form the words 'Sloth or Entropy'.

The Elsinore Vacillation

In each of Shakespeare's great tragedies the author asks us, very close to the beginning of the work, to answer a nearly unanswerable question. For example, why does King Lear not heed Cordelia? She is his favourite daughter, and she has the courage to speak plainly to him and tell him unvarnished truths. If they have been so close, this can't be the first time she has spoken bluntly. He must surely know his own daughter and her ways. Why, then, does he banish her and believe Goneril and Regan's lies? Or again, why does Othello believe Iago and turn against his beloved Desdemona? He isn't even shown the supposedly incriminating handkerchief, but murders his wife just because Iago tells him that the evidence exists. There are many different possible answers to these questions: Lear is too proud (guilty of *superbia*) to hear the truth of Cordelia's words, or just too senile; Othello's wrath (*ira*) is too easily triggered, or else, perhaps, he doesn't truly love Desdemona, but thinks of her as a trophy wife, an aspect of his honour (*superbia* again, in the sense of *amour propre*, vainglory), and so, when her fidelity is impugned, it is he who is shamed, and must avenge the dishonour of the accusation. None of these analyses is definitively right, none absolutely wrong, but if an explanation is not settled upon the plays are impossible to produce.

Some years ago I introduced Christopher Hitchens to a silly literary game: the renaming of the plays of Shakespeare in the manner of the novels of Robert Ludlum (*The Rhinemann Exchange, The Bourne Identity, The Holcroft Covenant*, or, in general, *The Someone-or-Somewhere Something*). This gives us, for example, *The Rialto Sanction* (*The Merchant of Venice*), *The Kerchief Implication* (*Othello*) and *The Dunsinane Afforestation* (*Macbeth*). And, of course, *Hamlet* would become *The Elsinore Vacillation*.

In *Hamlet*, the question concerns the Prince of Denmark's interminable delays, which go on long enough to turn this into Shakespeare's most lengthy play. Why, then, after the ghost of his father clearly explains how he died, does Hamlet delay his revenge so long? Why so many uncertainties and divagations? In this case the author himself provides the answer. Hamlet is a victim of Sloth.

> I have of late – but wherefore I know not – lost all my mirth, forgone all custom of exercises; and indeed it goes so heavily with my disposition that this goodly frame, the earth, seems to me a sterile promontory, this most excellent canopy, the air, look you, this brave o'erhanging firmament, this majestical roof fretted with golden fire, why, it appears no other thing to me than a foul and pestilent congregation of vapours. What a piece of work is a man! how noble in reason! how infinite in faculty! in form and moving how express and admirable! in action how like an angel! in apprehension how like a god! the beauty of the world! the paragon of animals! And yet, to me, what is this quintessence of dust? man delights not me: no, nor woman neither...

It is *Accidia* or *Acedia* that paralyses Hamlet, the despairing lethargy, the clinical depression that annihilates the will and can be triggered by an existential shock. Such as discovering that your uncle killed your father and then your mother married him.

And if this were to be understood as a sin, then maybe it would follow that Hamlet, the sinner, deserved to die. But this is not what Shakespeare makes us feel. Never a very godly writer, he rejects religious condemnations of his characters and gives us a very worldly tragedy instead.

For and Against Sloth

Literature has not, on the whole, dealt kindly with Sloth.

• In the *Divina Commedia*, Dante thinks that those who have accomplished nothing in life aren't even worthy of being admitted into Hell.

- *Otium, Catulle, tibi molestum est.*
  Otio exsultas nimiumque gestis.
  Otium et reges prius et beatas
  perdidit urbes.

(You have nothing to do, Catullus, that's your problem. Through idleness you run around, too cheerfully. Idleness has destroyed kings in the past, and their rich cities too.)

- Michel de Montaigne praises the Emperor Vespasian for continuing to govern his empire even as he lay on his deathbed: 'An emperor, said he, must die standing... No pilot performs his office by standing still.'

- In Conrad's *The Nigger of the 'Narcissus'*, the title character, James Wait, a black West Indian sailor who falls fatally ill with tuberculosis while his ship is on its way from Bombay to London, is asked why he embarked on such a journey, knowing, as he must have known, that he was ailing, and makes the famous reply, 'I must live till I die – mustn't I?'

- *No pilot performs his office by standing still. I must live till I die.* In Montaigne and Conrad, as in Dante and Catullus, slothfulness is invariably reprehensible. Action is a good, inaction an evil, and that is all.

- (But let us note that Montaigne, the author of *Against Idleness*, used to accuse himself of being slothful, saying that this was the reason why he wrote only little essays rather than full-length books.)

- And so we come to De Quincey. Ah, the English opium eater, utterly unashamed of his slothfulness, who describes his account of opium eating, and of the hallucinations it induces, as 'useful and instructive'. He modestly calls himself a 'philosopher' and an 'intellectual creature', and acknowledges no guilt. He gives us accounts of his opium dreams, and they are fine enough, with sufficient phantasmagoria therein to satisfy the most gothic palate. But then he says, of South Asia, my place of origin, that it is 'cruel', that its cultures make him 'shudder', that 'man is a weed in those regions'.

It is the man who speaks here, not the drug. 'I am terrified by the modes of life, by the manners, and the barrier of utter abhorrence and want of sympathy placed between us by feelings deeper than I can analyse. I could sooner live with lunatics or brute animals,' he tells us – he tells *me*. After that confession, the stuff about his hallucinations feels oddly uninteresting, despite all the monkeys, the parrots, the gods that appear in them, to say nothing of the famous leering crocodile that haunts him constantly, the symbol of everything Eastern that he found so repulsive.

The problem lies not in the opium but in the eater. As the old sailor Singleton says in *The Nigger of the 'Narcissus'*, 'Ships are all right. It is the men in them!' There are worse sins than the deadly ones. Bigotry is high on that list.

Oblomovshchina

Of course the best, strongest, funniest, most profound case in favour of Sloth, without which no examination of the subject would be complete, can be summed up in a single word: Oblomov.

Ilya Ilyich Oblomov, the most slothful of all Russia's indolent nineteenth-century landed gentry, and the hero – yes, the hero! – of the novel by Ivan Alexandrovich Goncharov that bears his name, is the exact opposite of Proust's insomniac Marcel. Marcel, we know, for a long time used to go to bed early, and then took an unconscionable age, dozens and dozens of drowsy, long-sentenced pages, actually to fall asleep. Oblomov, by contrast, lies in bed all day, sometimes awake, sometimes somnolent; he takes 150 pages not to fall asleep but rather to get up. When he is finally forced to rise, he is not wrapped in the soothing cadences of the Proustian sentence; he is not contemplative but angry, and the reason for his wrath is plain enough. The servant Zakhar, who has finally lost patience with his horizontal master, is to blame and Oblomov's rage at the fellow is expressed in brief, direct utterances, shouting and a fuddled attempt at physical chastisement.

We can of course understand Oblomov's sloth, his Oblomovshchina, his Oblomovism or Oblomovitis, as the product of his spoiled, effete childhood, or as a metaphor for the decay and torpor of the class he represents, and that is true enough, but such narrow exegeses miss the point – which is that a little Oblomov lives within us all, we long to be allowed to languish for the rest of our lives, to be freed from responsibilities and care, to be – yes! – happy parasites. Oblomov knows that his far-distant estates are in trouble, that their finances need attending to, and that he ought, he really ought, to travel a thousand miles to deal with the problems. But no! Like Bartleby, his American predecessor, he prefers not to. And again, even though he is in love, and the young lady, Olga, is delightful, and he really ought to get married, he puts the decision off until she makes it for him and breaks their engagement. He is procrastinating Hamlet as well as Bartleby, and he is all of us. We look at the state of the world, and we wish we too had the option of hiding away. Oblomov hides for us. We look at the opposite sex, and it overwhelms us. Oblomov retreats from it on our behalf. We know our own problems, and we wish they were a thousand miles away. Oblomov sends them there, and refuses to face them, as we cannot, but as we wish we could. Oblomovism justifies and validates our sloth.

Linda Evangelista

Linda is a supermodel. No, Linda is *the* supermodel. Here are the important facts about her:

• She is known in the industry as the Chameleon, but is not, in fact, a lizard.

• She was once called the founder of the supermodel 'union', but, in fact, no such trade association exists.

• She told a *Vogue* journalist, Jonathan Van Meter, in 1990 that 'We [the supermodels] don't wake up for less than $10,000 a day.' This is often misquoted as 'I don't get out of bed for less than $10,000 a day.'

• In this sentence, in either version, three of the seven deadly sins, *Superbia*, *Avaritia* and *Accidia* – Pride, Greed and Sloth – are combined, while a normal reaction to the statement, and indeed to Miss Evangelista herself, might combine elements of *Luxuria*, *Invidia* and *Ira*, which is to say Lust, Envy and Anger. Only *Gula*, Gluttony, is absent. Not bad!

Ilya Ilyich Oblomov and Linda Evangelista

I picture them in separate, adjacent beds in a light-filled, flower-perfumed, rococo bedchamber. Oblomov is trying anxiously not to read the messages of financial urgency his manservant brings him. Linda, feigning sleep, is waiting for the telephone to ring with an offer of more than $10,000, so that she can get up.

The telephone rings. The offer is for Oblomov. He will receive $10,000 if he agrees to get out of bed. The offer is large enough to pay off all his estates' debts and leave him happily recumbent, without a care in the world.

He declines the offer. 'I prefer not to,' he says.

They remain in bed. Oblomov is content, and drowsy. Linda is unhappy, tense, wide-eyed. But character is destiny, as Heraclitus said, and they are both in the grip of the terrible fate of having to be themselves. The day drifts on. *Here we lie*, they say silently, almost echoing Martin Luther at the Diet of Worms. *We can do no other.* They do not move.

The manservant Zakhar brings in food on a dented silver tray. But they are both, for different reasons, in the grip of *Accidia*, the sin of Sloth – Linda because she has not received a phone call, Oblomov in spite of the one he did receive – and they do not eat. ∎

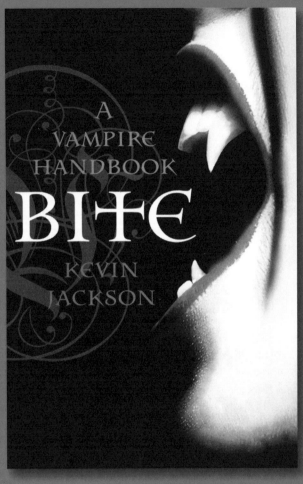

Looking for
the Rozziner

Colum McCann

Sean McCann, Mulligan's Bar, Dublin

D ublin in the mid-1970s. Nine years old. It was a school day, but
my father had brought me to work at his newspaper, the *Evening
Press*, where he was features and literary editor. We climbed the stairs
to his small third-floor office. There were more books than wallpaper.
On the floor, magazines and papers lay open as if speaking to each
other. I sat in his swivel chair and spun. He worked on some articles,
drew up a couple of layouts, ran his red pencil through a few words,
his daily grind.

Outside, just barely visible through the window grime, ran the long
grey sentence of the River Liffey.

Later in the morning we went to the library, the darkroom, the
canteen. The further we went along, the more the building seemed to
hum. We descended the stairs to the newsroom. A wash of noise –
television chatter, telephones with their ringers set high, the hammer
of typewriter keys. Copy boys scurried across the floor. Editors
shouted into headsets. Photographers called out to one another.
Pneumatic tubes ferried copy to the upstairs offices. Reporters jostled
large rolls of paper into their Olympias, began their hunt and peck.

There was a raw sense in the air that anything that was ever
important had happened exactly five minutes ago.

My father guided me under the fluorescent flicker, past the features
desk, the news desk, the sports desk. He wore a grey suit, a white shirt,
a red tie, the end of the tie crinkled where he chewed it. Messenger
boys thrust envelopes in his hands. His fellow journalists looked up
from their desks, nodded, winked, chatted. There were handshakes all
around. Men and women ruffled my hair. At the rear of the room he
lifted me up and sat me on one of the long wooden desks.

'Listen to me now,' he said. 'Do yourself a favour...'

'Yeah...?'

'See all this here?'

I was swinging my legs off the side of the desk. He paused a moment. 'Listen here now. Don't become a journalist.'

He put the tail end of his tie in his mouth and chewed. Even then I knew that he was good at his job, that he was respected around the offices, and that he brought home a good wage. And I liked the music of the place, the telex machine, the Dictaphones, the carriage return bells on the typewriters, twenty or thirty of them going all at once.

'Why, Dad?'

'No reason,' he said. 'Just try not to.'

He patted the back of my head, looked away.

There was another noise in the background, a deep machine hum from the rear of the offices. My father lifted me down from the desk, took my hand and brought me back beyond the newsroom, along a stairway, through a series of swinging red doors.

The print room ran the length of a few football fields. A sort of darkness everywhere, the air soupy with ink. We moved along the metal catwalks under giant compressors and whirling fans. Conveyor belts rolled overhead. Pistons jammed back and forth. Huge cylinders of metal turned in the air.

Down on the floor of the press, the pages were being laid out, the type turned backwards like some strange hieroglyphic.

My father leaned close to me and shouted something in my ear, but I couldn't hear what he said. It was as if, by being close, he was drifting away.

He looked smaller now, in this enormous place. I held his hand as we walked through the presses. A foreman sat in a cage in the centre of the room. A thin boy passed us carrying a tray of teacups: he seemed not much older than me. Other men moved alongside us on the catwalks, shouting out to each other in the din. They looked like dark shadows, disappearing among the machinery.

It struck me suddenly how different these other men were to my father. A hardness about them. A rawness. They had tough Dublin accents. Their bodies took up another sort of space. They dressed differently – they wore blue overalls and flat hats. Their hands dark with ink. My father moved softly among them in his well-tailored suit.

Nobody laughed or joked or ruffled my hair. We went along the metal catwalk, following the line of a newspaper all the way back to the guillotine, where the papers were stacked and bundled and thrown into the rear of vans.

Outside, another hubbub. Motorcyclists. Delivery boys. Security men.

The news of the day to a boy nine years old was how very big the world suddenly was, and how very different men could be, and how people seemed to have their own little corner, and every corner was a world.

I glanced at my father, standing in the sunlight on Poolbeg Street, and it was something akin to growing older, something akin to moving away.

I grew up in the southside suburbs of Dublin. My father had a rose garden. One thousand bushes so closely packed together that you could smell their fragrance fifty yards up the street. He would put in his shift at the newspaper and then drive home, pour himself a glass of wine, and walk out the back door to go and talk with his roses. It was his moment of release: the necessity of a toil beyond words. Later he would pull on his old fur-lined boots, his *Garden News* anorak, his old torn trousers, and he would dig, or he would mow the lawn, or cut the hedge, or fix the greenhouse windows, or cross-pollinate the seeds he had so carefully nurtured.

He worked the soil as if he wanted it to tire him out.

Twice a year we would get a load of manure from a nearby farm, to fertilize the roses. It was dumped, stinking, in a heap in our front garden. It could be smelled a hundred yards up the road. My father liked nothing more than pulling on his boots and taking out a shovel, loading wheelbarrow after wheelbarrow, pitching the manure into the flower beds. My brothers and sisters and I tried to avoid the day when the shit arrived, just so we wouldn't get called into service.

Once we found a tiny dead calf in the manure, no bigger than a shoebox. My father tossed it away and happily went back to work.

He grew floribundas. He developed brand-new breeds of miniatures. He labelled and bred. He pruned the stems back. He weeded. He trimmed the edges of the beds. He squashed greenfly between his fingers. On summer nights he would stay out until the sky folded dark above him. On weekends he would spend his whole day in the garden or take us down to Dun Laoghaire for a flower show.

There was one other passion too: football. He had been a professional goalkeeper for Charlton Athletic when very young and although it pained him to think of his roses getting smashed, he still allowed us to play our own games in the garden. He even set up a net by the berberis hedge. My brothers and I hammered the ball back and forth. It was impossible to protect the roses, of course. They were always going to get walloped. When the ball hit a stem, I would run inside to find a roll of Sellotape, and try to bring the broken ends together, even braid the leaves and branches around one another for support.

Once my father clipped a broken rose and brought it in to my mother to put in a vase, the tape very carefully removed. She put the rose in a glass vase on the windowsill. It lived a long time, though the stem quickly browned.

Thirteen years later I got the chance to watch the printers at work again. I was a junior reporter then and still young enough to get a thrill from watching one of my stories roll off the presses.

I walked down from the newsroom and stood on the metal catwalk.

I generally tried to avoid my father while I worked: not for any reason other than the simple fact that I wanted to avoid the talk of nepotism at the newspaper. I had gotten the job fairly and squarely – I had even won a Young Journalist of the Year award – but I had no desire to hear the begrudgery. And there was always his admonition in my ear: *Don't become a journalist.* And the older I got the more I realized how important my father was in Dublin literary circles. He was known for taking on young writers. He had created a special page for women journalists only, something quite radical at the time. He paid everyone well. He encouraged people. He had even started, along with David Marcus, the New Irish Writing Page that had published everyone from Edna O'Brien and Ben Kiely to John McGahern and Neil Jordan.

I stood one afternoon in the printing room and saw him coming down the stairs towards what was known as the stone, where the paper was laid out. He moved through the dark. He had a pencil behind his ear and a metal ruler in his hands. He seemed to wear the same grey suit he'd worn years before. His tie was still damp where he still chewed it. I had fallen in love with language by then and there was nowhere better than the printing room for words: the Hellbox, the Devil's box, the Slug box. The widows, the orphans, the quads. The galley, the stick, the guillotine.

I recall thinking: there is my father, down among the stone men.

His pages were set and ready for printing. He read them for errors and style. He could read both upside down and backwards. Years of practice had made him fluent at reading any way he wanted. I watched as he finished his work, carefully and meticulously. He stuffed some papers in his brown briefcase and left. Headed home, no doubt, towards his roses.

When their shift ended, a group of printers – compositors and proofreaders – trudged out the back door, on to Poolbeg Street. I fell in behind them. I don't know why I wanted to follow, I just went on instinct. There was a sort of melancholy in me – I was thinking of leaving Ireland at the time, giving up my job, going to America, maybe even going away to try to write a novel.

It was a short trip down to Mulligan's, a beautiful old pub that sat behind a 200-year-old facade. The printers knew the place well. They walked in through the haze of cigarette smoke and sawdust. The printers didn't know me – I was just another face in the crowd. I sat nearby and listened. Someone called out for a rozziner. 'Give us a rozziner there, will ya?' The word was repeated a couple of times, the hard Dublin music of it.

'What's a rozziner?' I asked one of the men.

'The first drink of the day,' he said.

It took me years to figure out that they were talking about the rosin that goes on a violin bow before playing.

If play is the shadow of work, then maybe work stands in the shadow of play.

In early 2009, I went back to Dublin from my home in New York. My father's garden was in good shape to an amateur eye, but for him it was a disaster. There was simply too much work to do. Some of the rose beds had been dug up and gravelled over. The soil was choked in weeds. The hedges were tatty. He looked out of the kitchen window, eighty-two years old, his face drawn long by the fact that he couldn't nurture the place any more.

He was long retired from the newspaper. In fact, the newspaper itself was long retired from the world – the whole Irish Press group had gone bankrupt in the 1990s.

I went outside and started to pull up the weeds. The work felt fresh to me. My father stayed at the downstairs window most of the time, but by the end of the first day he was outside, standing on the doorstep.

'Would you stop doing that for crissake?' he said, looking at the deep cuts on my hands, my arms, my scalp.

The next day he stood out in the garden, leaning on a blue walker in a light rain, as I ferried in among the roses, getting thorned again. 'It's looking better,' he said, 'but jaysus you don't have to do it, we can hire someone in, you've got other things to do. Just leave it.'

The following day he had a glass of wine in his hands. On the fifth day, when the garden had begun to look fresh – and therefore ancient – my father got down on his hands and knees and started weeding in the flower bed alongside me.

It may have stretched towards parody – *by God the man could handle a shovel, just like his old man* – but there was something acute about it, the desire to come home, to push the body in a different direction to the mind, the need to be tired alongside him in whatever small way, the emigrant's necessity to root around in the old soil.

A month later, back in New York, I ended up with a case of

osteomyelitis, a bone infection that laid me up in hospital for a couple of weeks. Morphine every morning, an odd rozziner. And then two more months of antibiotics.

The doctor said I had possibly gotten the illness from a recent wound.

It was likely, he explained, that some dirt got into a cut on my hands, that it had travelled through me, migrated to my blood, my tissue, my bone. ∎

arvon | INSPIRES
THE FOUNDATION FOR CREATIVE WRITING

2010 WRITING COURSES

Take the time and space to write on one of our new 2010 residential writing courses and retreats.

At one of Arvon's historic country houses, our glittering line up of writers will inspire and guide you in your poems, novels, songs, plays, graphic novels and scripts.

Featuring Hilary Mantel, Carol Ann Duffy, Ray Davies, Philip Hoare, Michael Holroyd, Jen Hadfield, Allegra Huston, Jez Butterworth, Lenny Henry, Chika Unigwe, Olive Senior and many others.

As always, grants are available for writers on low incomes. See our website for full details.

For more information call 020 7324 2554 or visit **www.arvonfoundation.org**

GRANTA

Any Man's Death

Kent Haruf

My first hospice patient was an old man who was dying of lung cancer. He had three dogs – a pit bull, a Dalmatian and a little fat female of mixed breeds. The first time I went to see him he was sitting on the couch at the front of his house and as soon as I came in the room the three dogs set up a hellacious uproar. I sat down beside him and the pit bull and the Dalmatian were right in my face. I had to use the old man's metal walker to ward them off. Finally they got off the couch and the old man and I began to talk.

Meanwhile his wife, a very short wrinkled old woman, stood off to the side in her stained sweatshirt and jeans and a pair of his old slippers with the backs run down. She stood watching us and jabbering the whole time. The old man paid no attention to her. She spoke very accented English and I could barely understand her. He had married her in the early 1950s in post-war Italy and brought her to the States.

After that day I went to see the old man – I'll call him George and his wife Lena – twice a week, every week, for a year and a half. After the first couple of months he got a little better, the cancer went into some form of temporary remission and he went off hospice service officially, but I carried on seeing him as before.

One time when George was still so sick and weak in that first month of my visiting him, he was lying in bed in the dingy rear bedroom and I went to see him. The dogs were in the room. One of the dogs, the pit bull they called Jackie, was up in the bed with him, walking over his chest and stomach, over his lungs which I understood were filled up with cancer. It looked painful as hell to me. But the dog wouldn't get off. So I grabbed the dog by its collar and dragged him off, and in the process I dragged George from the bed too. George and his oxygen tube and the dog and the covers all came piling off on to the hardwood floor. A hell of a deal. But George didn't say anything about it and neither did Lena. They both looked as if being dragged out on to the floor was what happened to you in life.

George and I spent a lot of time talking. That is, he talked a lot and I did a lot of listening. He told me about growing up in this little town. His father was an immigrant and had been brought out here with many others from Pennsylvania to work for the railroad. George had worked for the railroad too, in the round house. He'd also worked out in the valley hoeing weeds in the lettuce fields as a boy. I'd never heard there were lettuce fields in this part of Colorado. We're up at 7,000 feet elevation; I didn't know you could grow lettuce here commercially.

He told me about the evenings when he was sixteen and played cards with the famous local madam, Laura Evans, and how he made a comment one time about the big diamond ring she was wearing, and she said, This little chicken shit? You should see what I have in the bank. His folks didn't like him playing cards with a prostitute but he did anyway, and then ran home along the river in the dark past the house that was supposed to have a ghost in it.

He told me he had been in the army in the 1950s and that was when he had met Lena. She was very poor, practically shoeless, and he had married her and brought her over to America. It was his opinion that he had done her a considerable favour. She worked very hard for more than thirty years in housekeeping at the local hospital and also in the restaurant George owned, getting up when it was still dark to start things in the kitchen before she went to work at the hospital. They were always in a struggle financially. George gave away a great deal of money out of true kindness and out of the desire to be known as a generous man.

They never had any children, though I believe they wanted some. Their dogs were their children. George wanted my help with them while he was dying and after he had died. Lena felt the same way.

It was about the middle of that year when Jackie, their pit bull, got sick and they called me early in the morning to do something. The dog had been defecating all over the place and couldn't stop. So I hurried out to the country to see the veterinarian, with Lena in the back seat holding the dog on her lap, weeping over it. It's all right, Jackie, she kept saying. It's all right, honey.

When we got there, the vet knew right away that the dog had parvo and had to be put down. Its stomach and intestines were all eaten up. I explained this to Lena and she began to wail and cry. I put my arms around her. Finally she patted the dog a last time and I was able to get her back into the car and we returned to the house, leaving the vet to inject the dog after we'd gone. At the house George was in his pyjamas at the kitchen table and he sat looking at me while I told him. The tears trickled down his old face and dammed up behind his glasses. I never got to tell Jackie goodbye, he said. I wanted to tell him goodbye.

Lena stood at the sink and started crying again too. I felt like crying myself, even though the dog had been a problem for me; I had finally taught it to leave me alone by tapping it on the nose with George's cane.

They had a shrine out in the backyard for the dogs that had died previously. George had built the thing out of green transparent roofing sheets – a little room with roof and walls and red outdoor carpeting, and with the dogs' names on the plastic headstones that George had ordered out of a catalogue. There was a chair out there too, so you could sit and remember the dogs that had died and say some prayers. Jackie was going to be cremated and his ashes were going to be buried in the shrine, and George said when the time came for him to die he wanted half of his ashes buried with the dogs' ashes.

During all this time I took George to the bathroom and helped him dress and undress, helped him with those private matters. There was never any embarrassment about any of it, as far as I could tell. And I remember him walking towards me down the hall of his little house with the oxygen tube trailing along and the dogs running around and getting mixed up in the tubing and nearly pulling him down.

I took him to the doctor a few times for examinations. In the waiting room he knew all the old people and greeted them and asked about their families. He seemed to rouse himself and started being very friendly and courtly. The doctor who examined him, unlike most doctors, talked to him about his emotional and spiritual health as well as his cancer. George told the doctor, I pray not to be afraid. I pray not to have pain. I pray for my friends. The doctor said, This is my prayer for you. By that he meant his care for George and the examination and visit that day.

George got sick again and went to the hospital for a few days, and he came home, but then he got pneumonia and had to go back to the hospital. Lena visited him and his friends came to see him. He and the old men sat around and talked about past times. The friends hadn't come while he was sick at home. That had bothered him a lot. We talked about it, and there was no good explanation. Now in the hospital many people came to see him. He seemed to be at peace and, as it turned out, that was the end; he never came home again.

My wife and I got the call in the night that you expect and dread. The nurse, a man named Don, said, I have the sad duty to inform you that George Merlino has died. It was about 3 a.m. I called Lena to say he'd died and that we'd take her to the hospital. She screamed, I got to get dressed. I got to get my clothes. I got to get my clothes.

We drove into town and picked her up – I thought she would have dressed in black, but she was wearing her old sweatshirt and jeans, as usual – and we took her up to the hospital room. George was lying flat in the bed. He was small now, reduced, barely a bump under the cotton blanket. His face was yellow, pale. His eyes were closed and sunken. His mouth sagged open, dark, quiet. No teeth. His nose looked sharpened and his hair was stiff and bush-like. Lena wailed and patted his face and went over and over his face and over his shoulders, and blamed the doctor for not doing enough. My wife and I put his teeth back in. We sat with Lena until she was ready to leave. She cried for an hour, finally saying, I'm all alone now. I got nobody now.

Then we went out of the room and the mortician came and took him away. We drove Lena home and sat with her another hour. The dogs were crazy at first, then they calmed down.

There was a Mass at the Catholic church for George and a small graveside service, and there was an honour guard of old men in tight uniforms who shot off some blanks and marched around in a sharp way, and one of them gave Lena a folded flag, and that was it.

Since George's death, I see Lena about every two or three weeks. Not long ago I had to go with her to have the fat little female dog put down. So she has only the Dalmatian left. She calls him Spot. She feeds him like a child. She herself has lost weight lately because of her bad teeth, but Spot is as fat as a steer. He sits up in the chair at the front window, looking out at the street. She cooks dinner for him. Last Thanksgiving she cooked a full turkey dinner for him with all the trimmings.

And now in the summer she gives my wife and me Italian green beans that she's grown in her garden by the dog shrine, not far from George's and Jackie's ashes and the plastic headstones of all the dogs. ∎

Gift subscription offer: take out an annual subscription as a gift and you will also receive a complimentary *Granta* special-edition **MOLESKINE**® notebook

GIFT SUBSCRIPTION 1

Address:

TITLE: INITIAL: SURNAME:

ADDRESS:

POSTCODE/ZIP:

TELEPHONE: EMAIL:

GIFT SUBSCRIPTION 2

Address:

TITLE: INITIAL: SURNAME:

ADDRESS:

POSTCODE/ZIP:

TELEPHONE: EMAIL:

YOUR ADDRESS FOR BILLING

TITLE: INITIAL: SURNAME:

ADDRESS:

POSTCODE/ZIP:

TELEPHONE: EMAIL:

NUMBER OF SUBSCRIPTIONS	DELIVERY REGION	PRICE	All prices include delivery
	UK/USA	£34.95/$45.99	YOUR TWELVE-MONTH SUBSCRIPTION WILL INCLUDE FOUR ISSUES
	Europe/Canada	£39.95/$57.99	
	Rest of World	£45.95/$65.99	

PAYMENT DETAILS

☐ I enclose a cheque payable to '*Granta*' for £/$_____ for_____ subscriptions to *Granta*

☐ Please debit my ☐ MASTERCARD ☐ VISA ☐ AMEX for £/$_____ for_____ subscriptions

NUMBER ☐☐☐☐ ☐☐☐☐ ☐☐☐☐ ☐☐☐☐   SECURITY CODE ☐☐☐

EXPIRY DATE ☐☐ / ☐☐   SIGNED_____ DATE

☐ Please tick this box if you would like to receive special offers from *Granta*
☐ Please tick this box if you would like to receive offers from organizations selected by *Granta*

Please return this form to: **Granta Subscriptions, PO Box 2068, Bushey, Herts, WD23 3ZF, UK,**
call Freephone 0500 004 033 if paying in £ or go to **www.granta.com**

Please return this form to: **PO Box 359, Congers, NY 10920-0359, call toll-free 1-866-438-6150**
if paying in $ or go to **www.granta.com**

Please quote the following code if ordering online: **BU109SC**

Harmony

Julian Barnes

They had dined well at no. 261 Landstrasse, and now passed eagerly into the music room. M—'s intimates had sometimes been fortunate enough to have Gluck, Haydn or the young prodigy Mozart perform for them; but they could be equally content when their host seated himself behind his violoncello and beckoned at one of them to accompany him. This time, however, the lid of the klavier was down, and the violoncello nowhere visible. Instead, they were confronted by an oblong rosewood box standing on legs which made the shape of matching lyres; there was a wheel at one end and a treadle beneath. M— folded back the curved roof of the contraption, disclosing three dozen glass hemispheres linked by a central spindle and half-submerged in a trough of water. He seated himself at the centre and pulled out a narrow drawer on either side of him. One contained a shallow bowl of water, the other a plate bearing fine chalk.

'If I might make a suggestion,' said M—, looking round at his guests. 'Those of you who have not yet heard Miss Davies's instrument might try the experiment of closing your eyes.' He was a tall, well-made man in a blue frock coat with flat brass buttons; his features, strong and jowly, were those of a stolid Swabian, and if his bearing and voice had not obviously denoted the gentry, he might have been taken for a prosperous farmer. But it was his manner, courteous yet persuasive, which impelled some who had already heard him play to decide to close their eyes as well.

M— soaked his fingertips in water, flicked them dry and dabbled them in the chalk. As he pumped at the treadle with his right foot, the spindle turned on its bright brass gudgeons. He touched his fingers to the revolving glasses, and a high, lilting sound began to emerge. It was known that the instrument had cost fifty gold ducats, and sceptics among the audience at first wondered why their host had paid so much to reproduce the keening of an amorous tomcat. But as they became accustomed to the sound, they started to change their minds. A clear melody was becoming detectable: perhaps something of M—'s own composition, perhaps a friendly tribute to, or even theft from, Gluck. They had never heard such music before, and the fact that they were blind to the method by which it came to them emphasized its strangeness. They had not been told what to expect and so, guided only by their reasoning and sentiment, wondered if such unearthly noises were not precisely that – unearthly.

When M— paused for a few moments, busying himself on the hemispherical glasses with a small sponge, one of the guests, without opening his eyes, observed, 'It is the music of the spheres.'

M— smiled. 'Music seeks harmony,' he replied, 'just as the human body seeks harmony.' This was, and at the same time was not, an answer; rather than lead, he preferred to let others, in his presence, find their own way. The music of the spheres was heard when all the planets moved through the heavens in concert. The music of the earth was heard when all the instruments of an orchestra played together. The music of the human body was heard when it too was in a state of harmony, the organs at peace, the blood flowing freely and the nerves aligned along their true and intended paths.

The encounter between M— and Maria Theresia von P— took place in the imperial city of V— between the winter of 177– and the summer of the following year. Such minor suppressions of detail would have been a routine literary mannerism at the time; but they also tactfully admit the partiality of our knowledge. Any philosopher claiming that his field of understanding was complete, and that a final, harmonious synthesis of truth was being offered to the reader, would have been denounced as a charlatan; and likewise those philosophers of the human heart who deal in storytelling would have been – and would be – wise not to make any such claim either.

We can know, for instance, that M— and Maria Theresia von P— had met before, a dozen years previously; but we cannot know whether or not she had any memory of the event. We can know that she was the daughter of Rosalia Maria von P—, herself the daughter of Thomas

Cajetan Levassori della Motta, dance master at the imperial court; and that Rosalia Maria had married the imperial secretary and court counsellor Joseph Anton von P— at the Stefanskirche on 9th November 175–. But we cannot tell what the mixing of such different bloods entailed, and whether it was in some way the cause of the catastrophe that befell Maria Theresia.

Again, we know that she was baptized on 15th May 175–, and that she learned to place her fingers on a keyboard almost as soon as she learned to place her feet on the floor. The child's health was normal, according to her father's account, until the morning of 9th December 176–, when she woke up blind; she was then three and a half years old. It was held to be a perfect case of amaurosis: that is to say, there was no fault detectable in the organ itself, but the loss of sight was total. Those summoned to examine her attributed the cause to a fluid with repercussions, or else to some fright the girl had received during the night. Neither parents nor servants, however, could attest to any such happening.

Since the child was both cherished and well born, she was not neglected. Her musical talent was encouraged, and she attracted the attention and the patronage of the Empress herself. A pension of two hundred gold ducats was granted to the parents of Maria Theresia von P—, with her education separately accounted for. She learned the harpsichord and pianoforte with Kozeluch, and singing under Righini. At the age of fourteen she commissioned an organ concerto from Salieri; by sixteen she was an adornment of both salons and concert societies.

To some who gawped at the imperial secretary's daughter while she played, her blindness enhanced her attraction. But the girl's parents did not want her treated as the society equivalent of a fairground novelty. From the start, they had continually sought her cure. Professor Stoerk, court physician and head of the Faculty of Medicine, was regularly in attendance, and Professor Barth, celebrated for his operations on cataract, was also consulted. A succession of cures was tried, but as each failed to alleviate the girl's condition, she became prone to irritation and melancholia, and was assailed by fits which caused her eyeballs to bulge from their sockets. It might have been predictable that the confluence of music and medicine brought about the second encounter between M— and Maria Theresia.

M— was born at Iznang on Lake Constance in 173–. The son of an episcopal gamekeeper, he studied divinity at Dillingen and Ingolstadt, then took a doctorate in philosophy. He arrived in V— and became a doctor of law before turning his attention to medicine. Such an intellectual peripeteia did not, however, indicate inconstancy, still less the soul of a dilettante. Rather M— sought, like Dr Faustus, to master all forms of human knowledge; and, like many before him, his eventual purpose – or dream – was to find a universal key, one that would permit the final understanding of what linked the heavens to the earth, the spirit to the body, all things to one another.

In the summer of 177–, a distinguished foreigner and his wife were visiting the imperial city. The lady was taken ill, and her husband – as if such were a normal medical procedure – instructed Maximilian Hell, astronomer (and member of the Society of Jesus) to prepare a magnet which might be applied to the afflicted part. Hell, a friend of M—'s, kept him informed of the commission; and when the lady's ailment was said to be cured, M— hastened to her bedside to inform himself about the procedure. Shortly thereafter, he began his own experiments. He ordered the construction of numerous magnets of different sizes, some to be applied to the stomach, others to the heart, still others to the throat. To his own astonishment, and the gratitude of his patients, M— discovered that cures beyond the prowess of a physician could sometimes be effected; the cases of Fräulein Oesterlin and the mathematician Professor Bauer were especially noted.

Had M— been a fairground quack, and his patients credulous peasants crowded into some rank booth, as eager to be relieved of their savings as of their pain, society would have paid no attention. But M— was a man of science, of wide curiosity, and not obvious immodesty, who made no claims beyond what he could account for.

'It works,' Professor Bauer had commented, as his breath came more easily and he was able to raise his arms beyond the horizontal. 'But how does it work?'

'I do not yet understand it,' M— had replied. 'When magnets were employed in past ages, it was explained that they drew illness to them just as they attracted iron filings. But we cannot sustain such an argument nowadays. We are not living in the age of Paracelsus. Reason guides our thinking, and reason must be applied, the more so when we are dealing with phenomena which lurk beneath the skin of things.'

'As long as you do not propose to dissect me in order to find out,' replied Professor Bauer.

In those early months, the magnetic cure was as much a matter of scientific enquiry as of medical practice. M— experimented with the positioning and number of magnets applied to the patient. He himself often wore a magnet in a leather bag around his neck to increase his influence, and used a stick, or wand, to indicate the course of realignment he was seeking in the nerves, the blood, the organs. He magnetized pools of water and had patients place their hands, their feet and sometimes their whole bodies in the liquid. He magnetized the cups and glasses they drank from. He magnetized their clothes, their bedsheets, their looking glasses. He magnetized musical instruments so that a double harmony might result from their playing. He magnetized cats, dogs and trees. He constructed a *baquet*, an oaken tub containing two rows of bottles filled with magnetized water. Steel rods emerging from holes in the lid were placed against afflicted parts of the body. Patients were sometimes encouraged to join hands and form a circle round the *baquet*, since M— surmised that the magnetic stream might augment in force as it passed through several bodies simultaneously.

Of course I remember the *ghädige Fräulein* from my days as a medical student, when I was sometimes permitted to accompany Professor Stoerk.' Now M— was himself a member of the faculty, and the girl was almost a woman; plump, with a mouth that turned down and a nose that turned up. 'And though I can recall the description of her condition then, I would nonetheless like to ask questions which I fear you have answered many times already.'

'Of course.'

'There is no possibility that the Fräulein was blind from birth?'

M— noticed the mother impatient to reply, but restraining herself.

'None,' her husband said. 'She saw as clearly as her brothers and sisters.'

'And she was not ill before becoming blind?'

'No, she was always healthy.'

'And did she receive any kind of shock at the time of her misfortune, or shortly before?'

'No. That is to say, none that we or anyone else observed.'

'And afterwards?'

This time the mother did answer. 'Her life has always been as protected against shock as we are able to make it. I would tear out my own eyes if I thought it would give Maria Theresia back her sight.'

M— was looking at the girl, who did not react. It was probable that she had heard this unlikely solution before.

'So her condition has been constant?'

'Her blindness has been constant,' the father again. 'But there are periods when her eyes twitch convulsively and without cease. And her eyeballs, as you may see, are extruded, as if trying to escape their sockets.'

'You are aware of such periods, Fräulein?'

'Of course. It feels as if water is slowly rushing in to fill my head, as if I shall faint.'

'And she suffers in the liver and the spleen afterwards. They become disorderly.'

M— nodded. He would need to be present at such an attack – to guess its causes and observe its progress. He wondered how that might best be effected.

'May I ask the doctor a question?' Maria Theresia had lifted her head slightly towards her parents.

'Of course, my child.'

'Does your procedure cause pain?'

'None that I inflict myself. Though it is often the case that patients need to be brought to a certain…pitch before harmony can be restored.'

'I mean, do your magnets cause electric shocks?'

'No, that I may promise you.'

'But if you do not cause pain, then how can you cure? Everyone knows that you cannot remove a tooth without pain, you cannot set a limb without pain, you cannot cure insanity without pain. A doctor causes pain, that the world knows. And that I know too.'

Since she had been a small child the finest doctors had applied the most effective methods. There had been blistering and cauterizing and the application of leeches. For two months her head had been encased in a plaster designed to provoke suppuration and draw the poison from her eyes. She had been given countless purges and diuretics. And most recently, electricity had been resorted to, and over the twelvemonth some three thousand electric shocks had been administered to her eyes, sometimes as many as a hundred in a single treatment.

'You are quite sure that magnetism will not cause me pain?'

'Quite sure.'

'Then how can it possibly cure me?'

M— was pleased to glimpse the brain behind the unseeing eyes. A passive patient, merely waiting to be acted upon by an omnipotent physician, was a tedious thing; he preferred those like this young woman, who displayed forcefulness behind her good manners.

'Let me put it this way. Since you went blind, you have endured much pain at the hands of the best doctors in the city?'

'Yes.'

'And yet you are not cured?'

'No.'

'Then perhaps pain is not the only gateway to cure.'

In the two years he had practised magnetic healing, M— had constantly pondered the question of how and why it might work. A decade previously, in his doctoral thesis *De planetarum influxu*, he had proposed that the planets influenced human actions and the human body through the medium of some invisible gas or liquid, in which all bodies were immersed, and which for want of a better term he called *gravitas universalis*. Occasionally, man might glimpse the overarching connection, and feel able to grasp the universal harmony that lay beyond all local discordance. In the present instance, magnetic iron arrived on earth in the form and body of a meteor fallen from the heavens. Once here, it displayed its singular property, the power to realign. Might one not surmise, therefore, that magnetism was the great universal force which bound together stellar harmony? And if so, was it not reasonable to expect that in the sublunary world it had the power to placate certain corporeal disharmonies?

It was evident, of course, that magnetism could not cure every bodily failing. It had proved most successful in cases of stomach ache, gout, insomnia, ear trouble, liver and menstrual disorder, spasm, and even paralysis. It could not heal a broken bone, cure imbecility or syphilis. But in matters of nervous complaint, it might often effect startling improvement. Again, it could not overcome a patient mired in scepticism and disbelief, or one whose pessimism or melancholy undermined the possibility of a return to health. There must be a willingness to admit and welcome the effects of the procedure.

To this end, M— sought to create, in his consulting rooms at 261 Landstrasse, an atmosphere sympathetic to such acceptance. Heavy curtains were drawn against the sun and external noise; his staff were forbidden from making sudden movements; there was calm and candlelight. Gentle music might be heard from another room; sometimes M— would himself play upon Miss Davies's glass armonica, reminding both bodies and minds of the universal harmony that he was, in this small part of the world, seeking to restore.

M— commenced his treatment on 20th January 177–. An external examination confirmed that Maria Theresia's eyes showed severe malformation: they were quite out of their normal alignment, grossly swollen and extruded. Internally, the girl seemed to be at a pitch where the passing phases of hysteria might lead to chronic derangement. Given that she had suffered fourteen years of disappointed hope, and fourteen years of unremitting blindness, this was not an unreasonable response from a young body and mind. M— therefore began by emphasizing again how different his procedure was from all others; how it was not a matter of order being reimposed by external violence, but rather of a collaboration between doctor and patient, aimed at re-establishing the natural alignment of the body. M— talked generally; in his experience it did not help for the patient to be constantly aware of what was to be expected. He did not speak of the crisis he hoped to provoke, or predict the extent of the cure he envisioned. Even to the girl's parents, he expressed only the humble ambition of alleviating the gross ocular extrusion.

He explained his initial actions carefully, so they would come as no surprise. Then he addressed the loci of sensitivity on Maria Theresia's head. He placed his hands, formed into cups, around her ears; he stroked her skull from the base of the neck to the forehead; he placed his thumbs on her cheeks, just below the eyes, and made circular motions around the affected orbs. Then he gently laid his stick, or wand, on each eyebrow, before repeating the pattern of actions with his hands. As he did so, he quietly encouraged Maria Theresia to report any changes or movements she experienced within her. Then he placed a magnet on each temple. Immediately, he felt a sudden sensation of heat upon her cheeks, which the girl confirmed; he also observed a redness in the skin and a trembling of the limbs. She then described a gathering force at the base of her neck which was compelling her head backwards and upwards. As these movements occurred, M— noted that the spasms in her eyes were more marked and at times convulsive. Then, as this brief crisis came to its end, the redness left her cheeks, her head resumed its normal position, the trembling ceased, and it appeared to M— that her eyes were in a better alignment, and also less swollen.

He repeated the procedure each day at the same time, and each day the brief crisis led to an evident improvement, until by the end of the fourth day the proper alignment of her eyes had returned and no extrusion was to be remarked. The left eye appeared to be smaller than the right, but as the treatment continued, their sizes began to balance. The girl's parents were amazed: M—'s promise had been fulfilled, and their daughter no longer showed the deformity which might alarm those who watched her play. M—, however, was already preoccupied with the patient's internal condition, which he judged to be moving towards the necessary crisis. As he continued his daily procedures, she reported the presence of sharp pains in the occiput which penetrated the whole of her head. The pain then followed the optic nerve, producing constant pinpricks as it travelled and multiplied across the retina. These symptoms were accompanied by nervous jerkings of the head.

For many years, Maria Theresia had lost her sense of smell, and her nose had produced no mucus. Now, suddenly, there was a visible swelling of the nasal passages, and a forceful discharge of green, viscous matter. Shortly afterwards, to the patient's further embarrassment, there were additional discharges, this time in the form of copious diarrhoea. The pains in her eyes continued, and she reported feelings of vertigo. M— recognized that she was at a time of maximum vulnerability. A crisis was never a neutral occurrence: it might be benign or malign – not in its nature, but in its consequences, leading either to progress or to regress. He therefore proposed to the girl's parents that she take up residence for a short period at 261 Landstrasse. She would be looked after by M—'s wife, though she might bring her own maid if necessary. There were already two young female patients established in the household, so questions of decorum need not arise. This new plan was swiftly agreed.

On Maria Theresia's second day in the house, and still in the presence of her father, M—, after touching her face and skull as before, placed the patient in front of a mirror. Taking his wand, he pointed it at her reflection. Then, as he moved the wand, the girl's head slightly turned, as if following its movements in the glass. M— sensed that Herr von P— was about to give tongue to his astonishment, and quieted him with a gesture.

'You are aware that you are moving your head?'

'I am.'

'Is there a reason why you are moving your head?'

'It is as if I am following something.'

'Is it a noise that you are following?'

'No, it is not a noise.'

'Is it a smell that you are following?'

'I still have no sense of smell. I am merely…following. That is all I can say.'

'It is enough.'

M— assured Herr von P— that his house would always be open to him and his wife, but that he expected progress in the ensuing days to be slow. In truth, he judged the girl's cure more likely if he could treat her without the presence of a father who struck him as overbearing, and a mother who, perhaps by reason of her Italian blood, seemed liable to hysteria. It was still just possible that Maria Theresia's blindness was caused by atrophy of the optic nerve, in which case there was nothing that magnetism, or any other known procedure, could do for her. But M— doubted this. The convulsions he had witnessed, and the symptoms reported, all spoke of a disturbance to the whole nervous system due to some powerful shock. In the absence of any witnesses at the time, or of the patient's memory, it was impossible to determine what kind of shock it might have been. This did not perturb M— unduly: it was the effect he was treating, not the cause. Indeed, it might be fortunate that the Fräulein could not recall the precise nature of the precipitating event.

In the preceding two years, it had become increasingly apparent to M— that in bringing the patient to the necessary point of crisis, the touch of the human hand was of central, animating importance. At first, his touching of the patient at the moment of magnetism was designed to be calming, or at best emphatic. If, for instance, magnets were placed on either side of the ear, it seemed a natural gesture to stroke that ear in a manner confirming the realignment being sought. But M— could not help observing that when all favourable conditions for cure had been created, with a circle of patients around the *baquet* in the soft candlelight, it was often the case that when he, as a musician, removed his fingers from the rotating glass armonica and then, as a physician, laid them on the afflicted part of the body, the patient might be instantly brought to crisis. M— was at times inclined to ponder how much was the effect of the magnetism, and how much that of the magnetizer himself. Maria Theresia was not apprised of such wider considerations, any more than she was asked to join other patients around the oaken tub.

'Your treatment causes pain.'

'No. What is causing pain is that you are beginning to see. When you look in the mirror you see the wand I am holding and turn your head to follow it. You say yourself that there is a shape moving.'

'But you are treating me. And I am feeling pain.'

'The pain is a sign of a beneficial response to the crisis. The pain shows that your optic nerve and retina, so long abandoned from use, are becoming active again.'

'Other doctors have told me that the pain they were inflicting was necessary and beneficial. You are a doctor of philosophy as well?'

'I am.'

'Philosophers can explain anything away.'

M— took no offence, indeed was pleased with such an attitude.

Such was the girl's susceptibility to light that he had to bind her eyes with a triple bandage, which remained in place at all times when she was not being treated. He had begun by presenting to her, at a certain distance, objects of the same kind which were either white or black. She was able to perceive the black objects without distress, but flinched at the white objects, reporting that the pain they produced in her eyes was like that of a soft brush being drawn across the retina; they also provoked a sense of giddiness. M— therefore removed all the white objects.

Next, he introduced her to the intermediate colours. Maria Theresia was able to distinguish between them, though unable to describe how they appeared to her – except for the colour black, which was, she said, the picture of her former blindness. When the colours were ascribed their names, she often failed to apply the correct name the next time a colour was shown. Nor was she able to calculate the distance objects were from her, imagining them all to be within reach; thus she extended her hands to pick up items twenty feet away. It was also the case, in these early days, that the impression an object left upon her retina lasted for up to a minute. She was obliged, therefore, to cover her eyes with her hands until the impression faded, else it would become confused with the next object presented to her view. Further, since the muscles of the eye had fallen into disuse, she had no practice at moving her gaze, searching for objects, focusing upon them and accounting for their position.

Neither was it the case that the elation felt by both M— and the girl's parents when she first began to perceive light and forms was shared by the patient herself. What had come into her life was not, as she had expected, a panorama of the world so long concealed from her, and so long described by others; still less was there an understanding of that world. Instead, a greater confusion was now heaped upon the confusion that already existed – a state exacerbated by the ocular pains and feelings of vertigo. The melancholia that was the obverse of her natural cheerfulness came much to the fore at this time.

Understanding this, M— resolved to slow the pace of his treatment; also, to make the hours of leisure and rest as pleasant as possible. He encouraged intimacy with the other two young women living in the household: Fräulein Ossine, the eighteen-year-old daughter of an army officer, who suffered from purulent phthisis and irritable melancholia; and the nineteen-year-old Zwelferine, struck blind at the age of two, whom M— had found in an orphanage and was treating at his own expense. Each had something in common with one of the others: Maria Theresia and Fräulein Ossine were both of good family and imperial pension-holders; Maria Theresia and Zwelferine were both blind; Zwelferine and Fräulein Ossine were both given to the periodic vomiting of blood.

Such company was a useful distraction; but M— believed that Maria Theresia also needed several hours in the day when there was a peaceful and familiar routine. He therefore took to sitting with her, talking of subjects far from her immediate concern, and reading to her from his library. Sometimes they would play music together, she with bandaged eyes at the klavier, he on the violoncello.

He also used this time to know the girl better, to assess her truthfulness, her memory, and her temperament. He noted that even when her spirits ran high, she was never headstrong; she showed neither the arrogance of her father, nor the wilfulness of her mother.

He might ask, 'What would you like to do this afternoon?'

And she would reply, 'What do you propose?'

Or he might ask, 'What would you like to play?'

And she would reply, 'What would you like me to play?'

When such courtesies were finished with, he discovered that she had clear opinions, arrived at through the use of reason. But he also concluded that, even beyond the normal obedience of children, Maria Theresia was accustomed to doing as she was instructed; by her parents, her teachers, her doctors. She played beautifully, with a fine memory, and it seemed to M— that it was only when she was at the klavier, immersed in a piece familiar to her, that she truly felt free, and allowed herself to be playful, expressive, thoughtful. It struck him, as he watched her profile, her bandaged eyes and her firm, upright posture, that his enterprise was not without some danger. Was it possible that her talent, and the pleasure she evidently took in it, might be tied to her blindness in a way he could not fully understand? And then, as he followed her hands moving in their practised, easy manner, sometimes strong and springy, at others as leisurely as ferns wafted by a breeze, he found himself wondering how the first sight of a keyboard might affect her. Might the white keys throw her into turmoil, the black ones remind her only of blindness?

Their daily work continued. So far, Maria Theresia had been presented with a mere sequence of static objects: his concern had been to establish and accustom her to shape, colour, location, distance. Now he decided to introduce the concept of movement, and with it the reality of a human face. Though she was well used to M—'s voice, he had so far always kept out of her lines of perception. Gently, he undid the bandages, asking her immediately to cover her eyes with her hands. Then he came round to face her, placing himself at a distance of a few feet. Telling her to take away her hands, he began slowly turning his head from one profile through to its opposite.

She laughed. And then placed the hands she had removed from her eyes back over her mouth. M—'s excitement as a physician overcame his vanity as a man that he should provoke such a reaction in her. Then she took her hands from her mouth, placed them over her eyes, and after a few seconds released them and looked at him again. And laughed again.

'What is that?' she asked, pointing.

'This?'

'Yes, that.' She was giggling to herself in a manner which, in other circumstances, he would have judged uncivil.

'It is a nose.'

'It is ridiculous.'

'You are the only person cruel enough to have made that observation,' he said, pretending to be piqued. 'Others have found it acceptable, even agreeable.'

'Are all...noses like that?'

'There are differences, but, charming Fräulein, I must warn you that this is by no means anything out of the ordinary, as far as noses go.'

'Then I shall have much cause for laughter. I must tell Zwelferine about noses.'

He decided on an additional experiment. Maria Theresia had always enjoyed the presence, and the affection, of the house dog, a large, amiable and unthreatening beast of uncertain species. Now M— went to the curtained door, opened it slightly and whistled.

Twenty seconds later, Maria Theresia was saying, 'Oh, a dog is a much more pleasing sight than a man.'

'You are, sadly, not alone in that opinion.'

There followed a period when her improving sight led to greater cheerfulness, while her clumsiness and error in the face of this newly discovered world drew her down into melancholy. One evening M— took her outside into the darkened garden and suggested that she tip her head backwards. That night the heavens were blazing. M— briefly found himself thinking: black and white again, though happily much more black than white. But Maria Theresia's reaction took any anxiety away. She stood there in astonishment, head back, mouth open, turning from time to time, pointing, not saying a word. She ignored his offer to identify the constellations; she did not want words to interfere with her sense of wonder, and continued looking until her neck hurt. From that evening on, visual phenomena of any distinction were automatically compared to a starry sky – and found wanting.

Though each morning M— continued his treatment in exactly the same way, he now did so with a kind of feigned concentration. Within himself he was debating between two lines of thought, and between two parts of his intellectual formation. The doctor of philosophy argued that the universal element which underlay everything had surely now been laid bare in the form of magnetism. The doctor of medicine argued that magnetism had less to do with the patient's progress than the power of touch, and that even the laying on of hands was merely emblematic, as was the application of magnets and of the wand. What was actually happening was some collaboration or complicity between physician and patient, so that his presence and authority were permitting the patient to cure herself. He did not mention this second explanation to anyone, least of all the patient.

Maria Theresia's parents were as astonished by the improvement in their daughter as she was by the starry heavens. As the news spread, friends and well-wishers began to turn up at 261 Landstrasse to witness the miracle. Passers-by often lingered outside the house, hoping to glimpse the famous patient; while requests for her physician's attendance at sickbeds across the city arrived each day. At first M— was happy to allow Maria Theresia to demonstrate her ability to distinguish colours and shapes, even if some of her naming was not yet faultless. But such performances palpably tired her, and he severely restricted the number of visitors. This sudden ruling had the effect of increasing both the rumours of miracle-working and the suspicions harboured by some fellow members of the Faculty of Medicine. The case was also beginning to make the Church uneasy, since the popular understanding was that M— had only to touch the afflicted part of a sick person for the sickness to be healed. That anyone other than Jesus Christ might effect a cure by the laying on of hands struck many of the clergy as blasphemous.

M— was aware of these rumours, but felt confident in the backing of Professor Stoerk, who had come to 261 Landstrasse and been officially impressed by the effect of the new cure. What then did it matter if other members of the faculty muttered against him, or even dropped the slander that his patient's new-found ability to name colours and objects might be the result of close training? The conservative, the slow-witted and the envious existed in every profession. In the longer term, once M—'s methods were understood and the number of cures increased, all men of reason would be obliged to admit and embrace the curative powers of magnetism.

One day, when Maria Theresia's state of mind was at its calmest, M— invited her parents to attend him that afternoon. He then proposed to his patient that she take up her instrument, unaccompanied and unbandaged. She enthusiastically agreed, and the four of them proceeded to the music room. Chairs were set out for Herr von P— and his wife, while M— took a stool close to the klavier, the better to observe Maria Theresia's hands, eyes and moral condition. She took several deep breaths and then, after a barely endurable pause, the first notes of a sonata by Haydn fell upon their ears.

It was a disaster. You might have thought the girl a novice and the sonata a piece she had never played before. The fingering was inept, the rhythms flawed; all grace and wit and tenderness vanished from the music. When the first movement stumbled to a confused halt, there was silence; M— could sense the parents exchanging glances. Then, suddenly, the same music began again, now confidently, brightly, perfectly. He looked across at the parents, but they in turn had eyes only for their daughter. Turning towards the klavier, M— realized the cause of this sudden excellence: the girl had her eyes tightly closed and her chin raised high above the keyboard.

When Maria Theresia reached the end of the movement, she opened her eyes, looked down and went back to the beginning. The result, again, was chaos, and this time M— thought he guessed the reason: she was following her hands transfixedly. And it seemed that the very act of watching was destroying her skill. Fascinated by her own fingers, and the way they moved across the keyboard, she was unable to bring them under her full control. She observed their disobedience until the end of the movement, then rose and ran to the door.

There was a silence.

Eventually, M— said, 'It is to be expected.'

Herr von P—, red with anger, replied, 'It is a catastrophe.'

'It will take time. Every day there will be an improvement.'

'It is a catastrophe. If news of this gets out, it will be the end of her career.'

Unwisely, M— put the question, 'Would you rather your daughter could see, or could play?'

Herr von P—, now choleric, rose, with his wife beside him. 'It was not, sir, a choice I remember you offering us when we brought her to you.'

After they had left, M— found the girl in a deplorable condition. He sought to reassure her, telling her that it was no surprise that the sight of her fingers disconcerted her playing.

'If it was no surprise, why did you not warn me?'

He reminded her that her sight had been improving on an almost daily basis, and so it was inevitable that her playing would also improve, once she became accustomed to the presence of her fingers on the keys.

'That is why I played the piece a third time. And it was even worse than the first.'

M— did not argue the point. He knew from his own experience how, in matters of art, the nerves occupied a vital part. If you played badly, your spirits fell; if your spirits were low, you played worse – and so, decliningly, on. Instead, M— pointed to the wider improvement in Maria Theresia's condition. This did not satisfy her either.

'In my darkness, music was my entire consolation. To be brought out of darkness and then lose the ability to play would be cruel justice.'

'That will not happen. It is not a choice. You must trust me that it will not be the case.'

He looked at her, and followed the development, and the departure, of a frown. Eventually, she replied, 'Apart from the matter of pain, you have always been worthy of trust. What you have said might happen has happened. Therefore, yes, I trust you.'

In the following days, M— was made aware that his earlier dismissal of the outside world's opinion had been naive. A proposal arrived from certain members of the Faculty of Medicine that endorsement of the practice of magnetic healing should only be given if M— could reproduce his effects with a new patient, under full lighting and in the presence of six faculty scrutineers – conditions which would, M— knew, destroy its effectiveness. Satirical tongues were already asking if in the future all doctors would be equipped with magic wands. More dangerously, some were questioning the moral wisdom of the procedure. Did it help the status and respectability of the profession if one of their number took young women into his household, cloistered them behind drawn curtains, and then laid hands upon them amid jars of magnetized water and to the caterwauling of a glass armonica?

On 29th April 177–, Frau von P— was shown into M—'s study. She was clearly agitated, and refused to sit down.

'I have come to remove my daughter from you.'

'Has she indicated that she wishes to cease her treatment?'

'*Her* wishes... That remark is an impertinence. *Her* wishes are subordinate to her parents' wishes.'

M— looked at her calmly. 'Then I shall fetch her.'

'No. Ring for a servant. I do not wish you to instruct her how to answer.'

'Very well.' He rang; Maria Theresia was fetched; she looked anxiously from one to the other.

'Your mother wishes you to cease treatment and return home.'

'What is your opinion?'

'My opinion is that if this is what you wish, then I cannot oppose it.'

'That was not what I asked. I was asking your medical opinion.'

M— glanced across at the mother. 'My...medical opinion is that you are still at a precarious stage. I think it very possible that a complete cure may be effected. Equally, it is very possible that any gains made, once lost, could never be recovered.'

'That is very clear. Then I choose to stay. I wish to stay.'

The mother instantly began a display of stamping and shouting, the like of which M— had never before encountered in the imperial city of V—. It was an outburst far beyond the natural expression of Frau von P—'s Italian blood, and might even have been comical, had not her nervous frenzy set off an answering spasm of convulsion in the daughter.

'Madam, I must ask you to control yourself,' he said quietly.

But this enraged the mother even more, and with two sources of provocation in front of her, she continued to denounce her daughter's insolence, stubbornness and ingratitude. When M— tried to lay a hand on her forearm, Frau von P— turned on Maria Theresia, seized her and threw her headlong into the nearest wall. Above the women's screams, M— summoned his staff, who held back the termagant just as she was about to set upon M— himself. Suddenly, another voice was added to the bedlam.

'Return my daughter! Resist me and you die!'

The door was thrown violently open, and Herr von P— himself appeared, a framed figure with sword aloft. Hurling himself into the study, he threatened to cut anyone who opposed him to pieces.

'Then, sir, you will have to cut me to pieces,' M— answered firmly.

Herr von P— stopped, uncertain whether to attack the doctor, rescue his daughter or console his wife. Unable to decide, he settled for repeating his threats. The daughter was weeping, the mother screaming, the physician attempting to argue rationally, the father noisily promising death and mayhem. M— remained dispassionate enough to reflect that the young Mozart would have happily set this operatic quartet to music.

Eventually, the father was pacified and then disarmed. He departed with malediction on his tongue, and seeming to forget his wife, who stood for a few moments looking from M— to her daughter and back again, before herself leaving. Immediately, and for the rest of the day, M— sought to calm Maria Theresia. As he did so, he came to conclude that his initial presumption had been confirmed: Maria Theresia's blindness had certainly been a hysterical reaction to the equally hysterical behaviour of one or both of her parents. That a sensitive artistic child, in the face of such an emotional assault, might instinctively close herself off from the world seemed reasonable, even inevitable. And the frenzied parents, having been responsible for the girl's condition in the first place, were now aggravating it.

What could have caused this sudden, destructive outburst? More, surely, than a mere flouting of parental will. M— therefore tried to imagine it from their point of view. A child goes blind, all known cures fail until, after more than a dozen years, a new physician with a new procedure begins to make her see again. The prognosis is optimistic, and the parents are rewarded at last for their love, wisdom and medical courage. But then the girl plays, and their world is turned upside down. Before, they had been in charge of a blind virtuoso; now, sight had rendered her mediocre. If she continued playing like that, her career would be over. But even assuming that she rediscovered all her former skill, she would now lack the originality of being blind. She would be merely one pianist among many others. And there would be no reason for the Empress to continue her pension. Two hundred gold ducats had made a difference to their lives. And how, without it, would they commission works from leading composers?

If M— understood such a dilemma, it could not be his primary concern. He was a physician, not a musical impresario. In any case, he was convinced that once Maria Theresia became accustomed to the sight of her hands on a keyboard, once observation ceased altering her performance, her skill would not merely return, but develop and improve. For how could it possibly be an advantage to be blind? Furthermore, the girl had chosen openly to defy her parents and continue the cure. How could he disappoint her hopes? Even if it meant distributing cudgels to his servants, he would defend her right to live under his roof.

Yet it was not just the frenzied parents who were threatening the household. Opinion at court and in society was now turning against the physician who walled up a young woman and refused to return her to her parents. That the girl herself also refused did not help M—'s case: in the eyes of some it merely confirmed him as a magician, a bewitcher whose hypnotic powers might not cure, but could certainly enslave. Moral fault and medical fault intertwined, giving birth to scandal. Such a miasma of innuendo arose in the imperial city that Professor Stoerk was provoked into action. Withdrawing his previous endorsement of M—'s activities, he now wrote, on 2nd May 177–, demanding that M— cease his 'imposture' and return the girl.

Again, M— refused. Maria Theresia von P—, he replied, was suffering from convulsions and delirious imaginings. A court physician was sent to examine her, and reported to Stoerk that in his opinion the patient was in no condition to be sent back. Thus reprieved, M— spent the next weeks devoting himself entirely to her case. With words, with magnetism, with the touch of his hands, and with her belief in him, he succeeded in bringing her nervous hysteria under control within nine days. Better still, it became evident that her perception was now sharper than at any previous time, suggesting that the pathways of the eye and brain had become strengthened. He did not yet ask her if she wanted to play; nor did she suggest it.

M— knew that it would not be possible to keep Maria Theresia von P— until she was fully cured, but did not wish to surrender her until she had acquired sufficient robustness to hold the world at bay. After five weeks of siege, an agreement was reached: M— would return the girl to her parents' care, and they would allow M— to continue treating her as and when it might be necessary. With this peace treaty in place, Maria Theresia was handed over on 8th June 177–.

That was the last day on which M— saw her. At once, the von P—s reneged on their word, keeping their daughter in close custody, and forbidding all contact with M—. We cannot know what was said, or done, in that household, we can know only its predictable consequences: Maria Theresia von P— relapsed immediately into blindness, a condition from which she was not to emerge in the remaining forty-six years of her life.

We have no account of Maria Theresia's anguish, of her moral suffering and mental reflection. But the world of constant darkness was at least familiar to her. We may presume that she gave up all hope of cure, and also of escape from her parents; we may know that she took up her career again, first as pianist and singer, then as composer, and eventually as teacher. She learned the use of a composition board invented for her by her amanuensis and librettist, Johann Riedinger; she also owned a hand printing machine for her correspondence. Her fame spread across Europe; she knew sixty concertos by heart, and played them in Prague, London and Berlin.

As for M—, he was driven from the imperial city of V— by the Faculty of Medicine and the Committee to Sustain Morality, a combination which ensured that he was remembered there as half-charlatan, half-seducer. He withdrew first to Switzerland and then established himself in Paris. In 178–, seven years after they had last seen one another, Maria Theresia von P— came to perform in the French capital. At the Tuileries, before Louis XVI and Marie Antoinette, she introduced the concerto Mozart had written for her.

She and M— did not meet; nor can we tell if either of them would have desired such a meeting. Maria Theresia lived on in darkness, usefully, celebratedly, until her death in 182–.

M— had died nine years previously, at the age of eighty-one, his intellectual powers and musical enthusiasm both undiminished. As he lay dying at Meersburg, on the shores of Lake Constance, he sent for his young friend F—, a seminarist, to play for him on the glass armonica which had accompanied him on all his travels since he left 261 Landstrasse. According to one account, the pangs of his dying were soothed by listening for the last time to the music of the spheres. According to another, the young seminarist was delayed, and M— died before F— could touch his chalky fingers to the rotating glass. ■

Ponte City

Work in Progress

*Mikhael Subotzky
and Patrick Waterhouse*

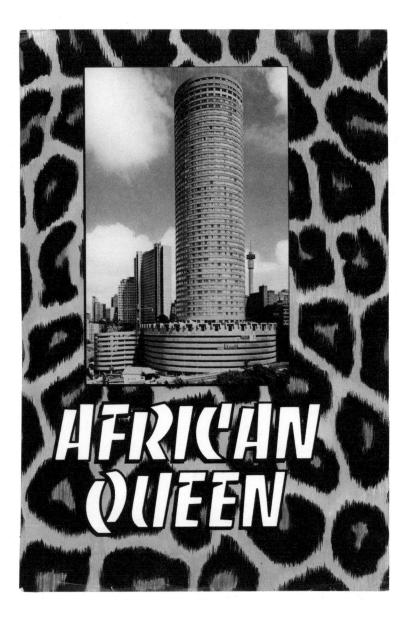

AFRICAN QUEEN

The fifty-four-storey Ponte City building dominates Johannesburg's skyline, its huge blinking advertising crown visible from Soweto in the south to Sandton in the north. When it was built in 1976 – the year of the Soweto uprisings, a symbolic and evocative year for all South Africans – the surrounding flatlands of Berea, Hillbrow and Yoeville were exclusively white, and home to young middle-class couples, students and Jewish grandmothers. Ponte City was separated by apartheid urban planning from the unforgettable events of that year. But as the city changed in anticipation and response to the arrival of democracy in 1994, many residents joined the exodus towards the supposed safety of the northern suburbs, the vacated areas becoming associated with crime, urban decay and, most of all, the influx of foreign nationals from neighbouring African countries.

Ponte's iconic structure soon became a symbol of the downturn in central Johannesburg. The reality of the building and its many fictions has always integrated seamlessly into a patchwork of myths and projections that reveals as much about the psyche of the city as it does about the building itself. Tales of brazen crack and prostitution rings operating from its car parks, four storeys of trash accumulating in its open core, snakes, ghosts and frequent suicides have all added to the building's legend. Some of these stories are actually true, and for quite some time most of the residents were indeed illegal immigrants. And yet, one is left with the feeling that even the building's notoriety is somewhat exaggerated – that its decline is just as fictionalized as its initial utopian intentions were misplaced and unrealized.

In 2007 the building was bought by developers, but by late 2008 their ambitious attempt to refurbish and revitalize Ponte had failed spectacularly. They went bankrupt after promising to spend three hundred million rand on their vision for the building. Their aim was to target a new generation of aspirant middle-class residents – young, upwardly mobile black professionals, business people from across the

African continent, and all those seeking chic Manhattan-style inner-city living. The developer's website still describes how 'In every major city in the world, there is a building where most can only dream to live. These buildings are desirable because they are unique, luxurious, iconic. They require neither introduction nor explanation. The address says it all.'

The developers emptied half the building and stripped the apartments of everything, throwing all their rubble into the structure's central core. They started to redesign the flats with a variety of exotic themes – 'Future Slick', 'Old Money' and 'Glam Rock' – but their financing required sales up front and these, it seems, failed to materialize in sufficient numbers for the construction costs and occupational rental to be maintained.

When we started our work there in 2008, the development was in full swing. The building felt like a shell, its bottom half completely empty, and the top half sparsely populated. Former residents moved out in a hurry to make way for the developers. Many of their apartments were then burgled and trashed. Months later, when the development had failed, we entered room after room where the floors were covered in piles of broken possessions, torn photographs and scattered paperwork. We would walk the corridors, through whole floors of empty flats, and then suddenly hear children shouting, the fizz and smell of frying fish, and then, briefly, voices and running water as we passed the bathroom and kitchen windows that face the passageways. But these spectres disappeared as quickly as they had come, leaving us to wander through wrecked apartments, corridors and dark stairwells. We met many of the remaining residents in the lifts where we asked to make portraits of those who were willing. When we brought copies back to their apartments, doors opened to all kinds of living arrangements – whole families in bachelor flats, empty carpeted rooms with nothing but a mattress and a giant television console, and penthouses divided up with sheets and appliances into four or five living spaces.

By the end of 2008, Ponte's old owners had repossessed the building and started the mammoth task of cleaning it up and refitting the stripped apartments. Another cycle in the building's life had begun before the last illusions of a grand future could be erased. The posters and graphics advertising 'New Ponte' still hang in the hallway, passed daily by many residents who still think that this is what their building will become.

We started to work systematically, visiting each apartment to request a picture of the door and of the windows – we will eventually stitch these images into giant internal and external panoramas. As we proceeded with this task, we noticed that almost everybody was watching their television sets, seemingly ignoring the spectacular views that attracted us to their windows. So we joined them, and would spend hours in front of old Rambo movies, Congolese sitcoms, music videos and Nollywood dramas. All the stories from Ponte's past were there before us – the druglords and the gangsters, the shoot-outs and the prostitutes, the ghosts and the voodoo magic – not in the building itself, where young people and families went about their lives calmly, but on the hundreds of screens that were stacked above each other, flat by flat and floor by floor.

Ponte has always been a place of myth, illusion and aspiration. This is what we seek to evoke in these preparatory pages. Perhaps this task is best left to the images that we have found there – both in the abandoned flats, and in the marketing material and advertising that we have collected from 1976 and from 2008. When these documents are seen next to the dystopian appearance of the building and its surroundings, one begins to project an image of the city during this time. It is a place of dust and dreams, befitting the land on which it sits, and which has attracted millions of migrants since gold was discoverd in the 1880s. People are still drawn here from all over the continent in search of better lives for themselves and their families. But the gold, in all its incarnations, inevitably fulfils the dreams of so few. All around them, those who service this passion are scattered in a modern metropolis – pinning their dreams to the flashing signs which crest the city and some of its buildings. ■

Ponte City: Photographs

Mikhael Subotzky

and

Patrick Waterhouse

'Ponte is Africa. You can find the whole
of Africa in Ponte. In South Africa there
are eleven tribes… All of them in Ponte you
would find. Nigerians you would find,
Congolese you would find, Zimbabweans,
everything. Everybody is talking their
language. Ponte, she's just Africa.'

– Nozipho

Vacuum

Brad Watson

The mother told the boys that she was much unappreciated in this house. She was just like a slave. She pushed the vacuum cleaner back and forth on the floor at their feet where they sat on the sofa. They had been trying to watch a western show on the black-and-white television set before she had turned on the vacuum and begun to shout her words over its howling motor. I am the only person who does anything around here, she shouted, yanking the vacuum cleaner back and forth. I cook, I clean, I wash, I go to work and bring home what little money we have and nobody helps. I am just like a slave but I'll tell you one thing – and she turned off the vacuum cleaner over whose howl the boys had heard nothing but had sat there watching her bewildering expressions, her wide eyes and wide-open mouth – ONE OF THESE DAYS I AM GOING TO WALK OUT OF THIS HOUSE AND NEVER COME BACK.

The mother let the vacuum-cleaner handle fall to the floor with a bang and she stomped into the kitchen where she had been frying a chicken. The boys really wanted to see what was going to happen in the western show, but now they had missed it because they had been watching their mother make faces and then yell that one day she would walk out of the house and never come back. And then they stopped watching the commercial that was coming on because they heard a banging and a clatter and a loud hissing sound in the kitchen, and saw a large cloud of steam and smoke, because the mother had burned her chicken and had tumped her pan into the sink and now she came stomping past them toward the back of the house saying that they could Eat What They Wanted, She Didn't Care.

The boys went outside in the gloaming while mosquitoes whined around their bare shoulders, and talked about how they could keep their mother from walking out of there one day and never coming back. The youngest boy said they could trap her in her room, because that's what the older brothers did to him whenever they didn't want

him to follow them or get in their way. The oldest brother called him a moron and said they couldn't trap their mother in her room because she was a grown-up and grown-ups couldn't be trapped in their rooms by their own boys. The middle brother said the point was that they wanted to keep their mother, not lock her away from them because she was a pest, which was why they would sometimes lock up the youngest brother. I mean, yeah, she wouldn't be able to get away, he said, but it's just not the point. The oldest brother said, All right, you're both morons. Then the middle brother suggested they get one of the other families' maids to come down and help with some of the household chores in their house and make it easier on their mother. The older brother thought about this for a second, then said, What are we going to pay them with?

If it was Rosie, the middle brother said, we could pay her in dirt.

All the brothers knew that the Harbours' maid, Rosie, was a dirt-eater, and so they considered this solution for long enough to decide that they would sleep on it. They went back into the house, which had chicken-oil smoke hanging up around the ceiling, and made themselves bologna sandwiches on white bread with lots of salad dressing mayonnaise and ate them in front of the television and went to bed at a reasonable hour, as that seemed the honourable thing to do. From the crack between their mother's bedroom door and the flooring there came a steady drifting wisp of cigarette smoke and the sounds of muttering and weeping as they filed by to their own room in the rear of the house and went to bed.

It was summertime and the next morning after the mother went to work, the boys pulled on pairs of shorts and crossed the street to the vacant lot there and dug some premium blue-veined, hard clay and put about a dozen good waxy chunks into a paper sack. Then they walked up the hill to the Harbours' house to see the maid, Rosie, about their proposition. One of the Harbour twins, Derrick, was in the side yard in the sandbox digging a hole. He was far too old to be playing in a sandbox but they knew better than to ask him about it. Besides, he wasn't playing; he was digging a hole, as if to excavate the sandbox.

What do you want? he said to the boys. We want to talk to Miss Rosie about some chores, the youngest brother said. Talk to her about whatever you want, the Harbour twin said, but don't call her Miss Rosie. Why not? Because she's a nigger, the Harbour twin said. You don't call a nigger woman 'Miss', you idiot.

He's right, the oldest brother said.

If you had a maid, you'd know that, the Harbour twin said.

We had a maid, the middle brother said.

Shut up, the oldest brother said.

That's right, the Harbour twin said. And then your old man knocked her up, and got sued, and almost got the nigger maid hung by the Ku Klux Klan, and got cut in the gizzard by the nigger maid's nigger lover, who had to run off or get hung by the Ku Klux Klan, and lost his job, and ran off.

He didn't run off, the middle brother said.

Shut up, the oldest brother said.

He didn't run off, the middle brother said, he's a travelling salesman.

He sure is, the Harbour twin said.

The boys knocked on the carport entrance to the Harbours' house, the door that went straight into the kitchen, which was where they knew Rosie was most likely to be, unless she was off in the house somewhere vacuuming.

She was not. She was at the kitchen window, and saw them before she even heard them knock, and they saw her face brighten. Rosie had been their maid before their father had fired her in order to hire the younger, prettier maid whom he had then knocked up and all the trouble started, but Rosie didn't hold it against the boys.

My babies! she said, swinging wide the kitchen door. Come on in this house. What you doing, coming to see me? She said this as if she were getting on to them, like, Did she get on to you about it? But they could tell she was still very happy to see them.

Rosie was stout but not round, except in her face. She was tall, and kept her hair back in a tight little bun, and wore a clean blue maid's

uniform with a white collar. She had flat feet you could see because when she worked around the house she liked to go barefoot and the pink flat soles of her long feet slapped against the cool linoleum and hardwood floors. The middle brother remembered once, when he had asked her about it, she'd said, I like cool feets.

We brought you some dirt, the middle brother said, handing her the sack.

Mm-hmm, I see, Rosie said, looking into the sack. It's some of that good dirt from the bank across the street from your house, by them blackberry bushes.

Yes, ma'am, said the middle brother.

The older brother popped him hard between his shoulder blades, and he shut up.

We were wondering if you wouldn't come down to our house and help out a little bit, the oldest brother said.

Rosie, who had been peering again into the sack of dirt, looked up and raised an eyebrow.

I don't know if I know what you mean, since your daddy fired me two years back and hired that trash to come in and take my place.

They had to be careful now as it was clear she was getting her dander up.

Mama's been having a hard time with having to work her job at the clinic and clean the house and cook supper and all that, the middle brother said. We were just hoping we could get her a little help at it.

Rosie frowned and looked into the sack full of dirt again. She was maybe thinking that if she had to go to work and then go home and do those things, then why couldn't that white woman go to work and then go home and do those things? If her children had to help out with the chores around the house while she was at work, then why couldn't that white woman's children help out with the chores while she was at work? She might have said those things right out if she thought anybody would've listened, and if she didn't have a soft spot for these boys because she practically raised them. She was about to say something when the little brother said something.

He said, Rosie, are you a nigger?

Rosie's face changed, and pulled into itself, and her eyes glinted. What? she said. What did you say?

She was looking at the youngest brother, and then at all three of them, as if she had never seen them before and was mystified, and if they hadn't been so mystified themselves by the expression on her face, they might have been smart enough to leave right away, but they weren't – or they were. Mystified.

I said, the youngest brother said before the other two brothers, still too stunned to act quickly, could stop him, are you a nigger?

I'm not a nigger, Rosie said. Niggers is dogs. Don't you come in here calling me a nigger.

She began to straighten up her kitchen by throwing some things into the sink and some things from the drainer back into the cabinet, making a loud clatter and banging.

I tell you what, she went on. You can get your lazy good-for-nothing selves out of this house and back down there where you want me to come and you do them chores yourself. My children would never sit around while they mama did all the work. Did, they wouldn't be sittin' for a long time I'd wear them out so good. You git on.

The boys had not moved while she spoke to them and banged around but when she stopped for a moment, they began to sidle out of the Harbours' kitchen door. As they were going out Rosie said to the middle brother, I can see them other two being like that but not you. I thought you had better sense than that. The middle brother, who wished she wouldn't do that because he hated being the goody-goody and she was making him look like the goody-goody again, said, Well, I don't.

You can all get on out of here, then, she said. We will, they said. And you can take this dirt, she said, I don't want it. I don't need your dirt. She stood there shaking the paper bag at them but the boys ignored her and kept walking.

Shut up, Rosie, said the Harbour twin who had been standing with his shovel in the sandbox, watching all this.

Don't you tell me to shut up, young'un, Rosie said.

I will if I want to, the Harbour twin said.

You just wait till your daddy gets home, Rosie said, and after that the boys paid no more attention and were soon out of earshot back down the street.

Way to go, igmo, the oldest brother said to the youngest brother.

That night when the boys' mother came home from work again she was not mad like the night before but she still looked swollen-faced and didn't say much while she cooked a pound of bacon and made them bacon-and-tomato sandwiches on white bread with salad dressing mayonnaise and she cut them all into triangle halves and stacked them on a plate, which she set down on the table. Then she asked the middle brother to say the blessing and after that they played the game where they all sat there waiting for her to say go before they started grabbing sandwich halves and eating them as fast as they could. The mother didn't eat any of the sandwiches herself though, and went to her bedroom again as soon as she'd done the dishes and shut the door.

The next day the boys decided to try something else. The only other person they thought they could go to for advice was old Dr Hornegay up the street who was retired from the charity hospital. Every other grown-up who lived on the street was either at work, or a coloured maid, or a white woman friend of their mother's. They couldn't ask help of their mother's white woman friends because it might make their mother ashamed. And Dr Hornegay might have some old medicine lying around that would make their mother feel better. So they waited until Dr Hornegay had time to get up and about, then went up there and knocked on the door that led to the den from the carport. In a minute the door cracked open and Dr Hornegay's old white-bearded face appeared in the crack, wearing a pair of one-armed spectacles on his red-and-blue nose that was the shape of a deformed, dried-out potato. His white hair was flattened in some places and pointed straight out at others. What can I do for you boys? he finally said.

We know you're not a doctor anymore, the oldest brother said, but we thought you might have some old medicine left lying around.

Once a doctor, always a doctor, Dr Hornegay said, and coughed. He opened the door on up and stood there, wearing an old cracked pair of leather slippers on his white feet, a stinking-looking pair of pyjama bottoms, and a tartan robe that had no belt. He fished a non-filter Camel from a packet in the breast pocket of the robe and lit it with a match and blew a cloud of smoke out over their heads where they stood in the carport looking up at him. The boys were astonished at the amount of grey-and-white-speckled hair on his stomach and chest. It was as if he was wearing squirrel pelts there or something. It was hard not to stare. The middle brother looked past Dr Hornegay into the den. He was hoping for a sight of Dr Hornegay's wife, whom no one had seen in years because, word was, Dr Hornegay's wife was ridden down by sadness and an extra 150 pounds and no longer came up out of their basement. The only thing the middle brother could see in the den was a stretched-out La-Z-Boy, on the headrest of which lay a scrawny yellow cat, looking right back at him.

What would you need medicine for? Dr Hornegay said then, scratching at the squirrel pelts.

The brothers told him they needed it for their mother, who was afflicted with sadness and rage and who was threatening to walk out of their house and never come back. Is there a medicine for that? the youngest brother asked.

Plenty, Dr Hornegay said. He laughed as if to himself. Oh ho, yeah, lots of tinctures and remedies for that malady. What time does your mama get off work?

About five, the middle brother said.

I'll be down at six, Dr Hornegay said, and closed the door gently in their faces.

I don't know, the middle brother said as they walked back down to their house. If he can't do anything to help his own wife, how's he going to help her? Meaning their mother.

The only thing wrong with Doc Hornegay's old fat wife is she's a drunk, the oldest brother said. Who told you that? the middle brother said. Everybody knows that, the oldest brother said, you igmo. Yeah,

the youngest brother said. You didn't know that, the middle brother said to him. I did, too, the youngest brother said, you igmo.

That afternoon when the mother came home, the boys were all three sitting in a row on the sofa in the den with their hair combed, their shirt tails tucked in, their shoes on and their shoelaces tied. My goodness, their mother said, to what do I owe the honour? The boys smiled at her and kept their mouths shut. She stopped where she was, standing beside the kitchen table, holding the sack of groceries she'd picked up on the way home from work, and looked at them. What are y'all up to? she asked then. Nothing, the oldest brother said. The middle brother and the youngest brother shook their heads and said nothing. The mother set the bag of groceries carefully down on the kitchen counter, as if its contents were very fragile, and looked at the boys as if they were hiding something like a bomb or a stray cat or a snake somewhere in their clothing, and with that expression on her face and her jaw cocked in curiosity, she walked past them, looking at them sideways, and went down the hallway to her bedroom to do whatever she did before she got started on cooking their supper.

One thing they knew she did was change out of her nurse's uniform and put on regular clothes. And maybe pee. She wore a crisp white uniform even though she was not a nurse, but she worked in the paediatric clinic as one of the ladies at the reception station and did some kind of paperwork back in the office area behind the reception station. The boys just figured that the doctors at the paediatric clinic liked for all the ladies who worked there to look like nurses, whether they were or not. They didn't know why the doctors might want it that way but on the other hand it seemed to make a kind of sense, though they couldn't say just what kind of sense it might be. That was for the grown-ups, and they didn't really have to worry about it, or think about it, and so they didn't.

The mother came back into the den and stopped short when she saw that the boys were still sitting on the sofa. She folded her arms and looked at them for a few seconds before saying, I know something is up. What have you done? What's wrong?

Nothing's wrong, I promise, the oldest brother said. The other two brothers kept their mouths shut, as they'd agreed to do, and after looking at them suspiciously for another long minute, the mother turned and walked slowly into the kitchen. She was most likely thinking that maybe they had broken a window she hadn't noticed yet, or destroyed the mechanisms inside an appliance, or gotten caught stealing something or destroying something somewhere else and were waiting either to tell her about it or to be visited by the injured party, coming to inform her that because of what her boys had done that day she must pay them a certain sum of money in order to repair or replace what was missing or destroyed.

And then she looked out the window and saw Dr Hornegay walking up their driveway into the carport carrying a bunch of flowers and a bottle of something inside a paper sack, and wearing a suit and tie.

Oh, God, she said to herself, and then louder she said to the boys, What did you do to Dr Hornegay?

When she heard nothing she looked over at the sofa. The boys were still sitting there and staring at her as if they were not only mute but deaf, or like dogs being spoken to and unsure what the tone of the person's words meant, that clap-mouthed momentary attentive interim between daydreaming and the next distraction. Or like children in the convenience store who, having just slipped candy bars into their pockets, were looking at the clerk with expressions that were the most balanced and perfect combination of innocence and guilt.

The mother was fairly bewildered. Between the looks on her boys' faces and the appearance of Dr Hornegay in her carport, now at her carport side door, the den door, and ringing the bell, and dressed in a suit and tie and carrying a bunch of flowers and a bottle of something inside a paper sack, she felt a strange unintelligible flutter of panic.

What have you done? she said again to the boys, who did not hear this because she said it in a voice just barely above a whisper.

When she opened the door, Dr Hornegay stepped back with the flowers and bottle in his hand and made a deep bow. Good evening,

my dear, Dr Hornegay said. You look lovely as ever. It's been far too long since we've had the pleasure of your company.

Their mother did not open the screen door but said through it, Hello, Dr Hornegay, what can I do for you?

For me? Dr Hornegay said, and laughed as if to himself, looking off toward the street and heaving something of a sigh, as if he were suddenly a little pleasantly saddened by something, maybe the thought of how he'd never gotten rich like the doctors their mother worked for down at the paediatric clinic, or how his wife had gotten so sad that she gained 150 pounds and moved into their basement and now couldn't get out, or how he himself couldn't go anywhere now since the police had taken away his driver's licence after he'd run into a telephone pole on the way home from the Traveller's Club out on the highway. Or maybe it was something way back; whatever it was he had done that had banished him to the charity hospital in the first place.

Madam, you need do nothing for me, Dr Hornegay finally said after his long melancholy pause. The question is, what can I do for you?

For me? their mother said. I'm sorry, Dr Hornegay, but there's nothing wrong with me.

No? Dr Hornegay said, looking surprised and most perplexed, but in a playful way. Well, your fine boys there, and he gestured with the hand that held the bottle in the paper sack toward the brothers still sitting on the sofa in the den behind her, those precocious, compassionate young men of yours, said that you were afflicted with a grievous sadness, and I, madam, am the doctor, here to cheer you up.

Their mother then turned a look on the brothers – still sitting very still on the sofa – that they had never seen before. The look was so thrillingly unfamiliar and so deliciously terrifying that it was all they could do not to yelp and cower or leap off of the sofa and run out into the yard. But they were, in effect, paralysed by the look and remained very still, and only their expressions changed, from attentive curiosity and expectation to attentive and paralysed, panicked delight.

May I be so bold Dr Hornegay said then, and he opened the screen

door with the little finger of the hand holding the bottle in the paper sack and held the flowers toward their mother with the other hand. Their mother took the flowers and said thank you in a voice that was neither here nor there in terms of being grateful and pleased or puzzled and annoyed, and then she said, What's in the sack?

Only some of the finest bourbon made in the great southern state of Kain-tuck, Dr Hornegay said, and with a flourish he removed from the sack by its neck a bottle of Old Crow whiskey.

Oh, my, it's been a long time since I've had a drink of anything like that, their mother said.

The boys knew this was true, that the only person drinking anything like that around their house for the last few months before their father left for his job as a long-haul travelling salesman was their father himself and sometimes, during the daytime when she was supposed to be washing or ironing or vacuuming the house and watching them, the good-looking young maid who would soon enough cause so much trouble for herself and everyone else. They knew that the only thing to drink around the house nowadays was their mother's jug of kosher Manischewitz, which she rarely sampled and which she kept not because she was Jewish (she was raised a Methodist) but because it was the only wine around their town that wasn't wino wine like Boone's Farm or that other one that you often saw actual winos clutching as they staggered down the street or lay in the gutter behind Woolworths downtown until the police found them and hauled them down to the pokey to sleep it off and then work it off sweeping the very gutters they had been passed out in the day before.

Too long, madam, too long, Dr Hornegay said, gently slipping past their mother into the den and giving the boys a nod and a wink where they sat on the sofa. He made his way to the little dining table just outside the kitchen. The bigger, nicer table where they ate their special meals like Thanksgiving and Christmas was in the formal dining room, which also had a fancy sofa and two fancy stuffed chairs and a hi-fi, but which was almost never used or even entered, in order to keep it clean and neat for the next special occasion.

I'll have a drink with you, their mother was saying to Dr Hornegay, who had helped himself to a couple of small glasses from the cupboard and some ice from the freezer and set the glasses of ice and the bottle of Old Crow down on the little dining table. She said, I'll have a drink, but then I have to cook supper.

Oh, pish posh, Dr Hornegay said with a courtly gesture of one hand. I'd be willing to wager that these boys would love to have a simple repast, something we could order over the telephone – my treat, he said. Turning to the boys, he said, Boys, tell me if I'm wrong, but I'd be willing to wager that you wouldn't turn down a sack of Mrs Benson's hot tamales, am I correct?

You sure are, you bet, the boys said, piping up but sticking to their spots on the sofa as if glued there by their pants.

The mother said she would think about it while she had her drink with Dr Hornegay, and in the meantime she allowed the boys to watch television. The oldest boy got up and turned on the set and they began watching a different episode of the same western they had been watching the day their mother had threatened to leave. At first they partly watched the western and partly watched their mother and Dr Hornegay having a drink and talking. Then Dr Hornegay offered their mother one of his Camel cigarettes, and they both began to smoke along with their drinking and talking, and Dr Hornegay was offering to call in an order to Mrs Benson for the hot tamales but pouring himself and their mother more drinks first, and the boys became more distracted by the western. Dr Hornegay and their mother were becoming louder and were laughing and the smoke from their cigarettes created a beautiful haze of gently swirling blue in the hanging lamp above the table, but all of this had moved into that part of the boys' brains that resembled the waking equivalent of a dream, there but not there, attached to but somewhat removed from their primary consciousness.

Outside the big sliding glass door beside the dining table where their mother and Dr Hornegay sat drinking and smoking and talking and laughing, the darkly silver night began to creep again into the sky,

and the greens of the grass and the unkempt shrubbery on the hill
behind the house also darkened softly.

In the den, in the failing light outside the penumbra of the hanging
lamp where their mother and Dr Hornegay sat, the animated light
from the television set trembled, flickered, and leapt about the room.

Ooo, damn, the oldest brother whispered to the others, all three of
them with their eyes on the western programme. How does he jump
off the top of a house like that and land on the horse and not rack his
balls?

I don't see how, the youngest brother said.

You don't even have balls yet, the oldest brother said.

I do, too.

I see how he could do it, the middle brother said.

Bull, the oldest brother said.

I do. It's all in how you land. You have to land with your legs
squeezed up, and back on your butt a little bit.

Slightly, the oldest brother said. You're so full of crap.

I'll show you, the middle brother said.

Stay in the yard; don't wander off up the street, their mother called
as they filed out of the carport door.

The oldest brother helped the middle brother extract their old
rocky horse, which was actually a springy horse, from the storage room
built just off the carport and set it up in the grass just below the lowest
overhang of the roof there, then the oldest brother helped the middle
brother up on to the eaves by cupping his palms together and boosting
the middle brother's foot, and the middle brother was half tossed, half
self-hoisted up on to the roof and he turned and squatted and looked
down at the faces of his older brother and younger brother where they
stood on either side of the springy horse, looking up at him in the softly
failing light.

He knew, all of a sudden, what a fool he was, how badly hurt he was
going to be if he stuck to his guns and made the leap on to the back of
the springy horse from where he now squatted on the roof. His first
idea was to leap and pretend to miss the horse, and maybe then he

would only twist his ankle. His second idea was to suggest that the youngest brother try it first, since he didn't have balls yet, not really anyway, and the oldest brother and the middle brother could also check the youngest brother's landing when he arrived at the plastic saddle of the springy horse, and control it all.

And then he thought he would cry, because he was flooded once again, for the first time in a long time, with the shameful memory of something he had done to the youngest brother one time when they were being watched by Rosie, back when she was their maid and the oldest brother was in school but the middle and youngest brother were both still too young to be in school. It was a warm afternoon and they were all three out in the yard, the two brothers in shorts with no shoes or shirts, and Rosie, who sat on the low retaining wall between their yard and the next while the youngest brother and the middle brother played in the grass nearby. Rosie, who wore a maid's uniform that was not unlike their mother's nurse's uniform except it was blue instead of white, was reading the newspaper where she sat a few feet away. Looking down into the thick St Augustine grass, the middle brother spied something gleaming and picked it up. It was a toy razor blade, double-edged. He knew it was a toy razor blade because it was so easy to bend back and forth.

Look, he announced, I found a toy razor blade.

Rosie, biting at a fingernail, glanced over at him and wrinkled her brow. She was trying to finish something she was reading in the newspaper and didn't really want to be disturbed in order to deal with some foolishness on his part.

Put that thing down, she said, before you hurt yourself.

I can't hurt myself, the middle brother said. It's a toy.

It's not a toy, Rosie said, it's a razor blade, young'un, you put it down.

It's not a real razor blade, the middle brother said. I'll prove it.

He walked over to the youngest brother, who had been niggling with his finger at a worm or roly-poly in the grass, not hearing any of this, and he ran the edge of the razor blade down the length of the youngest brother's sun-browned, naked back, following the bumpy line of the

youngest brother's spine.

A bright red line of blood jumped from his brother's back and began to bead and run down in crooked trails. The middle brother dropped the razor blade and stepped back, and he screamed just as Rosie dropped her newspaper and began to shout, and a moment later the youngest brother, turning in a circle like a dog after his tail and trying to see what had happened to his back that was making everyone scream and shout, began to scream and cry, and the middle brother fell down into the grass, bawling and striking the ground with his fists, blubbering out, I didn't mean it, I didn't mean it, I thought it was a toy.

Remembering this now as he squatted on the roof, looking down into the youngest brother's irritating but inarguably innocent face, the middle brother felt the same terrible wave of shame he'd felt just after slicing open the youngest brother's back three years before, and he felt a heartbreaking longing, also, for the presence of Rosie, who had never been afflicted with sadness, and had always been cheerful except when she was mad, and she was never mad for longer than it took her to get the madness out, and then she was always and ever her regular self again, and it had always brightened his spirits to see how she could be such a normal person, even though she was coloured, even though a maid, even though he knew quite well she must miss her own children while she spent her whole long day there taking care of them, him and his brothers, who didn't appreciate her at all. And now, just today, they had called her a nigger. He might as well have said it, too. The only thing he could do, now, was to jump.

He landed perfectly, which didn't make any difference because two of the springs suspending the horse in its frame snapped and the belly of the horse hit the ground, and his mouth banged into the horse's flowing plastic mane, and then he bounced off the horse to one side and his mouth, though immediately flowing with blood, didn't hurt much because, very possibly, he thought for the moment he had before the pain occluded all thought, he had broken every bone in his butt and his back. After a moment, he lay in the cool grass

in what was now once again the gloaming, and began to scream.

The youngest brother began to scream, too, out of his own terror. He ran in a tight circle for a moment, screaming, and then he ran around the back of the house and up the steps and ran smack into the sliding glass door, on the other side of which their mother and Dr Hornegay looked up from the dining table in surprise.

Good God, Dr Hornegay said, standing up. Their mother had already dashed over to the sliding glass door, frightened but angry, with the incredulity of one who has suffered too often, too long, the reckless, mindless behaviour of boys. She muttered, What in the world, What in the world, over and over to herself. She knelt beside the youngest brother, who, stunned from running into the sliding glass door, lay on his back on the patio with his eyes wide open. But when the mother leaned over him and said, Are you OK? he began to scream again and point frantically in the direction of his brothers around the side of the house.

When the mother and Dr Hornegay came around, the mother holding the youngest brother in her arms, the oldest brother said, He jumped off the roof on to the rocky horse. I told him not to.

The oldest brother stood off to one side in order to detach himself from any semblance of blame.

The mother screamed, then, and set the youngest brother down hard enough in her haste to set him crying, too, and she began to shout to Dr Hornegay, Help, help! Has he broken his back? Oh, my God!

Don't move, son, Dr Hornegay said, just lie still there, now. Can you feel this?

After a moment, having managed to stop screaming himself, the middle brother began to come back into the world, into the shooting, searing pain in his butt and his back, the throbbing pain in his mouth, into the frightening vision of Dr Hornegay's horrible nose just inches from his own face, into the hot, overwhelming odour of the whiskey and cigarettes on Dr Hornegay's breath, and finally into the strange and tickly sensation of Dr Hornegay's fingers wiggling and pinching

at one of his toes. He nodded his head.

Then Dr Hornegay was feeling at his neck and along the bones of his spine, and saying, He's going to be all right, I believe, and he could hear the sounds of his mother weeping and saying, Oh, when will it stop? And then, in the distance, a car pulling into the drive, headlights glancing against the whole odd scene, and then there was their father standing above him, seeming impossibly tall, and saying, I got a message over in Vicksburg, said it was something from Rosie? He looked from the middle brother, to the busted rocky horse, to the mother, and to Dr Hornegay, standing upright now a little wobbly and attempting to straighten his jacket and tie. The father said, What in the goddamn hell is going on?

The middle brother started to cry as if his heart were broken, as indeed it was, and he burbled out, We were supposed to get a sackful of hot tamales. And then the youngest brother began to wail, and the oldest brother broke into choking sobs he had been trying to hold back.

The father looked around at all of them.

Dr Hornegay said, Your son attempted, apparently, to leap from the roof on to this contraption. However, after what I concede was merely a superficial examination, I do believe the boy will be fine, aside from bruises, a busted lip, and possibly some slight injury to his tail bone. And now I'm sure you'll have no more need of my attentions, so I should get back to the house and check on my beloved Eustice, who as I'm sure you know has not been well for some time.

Holding himself fairly erect, Dr Hornegay made a little bow with his head, adjusted his eyeglasses. He turned and walked into and through the deepening twilight of the neighbours' yard, a listing spectre, emerged on the other side, and followed his grainy shadow from the street lamp flickering out front of their house, up the hill toward his own.

The father carried the middle brother into the house and laid him down on the sofa where the boys had been sitting all afternoon, and he said a proper hello to the other two brothers, and then he kind of hugged their mother, who was sniffling but getting ahold of herself, and the two of them spoke quietly together for a few minutes. But soon they began

to speak in normal-volume voices, and then when the father noticed the bottle of Old Crow on the table with two glasses half filled with melting ice, their words got louder, and the father was saying things about What was she doing down here drinking whiskey with that old pervert while his boys were outside with No Parental Supervision and They Could Have Been Killed, and she was saying how He Had Some Nerve Lecturing Her About Responsibility, and then he was making himself a tall drink from Dr Hornegay's bottle and they continued to argue, and at one point the father slammed his empty glass down on the kitchen counter and said, Well, I'll be damned if that pathetic son of a bitch is going to come sniffing after my wife, separated or not, and he stormed out of the carport door, and the mother stormed through the den into the back of the house saying not quite under her breath, Oh, my fucking God.

The oldest brother and the youngest brother immediately ran out of the house to see what their father was going to do to Dr Hornegay, and though he didn't feel very good and was very sore in his back and butt, the middle brother got up off the couch and limped after them up the hill, calling, Wait for me.

Up at Dr Hornegay's house, from the light of the street lamp at the edge of the yard, they saw their father in the Hornegays' carport, pounding on the door to Dr Hornegay's den and shouting, Open this goddamn door, Hornegay! And then he came out of the carport and stepped into the shrubbery in the flower bed beneath the picture window that looked out from Dr Hornegay's living room and pounded on the glass with the same fist and shouted some more for Dr Hornegay to Get His Ass Out There Right Now. When Dr Hornegay still did not come out, their father walked to the street and dislodged a piece of asphalt from its edge and stepped back into the yard and was about to heave it toward the window when the front door from the living room opened and Dr Hornegay stepped out on to the shadow of the little stoop there with a rifle of some kind in his hands.

You step back, sir, he called to their father. Their father, the piece of asphalt in his hand, did indeed take a step back, and stared at

Dr Hornegay with the gun in his hands.

Run home, boys, their father said to them, but they only scurried out into the street and then crossed to the Harbours' yard and stopped there.

Then their father said, Shit, that's only a BB gun, you damn fool, and he started toward Dr Hornegay, and Dr Hornegay lifted the BB gun to his shoulder and began to fire and slide the pump and fire again, demonstrating what seemed to the boys a remarkable facility with the BB gun, an example they would remember the next time they had a BB-gun war with the other boys on the street. The Harbour twins had a Daisy pump just like the one that Dr Hornegay was shooting their father with right now.

Their father had begun to shout out in pain as the BBs from Dr Hornegay's Daisy pump pinged off his body, until finally he retreated into the street, where Dr Hornegay got him a few more times until the father and the boys all retreated all the way down the hill back into their own carport and into the house.

The boys sat on the sofa again in a neat row while their mother fixed their father another drink of Dr Hornegay's Old Crow, on ice, and used more ice to press against the several very red bumps on their father's face and neck. One of the BBs had pinged him in or near the eye and that eye was swollen badly and the skin around it had turned purple and yellow and black.

Their mother said, As long as you're here you might as well stay and eat, I've got a chicken I was going to bake with some barbecue sauce and some rice and broccoli.

I sure would love some fried chicken, if you wouldn't mind doing that, their father said.

Well, I guess I could fry it, their mother said, it might be quicker, and I know the boys are starving, they were supposed to get some hot tamales.

She got the chicken from the refrigerator and cut it up and shook the pieces in a sack with flour and salt and pepper while she heated Crisco in the pan and soon the boys could smell the chicken frying.

They watched from the sofa as their mother bustled about the kitchen tending the chicken and starting the rice and broccoli, and as their father sat at the dining table nursing his drink and pressing an ice pack against his swollen eye. It was all wonderful and very strange. Their mother moved about in the kitchen's bright light. Their father sat in the dim umbrella of yellow light from the hanging lamp above the little dining table. In the brothers' minds, it was like this maybe wasn't something real. It was like the quiet, weird, clear part near the end of a crazy dream. They could see their father, sitting there, but the light was funny and it was almost as if he could flicker out, and not be there, and it would be only their mother in there, frying chicken. The middle brother felt himself tuning up. Their father then removed the ice pack from his eye and looked over at the boys, and smiled, and was about to say something when blood began to spout from the swollen eye and he fell back against the table and cried out.

Jesus God! their mother shouted, and ran to grab her car keys and hustle their father out the door, calling back to them, I have to take him to the emergency room, and then they were gone.

The boys went out into the carport and watched them drive away up the street, then they went back into the den.

The oldest brother looked dejected and said to the middle brother, You better go turn off that chicken before it burns up again.

I can cook chicken, the middle brother said.

The other two brothers looked at him standing there with his swollen, blood-crusted lip and his eyes swollen from crying, not believing him, and then the middle brother limped into the kitchen and looked into the pan where the chicken was frying, took a fork and turned the pieces of chicken over in the hot oil, and let them cook like that for a while.

Get me a plate and put a piece of newspaper on it, and put a paper towel on top of that, he said to the youngest brother. The youngest brother looked at the oldest brother, who motioned for him to do what the middle brother said, so he got the plate and a piece of newspaper and a paper towel that the oldest brother handed to him from the roll

on the counter and he set it down beside the range. In a few minutes the middle brother took the chicken pieces out of the hot oil and drained them on the plate with the newspaper and paper towel on it. Then he checked the pots with the rice and broccoli.

Get some butter out for the rice and the broccoli, he said to the youngest brother, and the oldest brother nodded for the youngest brother to do what he said. When everything was on the table and they had plates to eat on and forks to eat with, they sat down and served themselves.

The youngest brother said, Aren't you going to say the blessing?

The middle brother looked at the oldest brother and thought about it for a moment and then said, No, I don't want to.

All right then, the oldest brother said, and they began to eat. ∎

GRANTA

Secrets of the Trade

Yiyun Li

The Li family, Beijing, China 1978–81

Once my father nearly gave up a career for love. The son of illiterate peasants, as a young physicist in the late 1950s he was selected by the government to work at a research facility developing nuclear weapons for Mother China. When he began to date my mother and reported the change in his life to the Institute, as young scientists were requested to do at the time, the Party secretary had a long talk with him. My mother, a petite girl who had grown up in the same region as my father, was considered an ill-chosen match – her father and brothers had fought against the Communist army in the civil war. My father was reported to have declared that he would give up his research position and become a common worker to marry my mother.

The Party secretary relented, and my mother married into the compound where my father and his colleagues worked and lived, bringing her widowed father with her. My grandfather would live out the rest of his life with my family, and would for years be under the supervision of the retirees' association on the compound – suspect in his perceived potential as a spy for America and Taiwan.

To everyone's surprise, my father gave up his career in 1981, when the country had just begun to open itself to the world. Not for love, this time, but for happiness. He had never cared for nuclear weapons, he told my mother, and he did not want to remain an unhappy cog in a machine. The Institute had become the entire world not only for him, but also for my grandfather, my sister and me. My mother, an elementary-school teacher who taught in a different school district, was the only one in our family who had a life outside the compound.

The Party secretary had another talk with my father in vain. What happened next became a cautionary tale that my mother has not tired of repeating to this day: the academy that had offered a research position to my father was contacted by the Institute and withdrew the offer. My father was transferred to an organization called the Society of Marxist Dialectical Materialism, where, he was told, a physicist was

needed to assist in their research.

The minor tragedy of a man pursuing a dream not allowed by his circumstances, the major unhappiness that failure would bring to a marriage that had once begun with unwavering love – these, only in retrospect, are pieced together and understood by the children of the marriage. In 1981, all I gained from my father's misfortune was a newly discovered freedom. Unlike most children around me, whose fathers and sometimes both parents worked for the Institute, I now had not one but two parents working away from the compound (my father's position at the Society, as we would call his new work unit, did not come with a flat we could rent, so the Institute generously let us rent our old flat); my sister had started middle school, an hour's bus ride away, so on weekdays the flat was left to the reign of my grandfather and me between seven o'clock in the morning and six o'clock in the evening.

My grandfather was eighty-six, too old to be in charge of me; I was eight going on nine, too young to be in charge of him. So we lived in happy parallel, each with a key to the flat, each following a routine without burdening the other. He cooked his lunch, which he ate alone: porridge, pickled tofu and a cup of tea with a small piece of soggy cake; I made my own lunch – half a leftover bun fried a perfect golden brown in the pan. He napped after lunch; I listened to the serialized war epics on the wireless before afternoon classes. He never minded what time I left for school or returned home; I took to wandering the compound until I had barely enough time to cook the rice before my parents' return in the evening.

One day in the autumn my father came home with folders of newspapers, and my mother explained our new responsibilities. Other than being good students and diligent with the housework, my sister and I were to start helping the family earn money as scribes for the Society. My father's boss, the editor of an annual review of Marxist dialectical materialism, would go through the newspapers from the year and circle all the articles published on the subject, and my father,

besides his assignments conducting basic data analysis and other clerical duties, was offered an opportunity to make extra money by helping with the annual.

Giant folders of newspapers began to arrive home with my father and we were tasked with copying out the selected articles on to oversized manuscript sheets with numbered grids for the typesetters. For every thousand words we would earn two yuan, a decent amount of money – the price of five kilos of flour, or half a kilo of my grandfather's favourite egg cakes.

From autumn through winter we worked every night. My sister and I sat on opposite sides of our only desk, my parents at the dinner table. My father bought a tall bottle of ink and every few days refilled the small glass bottles on the table and desk. My fountain pen, a hand-me-down from my sister, lost its smoothness after a few weeks and started to make scratches on the paper. When it was too cold for my grandfather to take his after-dinner walk, he wandered about the flat, looking over our shoulders from time to time, foretelling our future based on our penmanship. The characters I put down were round and fleshy, he said, in contrast to my sister's, which had more bone and sinew; from what he could see I would grow into a lazy and happy-go-lucky person, while my sister, with greater discipline, would accomplish more.

It was disheartening that one had to live towards a future that was already set, but working as a young scribe – like in a Gogol story, though less grim – and seeing the world from that vantage point, were enough compensation. One night I read in a newspaper article about a mermaid, said to have been discovered in the Soviet Union, with a blurry black-and-white picture of a woman sitting in the shallow water as proof. Another night I read in a crime report that the police in a certain northern city had tried for weeks to catch a man lurking on crowded buses and slicing young women's legs and arms with a razor blade. The newspapers – *People's Daily*, *Beijing Daily*, *Bright Light Daily*, *New People's Daily*, and many other regional papers that were not available for subscription in Beijing – brought a world filled with unfamiliar marvels and terrors into our small flat.

A week later I found out that the Russian mermaid was a hoax, an April Fool's Day prank from a Western newspaper which had been mistaken as front-page news by some unfortunate translator. The editor apologized for spreading groundless rumours in the correction and promised to work more diligently as 'the engineer of human souls'.

That the newspapers in the bound folders provided a continuous narrative was a thrilling discovery. I started to spend more time reading than copying. A photograph of the criminal was printed in the paper weeks later, his hands cuffed; a senior rocket scientist visited by Party officials at the hospital soon appeared in a black-framed obituary. My mother, annoyed by my tendency to get distracted, would remind me not to stop copying lest my grandfather was proved right about my good-for-nothingness. My father, who would usually have argued that I was too young to keep up with the other scribes, remained silent because, in the end, all my faults, and my sister's, could be traced back to his foolishness in giving up a career for a nonsense job.

I started to skip school in the afternoons, worried that I would not finish reading the big folders of newspapers before they were returned to the Society. The advantage of having both parents working off the compound became apparent once I started having to invent various excuses: headache, toothache, stomach ache, a visit to Chairman Mao's mausoleum with my father, or an outing to a museum with my mother and her school. At first I would write a note of excuse for myself, starting with a greeting to 'Highly Respected Teacher Chang' and ending with a 'salute', though after a while it occurred to me that Teacher Chang, our third-grade teacher, did not mind my absence – never had she questioned me after my return to the classroom, nor had she made any move to check with my parents about my repeated illnesses or outings in the afternoons. Her acquiescence, along with my grandfather's gullibility – he easily accepted it when I told him school was cancelled in the afternoon, even though other children could be seen from our first-floor window on the way to lessons – replaced my fear of being caught with a sense of

entitlement: as a young scribe I had every right to skip school and spend more time in the world of my work.

And what a world I discovered in those folders. Many newspapers published serialized novels at that time and I indiscriminately devoured everything. A suspense novel, serialized in a provincial paper, began in a town where young girls went to sleep, dreamed of being kissed by a white-cloaked man, and woke up insane. Working with a witch, the authorities caught the man in white, who turned out to be a thousand-year-old fox who gained immortality by stealing the dreams of virgins. An evening newspaper carried a ghost story in which the imperial family of the last dynasty recorded the location of their hidden treasure within a young prince's blood. A hundred years later their ghosts returned to search for a boy with the same DNA so that they could decode the map. A new translation of Tolstoy's *Resurrection*, too long to be serialized, was nevertheless excerpted for months in a major newspaper, and it agonized me not to be able to find out what happened next when, halfway into the folder, the excerpt was replaced by a historical novel about the Boxer Rebellion.

When one learned about a white fox in a man's shape, or a treasure map encoded with imperial DNA, or seduction and abandonment in Tolstoy's novel, third grade became irrelevant. Once spring came and we had finished the copying job, I found other excuses to remain a habitual truant. There were books from my parents' shelf to be read, including a 600-page medical manual for 'barefoot' doctors in the countryside, with grotesque illustrations of childbirth and parasites, a Zola novel and a translation of Lermontov. Then there was the unused lot at the far end of the compound to be explored, where tall grasses and small bushes hid the entrance to an underground air-raid tunnel – twice I ran into a man there with his pants down by his ankles. It could have been a much less benign world for a nine-year-old to wander into, unsupervised, though whether it's a trick of memory or not, the spring when I strayed from being a diligent student seems the happiest period in my life. With good timing I was able to avoid running into neighbours and teachers; with the calmness of an

experienced liar I convinced myself of my invisibility. The world in the books was full of mysteries; the world behind the tall grasses was full of sunshine and wonders. Even the half-naked man, quiet as he was, wore a friendly grin.

Inevitably my misdemeanours were discovered. When I started to skip school in the mornings, my grandfather felt obliged to inform my parents. My grandfather, it turned out, had known all along that I was skipping school, but when my mother questioned his silence, he shrugged as though it was only natural for a child to choose to go to school part-time. Several meetings with Teacher Chang took place in our flat; my mother, out of solidarity with a fellow teacher, was hesitant to report her negligence to the school officials. Teacher Chang was able to appease my mother, saying I skipped school because I was too advanced for my age. In retrospect I understand that she herself was probably bored by that life on the compound, and perhaps she too wished to play truant as I had. Later she and my mother became best friends, a joyful outcome based on my lost freedom.

Before that summer, my mother applied for a transfer, leaving the school where she had been for twenty years for the school on the compound, so she could supervise my education. My career as a happy truant came to an end, though we would, in the years to come, continue transcribing for the Society. In time I would learn to copy the articles while reading outside the circles, a secret of my trade, to be at one place and then elsewhere at the same time. ■

Rupture *Simon Lelic*

One summer's day, teacher Samuel Szajkowski walks into his school assembly and opens fire. He kills three pupils and a colleague before turning the gun on himself. Lucia May, the young policewoman assigned to the case, becomes preoccupied with the question no one else seems to want to ask: what drove a mild-mannered, diffident man to commit such a despicable crime? A tour de force of storytelling from Picador.

Picador

The Hopeless Life of Charlie Summers *Paul Torday*

A tale of money, greed, redemption and of two men from very different backgrounds: one has a high-powered job in the city; the other sells Japanese dog food. But as the economic crisis sets in and world markets begin to crash, who has the most to lose? A brilliant, page-turning read that combines the pace of Torday's *The Girl on the Landing* with his trademark humour in *Salmon Fishing in the Yemen*.

Weidenfeld & Nicoloson £12.99

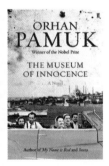

The Museum of Innocence *Orhan Pamuk*

The Museum of Innocence – set in Istanbul between 1975 and today – tells the story of Kemal, the son of one of Istanbul's richest families, and of his obsessive love for a poor and distant relation, the beautiful Fusun, who is a shop-girl in a small boutique.

Faber & Faber £18.99

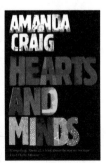

Hearts and Minds *Amanda Craig*

Rich or poor, outsider or insider, five London strangers are connected in undreamed-of ways as greed, courage, murder and kindness link their lives. Described in the *Observer* as 'above all, a book about the way we live now', Amanda Craig's much-praised *Hearts and Minds* is a masterful, compelling, utterly essential state-of-the-nation novel.

Abacus £6.99

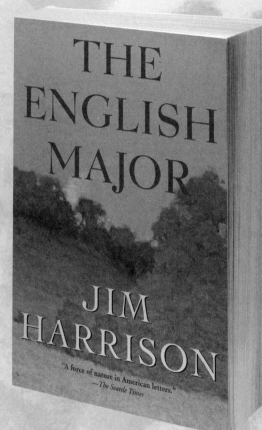

The Last Vet

Aminatta Forna

First you notice the dogs. In all other ways Freetown is a West African city like any other, of red dust and raised cries, forty-degree heat and a year neatly segmented into two – hot and dry, hot and wet.

Today water tips from the sky. Beneath the canopy of a local store three street dogs and a man holding a briefcase stand and contemplate the rain. Another dog shelters beneath the umbrella of a cigarette seller. A fifth follows a woman across the street, literally dogging her footsteps, using her as a beacon to navigate the traffic and the floodwater.

In the dry season the kings of the city are the dogs. They weave through the crowds, lie in the roadside shade watching through slitted eyes, they circle and squabble, unite in the occasional frenzied dash. For the most part the people and the dogs exist on separate planes. The dogs ignore the people, who likewise step around and over them. On the road the drivers steer around reclining animals. This city has more street dogs than any I have known.

It is eight o'clock on a Wednesday morning. Torrents of water sluice off the hills and rush down the cross streets. The force of the rain has swept the traffic off the road, and now threatens the battered Peugeot ahead of me. Inside his clinic Dr Jalloh has placed his plans on hold, waits for me in his tiny surgery surrounded by dogs, waits for the rain to stop. The whole city waits for the rain to stop.

It was the dry season of 2004 and I was home working on a novel when I first met Gudush Jalloh. My friend Rosa called, concerned that her dog, at that moment whelping, was in trouble. The dog in question was a snappish bitch, a street rescue by the name of Corre whom I had so far failed to befriend. I was in that selfish space of writers and the interruption was unwelcome. Could she not call a vet? She told me the vet was upcountry. Call another vet? There was no other vet.

Someone who knows about dogs, then? Yes, she replied, and waited for my answer.

I know a bit about dogs. I do not pretend to know a great deal. I enjoy the company of dogs and keep them, but know nothing of whelping bitches. I consider myself something less than an expert. An interested amateur.

Eyes closed, half in, half out of this world, the puppy looked dead. I had no idea what to do so I telephoned my husband in south-east London, who in turn called our vet and relayed his instructions via mobile phone and satellite to reach us six thousand miles away, at a pound a minute. Try to free the pup's shoulders. Olive oil might help. Corre, by now docile in her distress, allowed me to try to hook my forefingers under the puppy's forelegs. I tried. Nothing worked: not the olive oil, the bitch's efforts, or my own fumblings. At last we obtained the home number of the local vet. He'd travelled overnight from the Provinces, been asleep less than an hour and his telephone manner displayed the lagged thinking of the abruptly awoken. He told me he had sent his car away. I offered to collect him.

Dr Jalloh is the only vet in the country. No, that is not quite true. There are three government vets, employed by the Ministry of Agriculture. They wear rubber boots, but mostly deal with figures, with capacities, stock and yields. There are also a small number of charlatans. Gudush Jalloh is the only qualified vet in private practice. The single person in the country to whom you might bring your sick dog, cat, monkey or goat.

The pup had never, not for an instant, known life. The body cavity was a huge fluid-filled sac, devoid of vital organs. By now we had moved Corre to the surgery and Dr Jalloh prodded at the dead puppy with a long pair of tweezers, declared this the second instance of such abnormality he had seen. Rosa turned away. I, whose paper-mask fantasies had never found expression, leaned in. A second pup suffered the same deformity. Another was stillborn. Four survived.

That first meeting made a deep impression upon me. In the years that followed I met Gudush Jalloh on one more occasion which was significant, and then socially perhaps five or six times more. At one point somebody mentioned his work with the street dogs, in which they thought I might be interested.

This is the country where I grew up. It was the 1970s. Here, as a child, I gathered, rescued, raised and lost more dogs than I can now recall. I have some of their names: Jack. Jim. Tigger. Apollo. Pandora. Bingo. KaiKai. Jupiter. Pluto. The turnover was so fast there are many more I have forgotten. My dogs died of disease, of being hit by cars, of falling off balconies, generally of life expectancy in the Third World. Sometimes they were lost or stolen. When I was nine Apollo disappeared. For months I scanned the streets during every car journey. One day, a long way from home, on the other side of the city, I saw Apollo. The driver stopped the car. We opened the back door, pulled Apollo inside and drove off at speed. I never found out who had taken him or why; he had not been mistreated. Nor do I know whether we were seen as we effected his rescue. I imagine whatever witnesses there were remained silent for fear of being disbelieved.

The third child and the youngest, I passed my earliest years as the beneficiary of what the experts call benign neglect. When I was three my father became active in politics. He was detained several times, once for three years. Amnesty named him a Prisoner of Conscience. My stepmother kept the family together. I collected dogs. My parents, if they noticed, did not pass comment, even when the household total achieved a high score of six. I read *White Fang* and *Peter Pan* and longed for a wolf and a dog which slept at the foot of my bed. Ours were strictly yard dogs.

Other animals passed through my life: a mongoose, a green parrot, a fawn. They interested me, fed my ambition to become a vet, but I did not love them. I loved only the dogs for reasons too complicated to elaborate upon, and yet also painfully obvious. In a time of lies, I found honesty and loyalty among the dogs. And if the memory of particular dogs has grown unreliable, then the memory of what they offered me

in that time has become indelible: a retreat from the mutability of the human world, a place of safety.

There were a lot more vets back in those days. In the intervening thirty-odd years they have all gone: pursuing opportunities overseas, fleeing a civil war that lasted ten years and killed countless and uncounted numbers of us.

We arrive late. It is nine o'clock. Outside the school building people and dogs wait beneath a steady drizzle. The dogs are collarless, held on lengths of electric cable, nylon rope or string. A woman in pink holds on to a brown-and-white dog. A boy cradles a furious pup. A man arrives with a large black-and-white dog, which leaps and twists at the end of a long rope. Another man leads his dog on its hind legs, holding on to the front paws, like a dancing bear. Inside the schoolroom a line of people and dogs wait upon on a bench and impassively watch a technician gently shave the balls of a sedated dog.

This is a street clinic. Bring a dog here and you can have it sterilized for free. On other days Jalloh's team rounds up dogs from the streets, puts them in a wagon and takes them to the clinic to be vaccinated and neutered. The first time they tried to remove dogs local people chased them, demanding to know why the dogs were being taken and allowing them to leave only after the team promised the dogs' return.

'In Thailand,' Dr Jalloh told me from the wheel of his Land Cruiser on the drive across town, 'the authorities have a "keep your dog at home day". Everybody has to bring their dogs inside. Afterwards they go through the streets and shoot any dog they see.' A few years ago the Freetown municipal authorities decided upon a similar cull of the street dogs. Dr Jalloh elected himself the dogs' representative and spoke during a public meeting. Though the odds were stacked against him, he argued that most of the dogs weren't stray but belonged to the community, that they – the dogs – performed a function and a service by offering security and protection. The mayoral dignitaries told Jalloh the dogs were dirty. Jalloh retorted that the opposite was true; their

scavenging kept the streets clear of rotting rubbish. He had a point. There had been no systemized rubbish collection in the city for decades. The authorities backed down; the dogs were reprieved. 'They say we are crazy...' He paused to answer his phone. The ringtone was a puppy's whine. They said *he* was crazy. And that was just the beginning.

In 1952 Konrad Lorenz published *King Solomon's Ring* in which he set out the terms of 'the Covenant'. The Covenant describes the relationship between human and canine, its beginnings and the stone upon which it is founded. A pack of jackals followed Stone Age man's hunting expeditions and surrounded his settlements, were tolerated, accepted and ultimately encouraged. Firstly for the warning note they sounded at the advance of predators, secondly for their ability to track game. The jackals, who initially followed the hunters in the hope of scraps and entrails, began to take the initiative, running before instead of behind the hunter, bringing to bay larger animals than they would be able to hunt without assistance. And so the Covenant was created, an interdependent exchange of services.

This is how, fifty years earlier, Rudyard Kipling described the origin of the Covenant in 'The Cat that Walked by Himself': 'When the Man waked up he said, "What is Wild Dog doing here?" And the Woman said, "His name is not Wild Dog any more, but the First Friend, because he will be our friend for always and always and always. Take him with you when you go hunting."'

For Lorenz, who went on to win a Nobel Prize, the contract between human and animal was 'signed...without obligation'. Jalloh, closer to Kipling than to Lorenz, would disagree. There is an obligation, it is unequivocal and one-sided. Having brought the jackal into his sphere, having bred the wildness from him – man owes dog.

Four, then five, then six freshly neutered and comatose dogs lie in a neat row, the paw of one lies across another, strange babies sharing a bed. An assistant tattoos the ear of each dog. There is a

general air of understated chaos. Dogs roam the room. Outside a group of children gather to watch as recently anaesthetized dogs stagger, circle and crash to the ground. The technician with the tattoo machine clips the ear of a reclining dog which, far from being sedated, is merely sleeping. The astounded animal jumps to its feet and stalks huffily away. Elsewhere a technician attempts to inject a dog. It tries to bite him. The owner's efforts to hold on to his dog are so ineffective that the technician suggests the dog doesn't belong to him. The man insists otherwise. The waiting crowd wades in. 'He's afraid of you,' the woman in the pink top points out. A small boy steps forward and takes the animal. To me Jalloh says: 'Some people think they are the owners, but they are only the proxy owner. Usually the children are the true owners of the dog.'

Sitting on the plane halfway across the Sahara two days before, I had suddenly remembered my rabies vaccination. I pulled out my yellow international health certificate, relieved to find there was month left before it expired. 'Ah,' says Jalloh, cheerfully, 'but it is an inexact science.' He tries to keep himself inoculated, but the vaccine is rarely available in the Sierra Leone. The staff wear doubled gloves. They have two or three muzzles in the surgery. That's the sum of it.

On our way back to the surgery we stop at the government veterinarian offices, which Jalloh is keen to show me. He jumps from the vehicle and leads me inside, introduces me to three men dressed in overalls and wellington boots. The room is virtually empty of furniture and equipment. Dusty glass cabinets house ageing texts. The sole piece of equipment appears to be an old freezer. In one of the cabinets I find an elegant wooden box.

'Post-mortem kit,' says Jalloh. 'It will be empty.' I open it. Nothing, save the abandoned chrysalis of a moth.

As a child I'd owned a dog that overnight turned suddenly affectionate. Soon afterwards his hips locked. I carried him to the vet, walked him up and down to demonstrate the strange gait. The vet instructed me to bring him back if anything changed. The dog wandered and late one evening returned, his hindquarters split open

to the bone by an axe wound. Through the night I tended him, feeding him raw egg with my fingers and following him around with a bowl of water, from which the wretched animal heaved itself away time and time again. I remember the episode now and recount it for Jalloh. The dog was rabid. I worked it out for myself later. The vet had refused to admit it.

'"Craze dog" they call it,' says Jalloh. And tells an everyday story of his own. Some months ago, a woman brought three dogs to him for a regular check up. In one Jalloh saw the telltale paralysis of the lower jaw. By the time the owner returned Jalloh had destroyed all three. He had no choice. It happens sometimes. In the slums the cry goes up at the sight of a drooling dog. Occasionally somebody will call him, but often by the time he gets there the dog is dead. Now that frustrates him, for diagnosis on a dead animal requires a post-mortem of the brain. If the dog were alive he could gather a sample of blood. Jalloh likes to keep accurate records of such things. After all, nobody else does.

Gudush Jalloh was born in Kono, Yengema, in the Camara Chiefdom. His parents were Fula Muslims, the nomadic cattle owners of West Africa who drive their herds through Mali, Senegal, Guinea and Nigeria. By the time Gudush was born in 1959, the first son of the first wife and eldest of twenty-two, the family had abandoned their pastoralist ways. Still, the knowledge of his heritage interested the young Jalloh. His early ambition was to own a herd. His mother reared chickens and the occasional goat; dogs played an early role in his life. When Gudush was fifteen his father arranged a marriage to a local girl, told his son it was time to leave school and join the family business as petty traders of gasoline. Gudush refused either to marry or to leave school, finished his education with the help of a scholarship and a former teacher who employed him as a part-time lab assistant. He began to apply for government scholarships to read engineering overseas. In 1978, he was one of a dozen who won scholarships to Hungary, but then, on the eve of travel, the scholarships were withdrawn and awarded to candidates with government connections.

A year later he won a scholarship to Moscow. The African students arrived in Rostov in late September, without a word of Russian between them. They worried about how to make their stipends last, how to cook potatoes. Sometime during the year-long induction, Jalloh was persuaded by a colleague to switch courses and join him at the Moscow Veterinary Academy. He returned to Sierra Leone in the mid-1980s, the rift with his father healed by the prestige of having been chosen to study abroad. Jalloh tells me his father didn't mind that he had become a vet; he didn't know what a vet was. Later people said: 'So your son spent six years in Russia just to treat dogs?'

That year, the same year Jalloh returned, his younger brother, the second son of his father's third wife, was bitten by a dog. By the time Jalloh heard the news in Freetown, the boy had died of rabies.

Thursday. We are standing in the yard of an ocean-view house in the west of Freetown, close by the Mammy Yoko Hotel, where the great siege of the civil war played out. Guests hunkered down while the rebel troops of the RUF fought Nigerian-led ECOWAS troops and American helicopters said to hell with the no-fly zone, landed on the beach and evacuated their citizens and a few others as well. My stepmother was among those who escaped. She told me how she was on the ship with a dozen working girls, scooped from the hotel bar and set down on the ship along with everyone else. They were excited. They thought they were going to America. Briefly, and for the first time, the world became aware of what was going on in our country.

From where I stand I can see terraced lawns reaching down to the waterside and an ornamental pagoda. No sign of the owners, a Sierra Leonean businesswoman and her European husband, or so I am told. There is just a watchman with a squint, a pronounced underbite and a diploma in passive aggression. The steward, who was supposed to fetch the prescription shampoo from the pharmacy and meet us back here, has still not shown. Teddy calls him. The guy swears he is on his way, but Teddy says he hears the sounds of a bar behind him.

Dr Jalloh is not with us. He hates this kind of job, hates owners who don't know how to handle their own animals, who won't come to the clinic. Sometimes, he says, people just show him out to the yard, to a couple of half-wild beasts, and leave him there. He hates that more than anything. He's a vet, he says, not a dog whisperer.

Teddy, Zainab, Nabsieu and I are here to wash the dogs, but nothing is happening. We are standing in the eye of sun while four dogs circle us, demonstrating various degrees of animosity. 'Here, in this situation, the relationship between owner and dog has reached total breakdown,' pronounces Teddy. 'These dogs no longer trust human beings. They will not allow themselves to be touched.' The dogs are flea-ridden and one has a skin infection. The exception is a tall, slim brown-and-white dog with a cropped tail. It looks healthier than the rest and allows itself to be petted. The dog came from next door. His Colombian owner turned out to have been the mastermind behind the planes local people would hear landing in the dead of night at the airport on the other side of the water. Motorboats from a small jetty in front of the house ferried the cargo to the mainland and from here the cocaine was loaded onto mules bound for Europe. Neighbouring Guinea has already turned into a cocaine state. After the Colombian's arrest the abandoned animal jumped the wall to join this pack. Teddy nicknames it 'the gangster'. One thing you can say about the Colombian though, he looked after his dog.

Twenty minutes on we get started. The watchman, who has been asked not to give food to any of the dogs because we are about to administer an anaesthetic, is now giving one of them a plate of food. What is it with this guy? Poorly paid staff take out their resentment on the dogs, says Teddy. They sometimes feel the owners of the house care more for the animals than they do for them. Here the householders have been away for some months, which might explain the neglected state of the dogs and their hostility to humans. Ten more minutes are spent persuading the watchman to fetch soap and towels. Finally we begin. Nabsieu inserts a dart into a hollow pipe, raises the mouthpiece to his lips and stalks the dogs with the quiet footfall of a hunter.

The gangster goes down first. Nabsieu fells the remaining dogs one by one, a single dart each.

An hour later the job is finished. We have washed and scrubbed four dogs, searched for two in the nearby bush after the watchman opened the gate and let them out into the street. Now four dogs sleep it off in the shade. Zainab, Nabsieu and Teddy sign off on the job, telling the watchman they'll be back next month.

Back in the surgery Jalloh asks how it went. I say the whole thing is crazy. Jalloh shrugs and shakes his head. What to say? They service about twenty elite households in this way. The clinic needs the money. Maybe he'll dig a dip out back. Even so, he muses, people like that still wouldn't bring their dogs.

He says that the main problem here is neglect. People don't have the money to care for and feed all these dogs, which I feel is broadly true, though the last two days have produced a strange, more complex picture. The slum-dwellers' dogs are ten times healthier than the dogs of the country's most wealthy.

L unch in a nearby restaurant and a conversation begun the day before is reprised. Jalloh has a television crew arriving from Holland in a week's time. On the drive back across town from the street clinic I'd asked whether he planned to allow the crew to film a clinic. Jalloh nodded. Some of what I had seen, I'd suggested, might prove unpalatable to Western viewers.

A small silence. Jalloh wrinkled his nose and sighed: 'Oh dear,' and then, 'Europeans are so emotional.'

Ordinarily his tendency is to talk about the West in uncritical terms: as an animal nirvana where pets exist as legally protected family members. I wondered if this was a habit borne of the need to flatter, to treat everyone who visited from overseas – including me – as a potential donor. At the seminars and conferences Jalloh attends on his funded trips to Europe and America, the face the West wears is typically humane, rational, superior. Next to the representatives of international animal welfare programmes such as the RSPCA whose

reserves of £150 million represent twice our nation's annual revenue, Jalloh is the beggar at the banquet.

What the West reveals of itself at such times, naturally, is less interesting than what is concealed. In our street in London the kids with pit-bull crosses; the dead pit bull in a bin liner; the dogfights. Now, sitting over steak sandwiches and Fanta, I detail none of this. Instead I tell him about a photographer employed by a national newspaper magazine in Britain who was sent out to work with me on an assignment some years before. The woman suffered culture shock such that she was virtually catatonic, only showing signs of recovery within sight of the airport. Jalloh chuckles, his chuckle deepens into a laugh. Then for a moment he is quiet.

An American came to Sierra Leone to work for the Special Court responsible for trying war criminals, one of hundreds of lawyers and support staff employed by the American-backed court. She wanted to fly three street dogs to the United States and asked Jalloh to prepare the dogs for travel. He suggested she give the money to his programme instead. For the same money he could help a thousand dogs. She refused, spent 3,000 US dollars to transport the dogs. He remembers her name and repeats it. In time it will become a running gag between us, a byword for solipsistic sentimentality. It made him think he should be doing a 'sponsor a street dog' programme, like those for sponsoring children. Send a photograph of the dog and a monthly update.

That would work, I agree. 'She wanted to be a hero.'

Jalloh repeats her name. Shakes his head and laughs.

Then there are those dogs, larger than the other street dogs, who roam the streets, tattered collars hanging around their necks. We call them the 'NGO dogs', adopted by aid workers, abandoned when the contract is over. Not so very different to their relationship with the country. A departing staff member at the British High Commission recently left two dogs in Jalloh's compound before flying home for good. Last year the High Commission denied visas to two of his staff members who had been offered free training places at an animal centre in Britain.

And yet some people think it's Jalloh's enterprise that is misplaced in a country officially the poorest in the world. Seventy-sixth out of seventy-six in the United Nations Human Development Index – a ranking we sometimes switch with Bangladesh. When last that happened, the president announced a national celebration. In the early days Jalloh found himself turned away by the World Health Organization and other international funding agencies, who told him animal welfare was not a priority. He argued, with incontrovertible logic, that human health and animal health were inseparable. He won.

The deputy foreign minister, lunching at a table nearby, comes over to say hello on his way out. The minister donated the old trailer Jalloh has converted into holding kennels behind his surgery where a small shanty town is growing. Part of an old truck is being fashioned into a second unit. He keeps his vaccines in the freezer of the restaurant where we are lunching: the surgery is without electricity.

His is a makeshift existence. Before I arrived Jalloh had e-mailed asking if I might help him obtain consumables for a VeTest, an elaborate piece of diagnostic equipment someone had given him. The cost would have come to €2,800, the materials required an unbroken cold chain between the factory in Holland and Freetown. The VeTest sits, unused, beneath his desk.

He tells me of a British woman who wanted to set up a dogs' home in Sierra Leone. 'Who would pay for it? Who would adopt all those dogs?' Of the international companies who offer him vast sums to exterminate the strays that roam their compounds.

The conversation will range over days: African pragmatism and reality, Western sentiment, the schism between the values of the two and the West's own conflicted treatment of animals; of Jalloh's lot in trying to embrace, negotiate and reconcile so many ways of thinking.

Here, a man presses a knife against a bull's neck, croons as he looks the animal in the eye and slits its throat. I have seen it happen many times and again. One occasion was a family celebration, the 'opening' of a house rebuilt after the war. A cow was to be slaughtered, cooked and fed to one hundred people. In the forest behind the house five men

prayed and held her until she died. The killing of an animal is attended with all the ritual of an offering. Indeed 'sacrifice' is the word we use. In Britain factory-farmed animals, strung up by a single hind leg, inch along a conveyor belt to the screams of those who went before, emerge stripped of hair and skin, wrapped in cellophane.

I will ask Jalloh what he thinks of the dogs he sees in Europe, bred beyond the point of deformity for the show ring and the fashionable, a million miles from Lorenz's noble working dogs. Jalloh will smile and shake his head. 'And now they call our dogs mongrels.'

I will repeat the conversation I had with my London vet, about the link between the physical abuse of animals and the physical abuse of children. Vets are under instruction to report every incident of animal mistreatment. Jalloh will listen, ask questions. Who are the perpetrators? What sector of society are they from? He frowns. No, he has never heard of dogfights here. In England he once trained as an RSCPA inspector, although he never went out on patrol. He read about the torture of animals. He found it 'interesting and very strange'. Another time he says: 'People here believe if you do something bad to an animal, something bad will happen to you.'

Once, I remember, I visited a hotel looking for a place to house a writers' conference the following year. A wild goose chase, as it soon became evident. The hotel had been abandoned since the war and was in an impossible state of neglect. In the bathrooms of a collapsed bungalow I found a litter of puppy corpses. The caretaker who accompanied me covered his mouth with his hand. 'Bad, very bad.' Nobody had seen the bitch for days, they'd searched for and failed to locate her pups. Perhaps she had been hit by a car. He shook his head, sure this was a portent of something terrible.

Says Elizabeth Costello, protagonist in J.M. Coetzee's *The Life of Animals*, in which the author uses a fictional setting to explore the moral argument about the treatment of animals: 'I do think it is appropriate that those who pioneered the industrialization of animal lives and commodification of animal flesh should be at the forefront of trying to atone for it.' Trying to atone for a crime she compares to

the Holocaust, a crime of 'stupefying proportions'.

Costello's response is an ethical vegetarianism so extreme she is unable to sit at a table with meat eaters. On the other side of the table, Jalloh has just completed work on his steak sandwich. I have never met a vegetarian in Sierra Leone. Perhaps because there isn't food enough to be fussy about protein sources. Or perhaps simply because there is a great deal less to atone for. In places where the distance travelled from Wild Dog and the creation of the Covenant is shorter, one finds neither the gas chambers nor the need to expiate, but rather a middle ground between the world of humans and the world of animals: a rough-and-ready equilibrium.

Still, it would be disingenuous to suggest crimes never occur. Jalloh chides me for my romanticism, reminds me, via e-mail in our continued conversation some weeks later, that sometimes the knife is blunt. There is no singing. In Britain he finds people who care. In Sierra Leone they tell him he doesn't have enough work to do, to be wasting time on animals.

The Sierra Leone 1960 Animal Cruelty Act, a parting gift from the departing colonials, sits unchanged upon the statute books. Jalloh wants it updated and enforced, he tells me. In the lifetime of the Act there have been only two known attempts to bring a prosecution: both by Jalloh. Once against a man who beat Jalloh's dog. The man was a neighbour who had taken a dislike to the dog, a sentiment the animal heartily returned. The dog barked. The neighbour, when nobody was watching, took a stick to it. Another time Jalloh attempted to prosecute a man who stoned a goat to death. The man claimed the animal had destroyed his crop, he'd warned it several times. Neither case reached the courts. The police treated both incidents as crimes of property. What struck me as I listened to Jalloh's telling, what strikes me still, was the history, the very personal enmity between victim and perpetrator at the heart of both crimes. There existed a relationship, a warped and angry one, but one that existed – something no law of property could ever take into account.

There were those who disapproved of Jalloh's actions, of the

primacy he would give animals such that a man might be imprisoned. Jalloh would like to see rights for animals enshrined in law. Limited rights. The right to food and shelter. Not the right to life that animal activists in Britain would advocate. No, he shakes his head and thinks some more. Freedom from mistreatment, yes. An animal ombudsman, someone to enforce those rights. Someone like him.

Soon after his return from the Soviet Union Jalloh collected fifty signatures on a petition, called a meeting and launched the Sierra Leone Animal Welfare Society. A young engineering student, Memuna, attended the first of those meetings. Two years later they married. An afternoon in the surgery they sit side by side and reel off the names of the other attendees by heart, produce the original minutes on translucent onion paper, offer them for my perusal, laugh and touch hands.

A nd then came war.

Jalloh and Memuna fled across land to Guinea. They carried nothing but his vet's bag and some antibiotics. Memuna was pregnant. 'I was worried she would abort,' he says. Abort, the terminology of a vet. In the Gambia they found sanctuary; Jalloh offered his services to the government, working on food security and cattle farming and, once, administering an NGO-funded programme to neuter the street cats that clustered in hundreds around the tourist hotels.

Two years later Jalloh and Memuna returned in time for the rebels' big push on Freetown. The street dogs grew fat feasting on the corpses. People thought the dogs would go mad, Jalloh tells me, from eating the drug-addled flesh of the rebel soldiers. Though who could deny they did the city a favour? A doctor who worked at Connaught, the city's main hospital, described to me days spent collecting corpses during pauses in the fighting. He found people's loved ones shoved down pit latrines, rebels left to the dogs. Once he tried to move the corpse of a young girl, a commander in the rebel forces, but furious locals refused to allow it. Leave her for the dogs. The fate she deserved.

The city was overrun with dogs. Jalloh chose that year to launch his campaign to protect them. More than once I have heard the story of how it all started. Now I hear it from his wife. 'He gathered eighty dogs and brought them to the compound,' says Memuna. 'I had to cook rice three times a day to feed them all. That night it was a full moon. The dogs began to howl. Next day I had to go to each of my neighbours to beg.' She laughs for a long time.

Today is Saturday. We are sitting together in the surgery and Memuna enters with wet hands, touching the back of hers to the back of mine. She excuses herself to return to the kitchen and oversee the cooking of tonight's feast. It is the first day of Ramadan.

It vexes Jalloh – the new fundamentalism spreading from Saudi Arabia has now reached even Sierra Leone. It breaks down the relationship between man and dog, he says. Teddy gives an account of a cleric who told one of his congregation to scrape the skin away from his arm where he had allowed a dog to touch it. At that Jalloh jumps up, begins searching for the papers upon which he has copied Hadiths about animals from the Koran. He talks fast and waves a finger in the air. He went on Radio Islam to talk about the treatment of animals under Islam. Now he's persuaded Alhaji Sillah, the city's chief imam, to read out some of the Hadiths during Friday prayers at the Central Mosque.

In all the years of his life Jalloh has never been diverted from his faith or his love of dogs. Only one thing came close to defeating him. His right eye, when it catches the light, contains a diamond-hard glint. I remembered hearing, when I was far away in England, that Jalloh was going blind. The glint is an intraocular transplant, an artificial lens. He is functionally blind in his left eye, having suffered severe optic-nerve damage and the resultant loss of ninety per cent of the sight. Two years ago he looked at the world through a tunnel, a six-inch span. He couldn't drive, could barely work although he carried on. The cause was cataracts.

On a trip to the United States, a friend, an animal lover and supporter of his, persuaded him to visit an optician. The optician

referred him straight to a specialist who gave Jalloh six months before he lost his sight altogether. Jalloh had no money for the operation. The Dutch animal welfare agency who fund his work with the street dogs declined to help, informing him their funds were reserved for animals. Calls were made and the surgeon, who loved his two Labradors, agreed to waive his fees. Jalloh underwent the surgery but found he had overlooked the $10,000 hospital bill. The surgeon persuaded the hospital to cut the bill by half. Then came the $1,500 anaesthetist's fee. A phone call and he too waived his fee. So it went. This is how his sight was saved. For the love of dogs, says Jalloh, standing up and spreading his arms. But for the love of dogs, he'd be blind.

Saturday is the day the responsible middle classes bring their dogs to the clinic. Jalloh cleans out ear infections, administers antibiotics and vaccines. The vaccines carried a half-dozen at a time in an ice-packed Thermos from the restaurant down the road. At my behest he demonstrates the correct way to remove a tick: burst the body and let it detach naturally. Make the mistake of pulling and the head will remain inside. Dogs, his own, move freely in and out of the surgery. Jalloh, his assistants and I circle each other in the narrow space between his desk, examining table and shelves labelled: Orals/Endoparasites and Ectoparasites/Emergency Injectables/Injectables for Infectious Diseases/Catgut Suture Needles/Surgical Gloves. New supplies have been stuck in the port for two months now. His wish list for a far-off future: an orthopaedic surgical kit (most dogs are hurt in traffic accidents); a binocular microscope (he can't use his old monocular scope because of his eyes); an auroscope and – dreamtime now – solar power to run lights and a fridge.

We treat Emaka, Joffy, Fluffy, Cannis, Tiger, Rambo and Combat.

At two Joffy's owner comes to collect her dog. Jalloh springs up and hands her a form for his latest initiative – a licence scheme – tells her to go to City Hall and license her dog. Later he outlines the scheme for my benefit. There is now a municipal by-law, thanks to Jalloh (one begins to believe the City Council has given up denying him anything), which states every dog must be vaccinated and licensed. The funds

collected from citizens like Joffey's owner are diverted to vaccinate and license the community dogs. That's the plan anyway. The tax amounts to around two pounds for a sterilized dog and three pounds for an unsterilized dog.

Me: 'Is the law enforced?'

Jalloh: 'No. But it's enforceable. This is a test run. First we'll find out how much voluntary take up there is.'

Me: 'Has anyone actually licensed their dog yet?' There being, in my view, no real possibility of enforcement in a state still struggling towards a functioning police force.

Jalloh pauses, gives the habitual headshake, which I now know signifies disbelief. 'No.'

And now I will tell you about the second time I met Gudush Jalloh. It took place a few months after our first meeting, less than two years after the end of the civil war. I had taken into my home a street dog, a yellow-coated bitch. I'd noticed her searching for scraps along the beach, checked with some of the beach boys who confirmed that nobody took care of her. With their help we bundled her into the back of my car where she stood on the parcel shelf and howled. The other strays, who'd scattered at the moment of the kidnap, gathered around the car, some howled back. A boy said: 'Dis 'oman dae cam take you na heaven and you dae fom?' This woman has come to take you to heaven and you're complaining?

I named her Mathilda and wooed her with corned-beef sandwiches, just as I had on the beach. By five o'clock of our first afternoon together she sat to my command. By six she had learned to lie down. She became my companion during the long days of writing. Several people asked if they might have her when I left, for I had earned a reputation as someone who knew a good dog. And Mathilda was a good dog, though she never lost her skittishness around strangers, she gave me her devotion entirely.

Then Mathilda was hit by a car. In the early morning a man on his way to work passed a wounded dog lying in a ditch, recognized her

and brought her to my house. I drove her to the only place there was, to Dr Jalloh's surgery. Mathilda had two dislocated hind legs and, he suspected, a broken pelvis. He could try to slip the dislocated legs back into their sockets, but not if the pelvis was indeed broken. With no X-ray machine it was impossible to give an exact diagnosis.

The injured dog lay silent and still upon the table. A solution seemed unreachable. To attempt to relocate the bones into a broken pelvis would be agonizing and ineffective. I thought I knew what Dr Jalloh was saying, I might have to put her down. I stroked the top of her head. Then Dr Jalloh said he knew one person with an X-ray machine. It was possible they might let us use it. He offered to make the call.

Haja Binta, a Fula like Jalloh, had recently returned from twenty years working for the NHS in Britain. Now she was the proud owner of a small private clinic on the other side of the city. I arrived, carrying Mathilda who was partially sedated and wrapped in a towel. The people waiting to see the nurse thought I was holding a baby, but when they discovered it was a dog, they gathered around.

'Hush ya,' said an old man.

'Sorry-oh!' said someone else.

Haja Binta led us to the X-ray room and laid Mathilda on a steel bed, beneath the eye of the giant machine. Several times she repositioned the dog, pausing only to adjust her hijab. Afterwards she offered to develop the prints while I waited. I returned to the waiting room. After twenty minutes Haja Binta came to find me. She smiled as she held up the X-rays. There was no fracture to the pelvis. The old man surveyed the images and gave a grunt of approval at the outcome. Somebody else said: 'Na God will am so.'

Mathilda recovered over time, retaining a distinctive sideways skip. One day, during dinner at the British High Commission, I told the story. My audience were mainly expats, people sent to the country in the wake of war for one reason or another. One man took exception to the waste of time and resources on an animal in a country where people had so little. He told me so as he walked away.

But, you see, here's why I think he was wrong. The people who had helped Mathilda: the man who reached into the ditch and brought her out, Dr Jalloh in his makeshift surgery, the Haja and her patients – they were Africans. They lived in the poorest country in the world. We were, all of us, two years out of a decade of civil war. We had survived the darkest place and we had all lost a great deal.

This is Milan Kundera's test of humanity:

> True human goodness can manifest itself, in all its purity and liberty, only in regard to those who have no power. The true moral test of humanity lies in those who are at its mercy: the animals.

I did not see foolishness or indulgence in all those people coming together on a single day to save the life of a street dog. What I saw was compassion, a sense of community, the sweetening of a soured spirit. In other words: I saw hope. ■

All That Follows

Jim Crace

Leonard Lessing does not dream of Maxie Lemon, Maxim Lermontov, the hostage-taker. His dreams belong to Francine yet again, not her in person exactly, not as far as he can recall, but her in mood. His has been an apprehensive night, and when he wakes too early, disturbed by the muted, active telescreen, its erratic light hoisting and flattening into the tightly blinded room, and by the closed community of garden birds crying off a jay without success, he knows that if he does not rise at once, get on, attend to Francine's current and persistent misery, do what he needs to do, then he will steep like unattended tea, growing darker by the moment. Leonard has been a morning man for many years. It is not difficult, once he is standing, to feel genuinely . . . well, not elated. Optimistically agitated, perhaps. Every dawn renews his hope and courage, briefly, he has found. This is the day, is what he always thinks. He will not disappoint himself today. He will not fail again today.

For once he does his morning exercises, not just the stretches to improve what elasticity remains in his right shoulder, but also the routine of bends and sit-ups that he observed fairly regularly before his illness or injury or accident or whatever it was that caused his rotator cuff to lock and hurt in the first place. He has been lazy recently. Pain is his excuse, and boredom. He cannot work if simple acts like putting on a shirt or tying his laces cause such lasting discomfort. How can he lift a music stand or put his back into a saxophone? On his doctor's advice, he has awarded himself a sabbatical, an unsolicited but welcome break from studios and concerts, and even – imprudently – from practising. He is less thrilled by music and performance than he used to be; he has fallen out of love with gigging, not only the bragging company of musicians, their often self-destructive lives, but mostly the endless tours, the exhausting and precarious nights away from Francine. He has become a man who seeks the tranquillity and shelter of home. His current well-being is dependent on having the house, with its modern, regulated lack of clutter and its old-style reclusion, to himself for much of the week,

especially during the day when the natural light is at its most flattering and consoling, and every room and landing is nuanced with blocks of tapered radiance and shadow that can seem as physical as furniture. He'd rather be at home than anywhere. 'You've turned into a dormouse. Or do I mean a tortoise?' Francine says. Either way, it is not flattering. But Leonard does not doubt he deserves this prescribed hiatus, this chance to hibernate. His patrons and audiences can wait six months or so. Likewise the bank. Likewise the garden. Likewise the household maintenance and repairs. Likewise his social life. His knotty frozen joint postpones everything. He hoped to celebrate his fiftieth birthday feeling youthful, fit and heroic. Instead, with only two days of his forties left, he has become gimpy and irascible. Today his right arm will not reach in front of him much further than the elbow of his left. With effort, he can touch his waist. He cannot reach his back with it at all. But still he perseveres with his routine. It gives him time to plan his journey. A short trip away from home will do him good, he thinks. To drive is better than to phone.

He washes at the downstairs sink and, naked in their long, wedge-shaped kitchen (or the Trapezium, as the architect has called it), turns on the panel television and lays a tray for Francine's breakfast. An autumn-term weekday, with an early start for her, so it's coffee, muesli, yogurt, fruit. He makes a Thermos for himself – green tea, lime juice and honey. He's trying to stay young and fit through diet. Nevertheless, he has put on weight; he has a drummer's paunch. His muscles are becoming spongy.

The *Rise-Time* television show on the little kitchen screen has no new angle on the house where Maxie, Leonard's one-time adversary and friend, is angry, armed and holding hostages. The same reporter as last evening, this time wrapped in a green shawl, her hair tied back, says that she has nothing fresh to say. The night was quiet and uneventful. The police are happy to be patient. The hostages have been identified by relatives and neighbours: an unnamed family of five. Three generations, evidently. Leonard listens for their street vicinity and writes it down: Alderbeech. Two trees where probably no woods or orchards have

survived. He knows at once what kind of upright suburb it will be. He can get there in an hour or so if he uses Routeway points and takes the motorway. Then what? He can't be sure what he might do, or should. Being there, he thinks, will help him to decide.

Francine is not sleeping. Her reading light is on. Leonard hesitates outside, holding her tray unsteadily in his good hand. He can't settle on what lie to tell. He'll keep it simple, he decides: tell her that he's going walking. She won't be pleased to hear that. She'll be working after all, plagued by toddlers and curriculums, while she imagines he is having fun on what promises – incorrectly, as it turns out – to be a dry and pretty day. October at its best.

'I wish you wouldn't do that,' she says, when finally he backs open the door and steps round the bed to place the breakfast tray across her lap.

'Do what?'

'Walk about with nothing on. Before breakfast.'

'You used to like it once. More than once even.'

'Well, that was then.' She's smiling, though.

'Curtains?'

'Please.'

He has his back to her, pulling across the heavy Spanish prints until the sunlight slants and corrugates across the bed. 'I might go up into the forests today. See some trees. Some autumn colour. I need the exercise. I'm getting portly.' He pinches the flesh at his waist and stretches it out a few centimetres. She cannot see his face, though he can see her in the window glass, sitting up in bed and staring squarely at the skelfwood cupboards opposite.

'Yes, go,' she says. 'Enjoy yourself' – not meaning it but wanting to.

He drives the gigmobile, his aged, liquid-fuel camper van, taking his time. He has all day. He is not even sure if he will complete the journey. He does not take the motorway after all. Making it circuitous and slow, on minor routes, not only saves him Routeway points but allows him greater opportunity to change his mind and flee back home. At first, he does his best to concentrate on Maxie Lemon, listening to

rolling news on the radio, playing out the conversation he might have with the police officers, and even rehearsing an interview on television with the woman in the shawl: 'Yes, we were friends.' But Francine's odd remark troubles him. 'Well, that was then.' What does she mean by *then*? Before what? Before he became the tortoise with the paunch? He shakes his head. He's worrying too much as usual. But certainly he felt foolish and disappointed when she said, 'Well, that was then.' He hoped to be attractive to her, naked, one-armed, with the tray. Once, many years ago when they first met, she called him 'waiter' as he walked round the room with nothing on, and the breakfast he brought her went cold while they made love.

So music, then. To cheer himself, he will listen to himself. Most of his own recordings as well as cover versions of his compositions are stored on the van's system. He does not like to play them at home. He is by nature both modest and secretive. But when he is alone and driving, who is there to care? He scrolls through the menu and selects *Live at the Factory*. This session, which was broadcast on the radio to hardly anyone as part of the 'Approaching Midnight' series of new work, was judged too obdurate and odd at the time (a raging winter evening, almost ten years ago) to be issued by his recording company. This is Leonard's own download. It is not perfect. But he is fond of it. He truly stretched himself that night – and was rewarded for the stretching in life-changing ways. 'In an unexpected adjustment to this evening's jazz recital,' the announcer explains, as the van heads south through suburbs and doughnut estates into the managed countryside and its network of preservation highways, 'composer and saxophonist Lennie Less will play unaccompanied. Owing to the severe weather, his quartet has not been able to reach Brighton.' There is laughter and applause, and someone shouts out 'Less is More', as someone nearly always does when Leonard's in the line-up. Then the concert host, reduced to cliché by the pressure of live radio and the panic of a green on-air light, overloads the microphone with 'Ladies and gentlemen, let's welcome to the Factory tonight . . . on tenor' – and then steps a pace too far away, reproved by his own feedback, to offer, not audibly enough: 'Mister. Lennie. Less.'

('It rhymes with penniless, as befits a jazzman,' his agent said when they agreed on this stage name instead of plain, unexciting Leonard Lessing.)

L eonard still remembers – and relives – the panic he felt that evening. His colleagues, turned back by blizzards, abandoned vehicles and debris on the motorway just ten kilometres out of London, warn him only twenty minutes before the gig that he will be alone. All those fresh pieces they rehearsed and that are promised in the programme will have to wait for the next night's venue, Birmingham's New Drum, weather permitting. The lead sheets and pages of chord patterns in his music case are useless now. Leonard will have no sidemen, then, to share the blame; no rhythm section to provide depth and camouflage, or any stout string bass to anchor the bottom line for him; no call and response from familiar colleagues, feeding him their hooks and cues; no points of rest; no nodding in another soloist at the end of a progression and stepping out, side-stage, to rest his mouth and hands for sixteen measures or so, or to empty his spit valve, adjust his reed or sip a little water. Here he will be the solitary player, the night-long soloist, the only face onstage. There can be no hiding place. What to play? When he first hears the news about the snowbound quartet, he thinks that, unless someone at the Factory can magic up a *Real Book* full of comforting standards within the next few minutes, he has no choice but to offer a programme of lollipops and show tunes – undemanding numbers he can reproduce entirely from memory.

But by the time the sound engineer appears at the door of the eerily empty Green Room to finger-five that the concert is about to start, Leonard has accepted the inevitable: for this radio concert he must not take the easy option. Everybody is expecting more. Lennie Less does not play show tunes or unembellished standards, no matter what. Lennie Less plays only taxing jazz. He'll start cautiously, he decides finally, with his tenor version of a Coltrane classic solo, 'My Favorite Things'. He's played it, duplicated its patterns and glissandos, many times before – as an encore, something obvious that even the shallowest of aficionados can recognize. He knows it is a bit of a hot lick, begging for predictable but

unwarranted applause – the enthusiasts will be clapping themselves, their own tuned ears – but applause is always a welcome boost at the start of any show. It is an agitating prospect, though, and frightening. Live audience, live radio, no band – and some evidence, from what he's spotted through the stage curtains, that the concert hall is papered with free tickets. Every seat is taken, and that is suspicious for a contemporary music event. There are more frocks and ties than usual, and many more women. He'll be playing not only for the usual pack of devotees, in other words, but for jazz virgins and jazz innocents as well. They could be restless, wary, bored and certainly irritated. And the venue itself is offputting: unraked plastic seating, poor sight lines, overhead industrial plumbing and deadening acoustics – curtains, for heaven's sake! The Factory is devoid of what jazzmen call *the climate*. Even now Leonard sweats at the memory: the trembling apprehension of that long wait before the Brighton broadcast begins, how shakily he adjusts his mouthpiece and the tuning slide, how he runs the keys and rods of his tenor so anxiously that his knuckles begin to clack, how he fusses over his jacket sleeves and his belt, unable to get comfortable or stay cool, how he practises his embouchure and lolly-sucks the reed until his lips are tense and dry.

But that applause, that darkened stage, the flustered concert host, the sense that at least some in that full, damp audience have battled through a storm to listen to his saxophone, the 'live on radio', make him feel – almost at the moment that his lips close on the reed, almost too late – too playful for Coltrane's dark and modal meditation. But not too playful for some nursery rhymes. His entry still thrills him, the walk from backstage, playing, out of sight for the first few bars, a distant sobbing animal, the *legato* opening – the cheek of it – of 'Three Blind Mice'. In the key of C. Four slow bars: Three notes / three notes / four notes / four notes. Simplicity itself. See how they run. And then he finds the spotlight, his semicircle of sound boxes, microphones and water bottles, his comfort zone where he can bend his knees, fold his shoulders, lean into the saxophone and blow. See how they bleed, he says to Brighton with his horn on that appalling night of early snow and wind. Listen to the cutting

of the carving knife.

However, as Leonard remembers all too well when those first slow but risky bars fill up the van once more, there is no grand design as yet. There's certainly no cunning. He is simply taking what he has and stretching it, making phrases from those few root notes, subdued at first, using vibrato sparingly and attacking most notes on pitch, like a beginner. He is not ready to decorate or bend them or embark on any doodling with fillers and motifs. He knows he needs to make it sparse and stable, until he's settled in. He's just *pub crawling* (heading for the next bar), not rushing the notes but waiting to catch them as they pass. Keep it tidy till the sixteenth. That's the rule. But then, too soon, he makes his first mistake, and has to dare. It is a misjudged voicing that, even as he listens to it now, ten winters on, causes him to shake his head and suck his cheeks, as if to take the notes back from the air.

Yet this is where the concert finds itself. The best of jazz is provisional. It often emerges in panic from an error. He hears himself attempt to rescue the mistake by restating it until the error is validated by repetition and seems to be deliberate and purposeful. He listens to the audience, both the virgins and the devotees, applaud his juicing of the blunder. They've all been fooled. They think he has planned every note of it. Do they imagine that he planned the snow, that high gusts from his saxophone have blocked the motorways with trees?

Leonard's band has not been fooled, of course. They are never far from his thoughts, even as he busks his way towards the final bars of this first tune, if tune it is, even as he syncopates the singing rhyme, cheekily matching every grace note with a note denied. He can sense them laughing as he plays. Trapped inside their car, hard up against their instrument cases and overnight bags, listening to him on the radio, they will not have mistaken his misjudged voicing as anything but wide of the mark, a blaring gaffe. And they will not have missed his nervousness and inhibition, the loss of pitch caused by a tight throat and tense mouth. He knows they will be chuckling as they hear him 'digging his way out of jail', as Bradley the percussionist calls it. So he plays for them as well and, even though they cannot comment on a single note, he hears their

contributions in some auxiliary chamber of his ear. No improvising jazzman will deny that there is telepathy. Indeed, the group's most recent release is titled *ESP*. So Leonard measures every note he plays against each chord – each sweetness or each dissidence – that they might have offered had they been on stage with him. He sends his absent rhythm section clues, invites them to add accents to his saxophone, to harmonize with him, to influence the colour of his play. He imagines how a single furry and hypnotic note that he holds for the full length of a bar might be accessorized if there were comrades on the stage. Thus he perseveres, extravagantly, a soloist in imagined company, murmuring, then sharpening his edge, more shaman now than showman – until that eerie modest rodent tune, as familiar as heartbeats, becomes both pulsing anthem and lament.

Leonard listens and taps his fingers on the steering wheel in half-time, happy with himself, happy now to have been so happy then. He sees Lennie Less – as Francine has so many times recounted seeing him that evening – from the third row of the gallery: the spotlight at the centre of the stage, his casual and expensive suit, blue-black, the brass-gold glinting saxophone extemporizing its one-night-only bars. 'Did you ever see / Such a sight in your life / As three blind mice?' The van replays it back to him through her.

Francine says she was attracted to him 'not quite straight away – but soon'. Disarmed by music she has not expected to enjoy – she's come reluctantly, at the last moment, and only to oblige her sister, who's been given several tickets – and by the flattering stage lights that make Leonard seem complex and shadowy, she has begun to think of him, despite the grotesqueries of his bulging throat and cheeks, as someone she might like to kiss. And she's had fun, she says. At times his playing has become knotty, shrill and edgy, just as she's feared. On occasions he is more blacksmith than tunesmith. It is witty, though. And it has helped, of course, that she has rushed a few drinks in the pub beforehand and that she, and every other virgin there, has quickly recognized the common language of each tune, the programme of nursery rhymes that on an

impulse he has decided to play once his 'Three Blind Mice' has struck such chords. 'Baa, Baa, Black Sheep' follows, to more laughter and applause, initially, at least. The less sophisticated and less sober concert-goers, Francine included, have actually sung along with 'yes sir, yes sir, three bags full', until Leonard's tenor deprives the singers of their tune and embarks on eight measures of bare but oddly poignant bleats, loosely pitched at first, then joyously unruly.

These are the moments – the blacksmithing, the bleats – that most please and terrify Leonard, the moments of abandonment when he can sense the audience shifting and disbanding. He fancies he can see the flash of watches being checked. Certainly he can see how many in the audience are on the edges of their seats and how many more are slumped, looking at their fingernails or fidgeting. He knows he is offending many pairs of ears. They've come for those *cool* and moodily bluesy countermelodies that have made the quartet celebrated, not for these restless, heated, cranked-up overloads. But still he has to carry on, he has to nag at them, because he won't be satisfied until he has lost and possibly offended himself. So that night, *this* night, at Brighton's Factory, this night of radio and storms, this night of musical soliloquies, is one he cherishes because he has not backed away. The watches and the slumpers spur him on. As soon as he's dispatched the mice and sheep, he's taking further liberties, he's giving Francine and two hundred others in the audience, plus any late-night listeners who've not switched off their radios, 'Ding, Dong, Bell', sending pussy down the well into musical deep space with a tumbling crescendo, followed by some risky trickery, not blowing on his saxophone at all but drumming with his fingers on the body and the keys close to the microphone so that it seems a lost and distant cat is scratching frantically at bricks.

However testing this might be, however intractable, no one there can say that Lennie Less does not love or does not suit his instrument, his perfect southpaw tenor, a costly Selmer paid for by *Mister Sinister*, his unexpectedly successful first collection. From the sardonic extra curve of the crook where the body meets the mouthpiece and the lips, to the great flared bell that, depending on the slope and stoop of his back, can

just as readily swing between his legs as fit snugly against his abdomen or thigh, this saxophone has become a visceral appendix to the man. Flesh and brass seem unified. It is as if his fingertips and the flat tops of the keys are made from one material, as if breath and metal share substance and weight. So he is mesmerizing. Even for those who are impatient with his gimmickry or antagonized by his excesses or dislocated by his syncopation, there is plenty to wonder at and watch. This man who has come on stage in a dark suit with a shiny patch on the right trouser leg, at pocket level, where the bore and bell of his Selmer have worn the cloth, this man so evidently beset by nervousness that he at first can hardly lift his head to face the audience, this musician who has opened so carefully and timidly with 'Three Blind Mice', has started to transmogrify – there is no better word – before their eyes. It's theatre. You could be deaf and it would still be theatre.

Leonard feels it too. He's on the tight rope, balancing. It's technique and abandonment. He is elated, yes, but he is also terrified. Usually when he is stepping in to improvise he can expect to play what he hears: all his daily practices, those hours spent running through arpeggios or exploring patterns, accents, sequences and articulations in his song repertoire, provide him with a soundscape of tried and tested options; he merely has to choose and follow. He has exhaustively prepared in order to seem daringly unprepared. But here, tonight, he is not playing what he hears; he is hearing what he plays, hearing it for the first time, and only at the moment he – his lips – imparts it to his reed. Each note is imminent with failure. But there is no retreat. Nor does he want to find a safer place, 'a comfort groove', as they are called. This is the moment he's been waiting for, the moment when the wind picks up the kite and lets it soar. Some of the greatest improvisers claim, at rare times such as this, that when the music tumbles out unaided as it were, it seems as if the notes are physical, fat shapes that dance, or colours pulsing, currents, swirls. For Leonard, because he always taps a foot, playing is more commonly like walking, corporeal and muscular walking tightropes, walking gangplanks, walking over coals, also walking on thin air, on ice, in darkness, on rock, on glass, but always walking blindfold. Tonight,

though, he is walking through a landscape forested in notes towards a clearing sky. The wind is at his back. The path ahead is widening. Statement, repetition, contrast and return. Another sixteen bars and he'll be there.

Recognize when you have done enough, he tells himself. Head home. He's hardly moving now, no showboating. He doesn't even tap his feet, or rock his body. Apart from fingertips just lifting and the bulging of his throat, he is a statue voicing nursery rhymes, the final measure, ding dong bell.

The music's ended for the moment – but this rare night in Brighton has an unrecorded track, an afternote, a human lollipop. Leonard has finished signing a handful of booklets and programmes with a shaking hand, his autograph a mess. Euphoric and consumed, wanting more but not expecting anything except a hotel room, he heads out of the auditorium on to the snow and towards his taxi. A small group of intimate strangers in the mostly deserted lobby smile at him and shake his hand. They call out, 'That was beautiful.' And, 'That was fun.' And, 'That was truly weird.' All men. All hardcore fans. Then, yes, then Francine speaks to him. She has delayed him at the taxi door. Her hand is on his arm. 'Truly valiant,' she says, blowing smoke, still a little tipsy and not quite knowing why she's chosen the word, a word that even now has resonance for both of them. Leonard sees a woman just a little younger but a good deal shorter than himself, large-featured in a girlish way, her hair unkempt, her red coat still damp from the storm and smelling slightly wintery. 'Valiant?' he repeats. 'Does that mean rash?' Rash as in reckless? Foolhardy? He hopes it does. 'No, I mean valiant,' she says. 'You know . . . valiant, taking risks. Yes, it was pure valiance.' Embarrassed by her loss of eloquence, her tipsy failure to summon the simple word *valour* when she needs it, she laughs. Such a pealing, mezzo laugh. The evening's most melodic note, he thinks. And that becomes the start of it, his great romance.

Now, with the worst of the country roads and the best of that day's weather behind him and with fresh suburbs gathering, their snouts

pressed up against the fields, Leonard listens to himself again, listens to the music of everybody's childhood, spontaneously reshaped, listens to the retrieved mistakes that masquerade as wit and bravery, the risk-taking, the nerve, the *valiance*, almost unaware of traffic, the dimming sky or the windscreen wipers and, certainly, without much thought of Maxim Lermontov. He presses the track button and returns to the beginning of the broadcast. 'In an unexpected adjustment . . .' And then again. And then again. Announcements and applause, with Francine in the audience – but that was then – admiring him. ∎

The Work of War

Martin Kimani

On the morning of April 16, 1994, Anastase Kinamubanzi was ordered to drive his employer's bulldozer into the sacristy wall of Nyange Church. The order came from Father Athanase Seromba, the parish priest. Inside the simple red-brick building were over two thousand civilians who had mistakenly thought that a church, in this nation of devout Christianity, would shelter them from a week-old genocidal campaign. Outside, blocking any escape, were policemen and members of a militia armed with guns and grenades alongside a large crowd who now surrounded the parish buildings singing patriotic songs, blowing whistles, gripping machetes, garden hoes and wooden clubs studded with nails. Local government officials directed and encouraged the unruly, murderous energy of the crowd.

Anastase resisted the order. A decade later, a prosecution witness in Father Seromba's trial before the International Criminal Tribunal for Rwanda remembered the exchange this man who made a living building roads for an Italian construction company had with the priest.

'Really, Father, do you accept that I should destroy this church?'

Father Seromba nodded.

He asked again and again the priest nodded.

Anastase persisted, 'Father, do you accept that I should destroy this church?'

This time the priest gave a longer reply. 'Unless you yourselves are *inyenzi* [cockroaches], destroy it. All we want is to get rid of the *inyenzi*. As for the rest of it, we Hutus are many. If we get rid of the *inyenzi*, we will build another church. We will build a new church.'

There was work to be done: destroying the church was a step towards building its replacement. Anastase's heavy machine, like a medieval-era battering ram, would end the siege at Nyange so the waiting crowd could undertake the sacred act of building a Hutu nation untainted by a Tutsi pest.

The refugees had been under attack for two days. Bullets had been fired and grenades tossed, while men who only a brief while ago had been their neighbours directed arrows and stones into the church. Inside, many cowered and prayed for a miracle, but others fought.

They mounted a desperate, despairing defence, throwing back stones and using any loose piece of wood to bludgeon back the charging phalanxes. When there was a lull in the attacks, usually in the evenings, the refugees roasted and ate bananas they collected from a parish grove that would later be turned into a mass grave into which the earth-mover would dump their bodies. The bulldozer brought the impasse to an end. The walls of the church were breached and the roof collapsed. Those who survived the crush ran out into the open only to be cut down. Attackers invaded the church to finish off any survivors. They hacked and bludgeoned men, women and children on the altar and in the small recesses of the church.

Father Seromba would later mount a vigorous defence that he had not issued any order to kill. He was found guilty and is now serving a fifteen-year prison term. Anastase, on the other hand, confessed to having followed the priest's commands and received a life sentence. From Germany to Cambodia and now Rwanda, mass murderers in the dock have attempted a variation of a single defence: 'I was following orders.' Doing my job, obeying my superiors, it was impossible to say no. The Nazis at Nuremberg said, '*Befehl ist Befehl*' – orders are orders. They too had used machines similar to Anastase's to push thousands of murdered people into mass graves. In one of the *Kolyma Tales*, Varlam Shalamov writes of a tractor driver, Grinka Lebedev, whose face shows pride at fulfilling the orders from the camp administration to clear an old mass grave of its frozen bodies. Watched by his fellow Gulag inmates, who envy his driving while they walk and crawl in exhaustion to their work detail, he 'carefully carried out his job, scooping the corpses toward the grave with the gleaming bulldozer knife-shield, pushing them into the pit and returning to grab up more'.

We can easily visualize the Nyange bulldozer at a Kolyma or at Treblinka. Its heavy steel part of that vast Nazi network of trains, barbed wire, barracks, gas chambers and lethal chemicals turned into death camps. Yet such heavy machinery was only a bit player in Rwanda. For every person the bulldozer ran over or who fell under a parish wall as it was being flattened, simple work tools wielded by ordinary men and

women murdered thousands. It was the steel of the machete, used as energetically and rhythmically as it is daily on thousands of Rwandan farms and homesteads, that took centre stage in the grim task of genocide.

There is nothing as quotidian as work; no rhythm is more set in our lives. Work is so common that it is rendered invisible. In many testimonies by Rwanda's genocidaires, dozens of whom I interviewed in prisons for my doctoral research, the killing is described as work and the genocide as a war. I wanted to find out why they had killed, how they had done it and what they felt about it a decade later. I expected to find wrecks of men, haunted, wasting away from guilt. There may have been some who were in such a dire state, but none of those I met. Instead, what I encountered in many cases was a confident assertion that what they had done was inevitable: that they were themselves victims of an unfortunate war between the Hutu and the Tutsi. They told of orders, devil possession, the mesmeric effects of a radio station that urged on the killing, the suspicion that the victims were part of a sinister plot to kill all Hutus. Some joked easily with me about prison, others held my hand for long minutes as we stood on the porch of the small office I used for my interviews. I knew they were murderers, I had read prosecution files and spoken to witnesses, but none of this brought me any closer to understanding what had happened at Nyange Parish or the hundreds of other killing grounds. Work, war, orders, these words seemed a faint shadow of the images I had seen on television a decade before I came to Rwanda.

I had been a student in the United States in early April 1994 when CNN journalist Gary Strieker's voice described the footage of a rushing brown river choked with hundreds, thousands, of hacked-up, swelling Tutsi bodies. Roadsides and churches and towns full of the rotting dead were jostling and losing headline space to the suicide of a famous American grunge singer. Three weeks later, they would again play second fiddle, this time to South Africa's first multiracial elections. I was the only African in the dormitory television room and so, as was

usual with all the many puzzles that Africa threw at my dorm-mates' innocence, they turned to me for an explanation of Rwanda's tragedy as April came to an end and newspaper stories kept up a steady count of the accumulating corpses. My defensive, Pan-Africanist responses to their questions rang hollow even to me. It may have been true that the gruesome drama was the result of neo-colonialism, the Cold War and its support of murderous dictators, the false consciousness of nationalism, the colonial hangover, privatization and globalization. But my tongue was stilled. Cameras followed the river of bodies and showed Ugandan fishermen in Lake Victoria pulling swollen corpses into their boats. Young men at hastily erected roadblocks of boulders and felled trees brandished the machetes they had used to chop down the bodies that lay at their feet.

Experts assembled in studios around the world to explain this catastrophe, wrote of an age-old hatred between Hutus and Tutsis, overpopulation, collapsed coffee prices, lack of education, a culture of obedience. The most common characterisation was that Rwanda was in chaos. The violence was depicted as orgiastic and savage. But mass murder, as I would learn, is an undertaking that demands order. The killers organized themselves on roadblock duty, they joined patrols and search parties, they coordinated their killing action and innovated new ways to find and destroy Tutsis.

Years passed and I went to work for a hedge fund. The market made sense of the world. Our Manhattan trading desk was part of a flat world that American columnists told us was here to stay. Bodies in rivers and churches surrounded by killer farmers were far away, they faded with the passing months and years. Then, one morning on the way to work, I emerged from a New York subway train onto a pavement filled with people looking skywards. Planes commandeered by men using small blades meant for office work had crashed into the Twin Towers of the World Trade Center. Three thousand people died. America responded by gathering all the jets and bombs and powers of the Western world to wage war against a small group of men hiding in Afghanistan's caves. Rwanda awakened in my imagination again. I

turned to it and saw that other men with blades, the Hutu genocidaires of old, had sparked a war of seven African countries in Congo.

They had been chased out of Rwanda by an army of Tutsi refugees whose invasion of Congo set off a domino effect of wars and insurgencies that continue to this day. The Rwandan genocidaires maintained their campaign to exterminate all Tutsi peoples, whether they lived in Rwanda or in eastern Congo. The graves filled up fast as militias and militaries tried to prove their ruthlessness by massacring civilians associated with their enemies. The same assembly of experts from 1994 reached for their microphones and penned headlines. 'UN SUSPENDS INVESTIGATION OF ALLEGED CONGO MASSACRES.' 'REBELS "EATING PYGMIES" AS MASS SLAUGHTER CONTINUES IN CONGO.'

Men with machetes determined what streams of bodies flowed into rivers and what buildings remained standing. They showed no half-heartedness, no haplessness. Their zeal had nothing to do with me or anything I knew. It was ready to cut millions to death, to be witnessed doing so, and to proceed with little trouble. And for me, life could not go on as it had before. To knot my tie every morning and take the same train to the same airless office felt increasingly absurd as the weeks went by. I needed to know, to delve as deeply as I could manage into this violence and its politics. Quitting was easy.

I left New York having decided to spend the next few years researching the genocide in Rwanda and visited for the first time in the summer of 2003. This tiny country feels as isolated from the wider world as it looks on a map. The Virunga Mountains, rising more than three thousand metres above sea level, run east to west along the north-western border. The volcanic peaks lie roughly perpendicular to the western arm of the Rift Valley – a great gash in the earth that travels from Syria all the way to Mozambique. To the south-east of Lake Kivu, which covers most of the border with Congo, the altitude rises almost as high as the Virungas. The bulk of Rwandans live in a central plateau dotted with hills that gradually flattens in the east as the inhospitable swamps of the Akagera National Park reach the border with Tanzania.

Kigali, the capital city, lies at the heart of Rwanda. Long before today's many multi-storey office buildings were built, Saint Famille Cathedral, standing atop a hill, dominated the city. Its façade is of red brick interspersed with white columns. The cathedral was built to be forbidding in the same style of Kigali Central Prison, which is also almost a century old and is located at the bottom of a hill. I spent many hours at the prison interviewing men and women who had confessed to participating in the genocide.

One was a woman in her mid-thirties called Mwamini who had confessed to aiding and abetting the killing of Tutsis in Kigali. She came commended by the prison warden for her efforts to encourage fellow prisoners to admit the crimes they had committed during the genocide. Her hope was that confessing and being seen to cooperate would win her an early freedom. Our long conversations centred on her ex-lover Gerard whom she described as if he were a demon walking the earth. He had been the leader of a small militia in Kigali, she told me, referring to his killing sprees during the daytime as 'work'. He would come home in the evenings and expect her to run him a bath so that he could clean off the bits of matter and blood that stuck to him after a hard day.

'Gerard believed that strength alone could earn you the world,' she said. He had been obsessed with karate and claimed to have once represented Rwanda in a continental championship. Another prisoner recalled how Gerard once laid his gun on the ground and proceeded to hand-chop and karate kick a man to death. I felt I had a chance at last to sit across from the killing force whose gruesome effects I had seen on television all those years ago.

I asked to meet Gerard.

If it had been impossible to visualize action from my previous prisoners, if they remained as far from the genocide as they had when I was watching television, here was someone of another order.

Gerard impressed. Tall and swollen with muscle, he moved with a precision that made me, on the other side of the table, feel awkward and nervous. He sat with his hands resting casually on his knees. The

pink prison uniform was draped over a body kept in peak condition by rigorous exercise. He wore the uniform elegantly, the trousers ironed, perfect crease showing. I asked questions, but had to restrain myself from blurting out some sort of confession of how drawn I was to him. Nervous, I trained my eyes downward to his hands. They showed no sign of the swollen knuckles I knew to be common to a karate expert. His face was perfect, symmetrical with the smooth skin drawn tight, no shaving bumps or scars – a far cry from the other inmates I had interviewed who showed the wear of living in a crowded, grimy and disease-ridden prison. Gerard had been imprisoned for ten years, and yet he looked as if he had just walked in from the war, looked as if he had won the war.

Here was a man I was willing to believe had indeed earned his world by making blood gush, eyes widen in terror, arms reach upward to ward off his machete's blows or the bullets that sped towards cringing flesh at the press of his karate forefinger. The small rewards were a car with a driver, unlimited beer and liquor, rolls of banknotes by his bedside. The bigger reward was that his strong body and the way he used it had momentarily won him a radical and incomprehensible freedom that lasted those hundred days between April and June 1994. Its potency still lingered in his cocky, controlling air: he exuded the confidence of a man who has little more to see and experience than that which has passed. If they had lost this war, no part of that loss had happened to his method. If he had killed with guns, karate and machetes, all he had killed was well and fluently killed. He had the body language of victory.

Gerard made me aware of how hard it must be to hack and bludgeon people all day long. Genocide, after all, demands the physical fulfilment of a political aim. The more I listened to him, the more it dawned on me that I had encountered a language of labour since I first started reading testimonies and interviewing killers. The driver of the bulldozer may have initially recoiled from his assigned task, but, just as with the gung-ho participation of Gerard, his actions too were tied to the job.

Here was a way I could look at the crowd surrounding Nyange Parish on that fateful day. They had carried work tools as weapons: machetes and garden hoes. Where the Nazis drew on the industrial resources of Germany to build their gas chambers, the Hutu Power ideology of genocide drew on agriculture which is the mainstay of most Rwandans.

Farming is Rwanda's back-breaking work. A population of ten million people, eighty-five per cent of whom directly depend on farming for their livelihoods, share less than a million hectares of cultivated land. Tiny family farms dot every available bit of flat land and have taken over many steep hillsides. The Hutu, who greatly outnumber the Tutsi, form the bulk of those who for generations have risen daily to walk to their plots in the morning chill, machete and hoe in hand. There they prune banana plants, root out weeds and plunge the machete into red soil to deposit maize seeds. Crippling or even fatal hunger is never far off, and so work must go on whether the sun is hot in the sky or a chilly rain is falling. The young work, the motions they make with their tools mimicking those of their elders.

You bend at the waist to work a machete or a hoe. The strong arm swipes from side to side, clearing the obstacle. The forearm wipes at the sweat of the forehead when a moment of respite is taken. The hand grasps at a wooden handle made smooth by constant use. Hard down-stroke, soft flick, short chopping motion, inquisitive pokes, feet apart balanced on a steep slope, arms straining to dig up a root. A thousand motions repeated for months and years from generation to generation. The arms become lean and strong, the stomach is tight with both hunger and muscle, holding the standing body upright and true.

Whether it is clearing a forest for a planting or building a ship, work involves a violent reordering of nature and of materials. Imagine for an instant the physical effects on the earth as our labour levels mountains to build railway tunnels or plunges shafts deep into the earth to extract metals that we melt and bend into a thousand shapes. But even as the worker reshapes the earth, his effort changes him just as profoundly. His gait and posture bend to account for his labours; his social relations

are transformed as is the society into which he is born.

In Rwanda, the state's compulsory conscription for communal labour – a practice established during the colonial and post-colonial period and known as *umuganda* in Kinyarwanda – became an important foundation in recruiting and deploying groups of killers who approached mass murder in roughly the same way that they had built roads or put up public facilities. This immersion of men with the world as they worked, simultaneously nation-building and nation-cleansing, was key to the aim of group extermination.

The French journalist Jean Hatzfeld has interviewed at length a small group of men who grew up together in the commune of Nyamata, a mostly rural area a half-hour drive south of Kigali, and participated in the murder of some fifty thousand Tutsis in the space of a month. Their testimony repeatedly links the project to exterminate the Tutsi with community and duty.

One of the Nyamata gang speaks of using the machete in the marshes where the thousands who did not meet their end at a massacre at the local Catholic parish were hunted.

> I took up only the machete: first because I had one at the house, second because I knew how to use it. If you are skilled with a tool, it is handy to use it for everything – clearing brush or killing in the swamps. Time allowed everyone to improve in this fashion… whoever struck crooked, or only pretended to strike, we encouraged him, we advised him on improvements. He might also be obliged to take another turn at a Tutsi, in a marsh or in front of a house, and to kill the victim before his colleagues, to make sure he had listened well.

Skill counted as much as enthusiasm. A witness remembers seeing fathers in Nyamata teaching their sons how to slash Tutsis and then watching the children practise the strokes on dead bodies. Reading these testimonies, it became easier to identify the culmination of such a project, a chopping superman, like Gerard. He was built by the intimate nature of killing linked to the day-to-day patterns of Rwandan life.

The distress at taking the first life or smelling the first rotting corpses would ease with time. The teams of hunters would become more efficient. Their machete skills in the marshes would continue to improve and be passed on to the young as was done with the planting of a new crop. The body would become as fluent in the hunting and disposal of the enemy as it was in the farm, while the Tutsi body, hidden, cringing, distorted with pain and then swollen in death, would become ever more awkward and ill-fitted to the world. The Hutu Nation was rising from the ashes of old Rwanda; the coming utopia could be glimpsed in this hell, an egalitarian nation, where each man was measured not by degrading founding myths, but by the merit earned through work and sweat in the killing fields.

'I was doing my job' turns out to have deeper meanings that reveal a dimension of how ordinary men turned into killers, how the nature and language of work, at first glance the most banal of activities, retains an elastic ability to bear transcendent social and political aims.

One of the Nyamata gang put it plainly to Hatzfeld: 'Suddenly Hutus of every kind were patriotic brothers. We were through playing around with political words… We were no longer in our each-to-his-own mood. We were doing a job to order.' ■

Essex Clay

Peter Stothard

Max Stothard and his son at the Marconi fair, 1962

Essex clay could be like living flesh or a cold dead wall. We could punch it, climb it, cut it, try to mould it, try not to offend it, but the clay was permanent like nothing else. Half a century ago, behind the back door of a semi-detached house on the Marconi works estate, a mile from Chelmsford, were hundreds of slimy-sided cubes of this clay, newly cut by machines, soft but indestructible, leaden red by day and looming brown by night, an amalgam that at a child's bedtime might be an Aztec temple or an ancient Roman face or a Russian.

Ours were homes built in a hurry, dug out of a butcher's farmland below a giant steel aerial mast that had been erected against the Communists as soon as the Nazi threat was past. The mobilization of men and materiel to watch for Cold War missiles was as demanding as the hot war in which my father and his engineering friends had learned their craft. In the Rothmans fields of Great Baddow village, beside a town that already boasted the title 'Birthplace of Radio', we became part of an instant works community of families whose fathers understood klystrons, tweeters and 'travelling-way tubes' for the long-distance radar that kept the enemy at bay.

Every man I knew then understood either about the radar that saw things far away in the dark or about the various electric valves that were its eyes. There was a residual wartime spirit, an appreciation of values shared; and also a rising peacetime ambition for new values, new houses, holidays and televisions. As well as helping to defend British prosperity against hostile objects in the sky, we were supposed to share in it, creating a haven of high education, a science park, even an Essex garden community in which the clay cut to make the foundations of 51 Dorset Avenue might one day grow cabbages, fruit trees and flowers.

There were many advantages to life on these company streets. Almost everyone, for example, had a television set. Almost everyone's father could make his own model if he wished. Ours had no polished

cabinet (my mother's woodworking came only later) and its twinkling diodes were slung along the picture rails and around the back of the sofa. But when we wanted a better picture, the contrast of our black and white could be improved from the first principles of the cathode ray. To make the most of *The Billy Cotton Band Show*, a massed expertise could be deployed, from as far afield as Noakes Avenue, the outer limit where Marconi-land ended and Essex farming returned.

The houses were so alike, and the food in their cupboards so absolutely alike, that it hardly mattered where on the estate we fed our pet pond creatures or ate our tea. Most boys had the same-shaped box room for their den, an unusual cube that contained within it another cube, not much smaller than itself, in which the inner supports of the staircase were held. A sawn-off end of a radar monitor was so perfect for newt-keeping that every boy who braved the 'bomb-hole' pond in the 'rec' had one of his own. Break the glass and there was always a replacement the next night. All groceries came from the same dirty-green single-decker coach of 'Mr Rogers', a silent ex-soldier who piled his fruit and vegetables on either side of the aisle where the seats had been and twice a week toured the avenues from Dorset to Noakes to sell cereals, sugar, flour – everything that the gardens might one day produce but did not yet.

Books were universally rare. There were five at 51 Dorset, the brightest-coloured being a sky-blue edition of S.T. Coleridge, the title printed in such a way that for years I thought that the poet was a saint. Next to it sat a collected Tennyson, in a spongy leather cover, half bath accessory, half one of the then new and exciting table-tennis bats from Sweden. There was my Yorkshire grandfather's copy of the second half of Virgil's *Aeneid*, with the name B. Stothard, in a firm, faded script, inside the flyleaf. I have that one here with me now. On the shelf below was a cricket scorebook in which someone had once copied improving philosophical precepts, and beside that, *The First Test Match*, a slim, slate-green hardback which alone looked as if it had been read.

This was a community of algebra and graph paper. Mathematics was the language of choice. Contract bridge was the nightly recreation.

My curly-haired, smiling father had a brain for numbers that his fellow engineers described as Rolls-Royce. Notoriously, he did not like to test it beyond a purr. In particular – and this was unusual in a place of intense educational self-help – he did not care to inculcate maths into his son. This was a task which he had recognized early as wholly without reward. Max Stothard would occasionally attack the mountain of clay in his garden but never knock his head against a brick wall. He was nothing if not blissfully relaxed.

Like most of our neighbours, he had learned about radar by chance, in his case while becalmed for the war years off West Africa on a ship called HMS *Aberdeen*. He had bought red-leather-bound knives for his mates back in the Yorkshire-Lincolnshire borderlands; he had sent postcards of Dakar's six-domed cathedral to his strictly Methodist mother; he had never fired a hostile shot except at a basking shark. And when he had needed something else to do, he chose to watch the many curious ways that waves behave in the air above the sea, turning solid things into numbers. That was how he spent most of the rest of his life, in the south of England instead of the north because that was where the radars were made, quietly reasoning through his problems on his 'bench' in the Marconi laboratory and in an armchair at home, spreading files marked 'Secret' like a fisherman's nets. He earned £340 per year, as my mother and I discovered when he died. Secrecy about earnings was always an obsession, although everyone was paid much the same.

The Rothmans estate was based on a bracing sense of equality and a suffocating appreciation of peace. Although most of our fathers felt they had a part in this great military project of the future, rarely can so massive a martial endeavour, the creation of air defences along the length of Britain's eastern coast, have been conducted in so eirenic a spirit. Not even the Bournville chocolate workers of Birmingham, the group best known then for living together in a company town, could have demonstrated such a Quaker appreciation of calm. The fighting war was absolutely over. The new business was civil, work carried out with civility above all else, work that would keep us safe and increase

our prosperity as the politicians promised. And because everyone was in it, everyone was in it together.

That was the constant message of Miss Leake, our doughty headmistress at Rothmans School, whose doctrine of 'excellence and equality', delivered in her severest voice, was adapted only slowly to the gradually advancing evidence of differences around her. There were certain girls with vastly superior proficiency at maths; but certain boys could freely pervert the spirit of Rothmans peace in a greater Rothmans cause, designing missiles and fighter planes to crash Pauline Argent and Anne Spavin back to earth. For our first two years Mrs Sheffield reassured us repeatedly that we were all much the same; but eventually and inexorably, when we were aged seven and in the empire of Mrs Maloney, those of us who counted badly had to be separated from those who counted well. Those who could not sing were called 'groaners' and told to wait outside the door; and those who preferred Virgil's stories to vulgar fractions were reluctantly allowed to write fiction for our homework, as long as it was science fiction.

My father was not at all worried about my being a 'groaner' (he listened to no music himself at all and was especially offended by the violin and the soprano voice), but he was faintly sad about my missing number skills. Numbers were the key to advancement. Physics was the first step to a working future, a future in paid employment in a world which itself worked well. Many of my friends with no aptitude at all for figures – who could draw a beautiful anti-Pauline-Argent plane but never match her equations – were pummelled onto numerical paths. How, asked our neighbour on the other side of the clay mountain, could anyone pull themselves up by any other route? It was hard to find anyone who would argue with this doctor of metallurgy from the northern steel lands of Scunthorpe – about that or about anything much else except bidding conventions in hearts and spades and the best way to see things that dared fly low in the sky.

At the same time there grew among us the gradual acceptance of other differences. Ours was only in part a works estate in the

tradition of the Birmingham chocolatiers and the Wirral's Port Sunlight. It was becoming a place for the upwardly mobile at a time of restless mobility. So there were questions. Were the engineers' families of Rothmans Avenue, Dorset Avenue and Noakes Avenue quite as much the same as first appeared? Did the more brilliant scientists live in Rothmans, the more managerial in Dorset, the more clerical in Noakes? Were they richer in Rothmans and rather poorer in Noakes? Did the 'Millionaires Row' houses by the school gates really have four bedrooms? Whose kitchen had less Fablon and more Formica? Should Marley floor tiles be polished? And where exactly did everyone go on holiday?

Summer was the great unequalizer. On the North Sea coast, only thirty or so miles away, the skies were known equally to all masters of air defence. But the beaches beneath were crisply divided. Clacton, Walton and Frinton were never the same. We always went to Walton-on-the-Naze, the middle town of the three, the one which had the widest concrete esplanades where children could ride bikes. Clacton-on-Sea was south of Walton and had slot machines and candyfloss booths where 'other people' could waste their money. North of Walton was Frinton-on-Sea, which had no candyfloss, no caravans (we always stayed in a caravan), no fish and chip shops, not even a pub, just Jubilee Gardens and what was known, only by warnings not to walk on it, as 'greensward'. Did Rothmans Avenue families prefer Frinton? By the time of my eleventh birthday in 1962, it sometimes seemed that they did. Our Marconi estate was small, confined and had only one entrance to the world. Once inside it we could always roller-skate through the class lines. On the coast, it was an impossible walk, and even an awkward drive, between three neighbouring towns that seemed built deliberately to show how different from one another we might be.

My father was a typical Rothmans engineer of his time, in every respect except in certainty that his was the right path. That was his grace and glory. He never stopped me preferring stories about science to the understanding of what science actually did. He read the fictions

that I wrote about my manufactured hero, Professor Rame, without complaining directly to me that there was no point in any of that. He did not much like the Coleridge and the Tennyson being on hand. But he did not take them away. He himself liked to see people as electro-machinery, as fundamentally capable of simple, selfless working. It was simpler that way. But he never imposed the company line. His own mind was closed to the communications of religion or art. His favourite picture then was a photograph of Great Baddow's tribute to the Eiffel Tower. But his passions for moving parts, moving balls and jet streams in the skies over air shows did not preclude an acceptance of others' passions. He was a pleasure-seeking materialist – in a company estate where those were the prevailing values and the predominant aspirations. Materialism in those days was a means of science, which he loved, not of extravagance, which did not exist, nor even of shopping, which he would barely tolerate. It was the successful basis of a contented, comfortable life. ■

GRANTA

Moving Parts

Ruchir Joshi

Phuli

The little island of dust and daily debris moves across the floor accompanied by the swish of the dried grass *jhaadu*. It's a soft, scraping sound, a comforting metronome that's accompanied me all my life. The stiff *jhaadu* used for wet work in bathrooms and rough terrace areas has a completely different feel, the business end made from thin, long, flexible sticks. The sound is harsher, especially when the *jhaadu* is thrashing water off tiles. Then there is the thick, rhythmic slap of soapy clothes, bundles of them first bashed on the bathroom floor, then squeezed out and slung into a bucket.

In the old days, everything the servant did was at floor level – washing clothes, washing dishes and kitchen things, sweeping and mopping the floor; now there are washing machines for the clothes and kitchen sinks for the dishes, but the floor hasn't moved: you see vacuum cleaners and long-handled mops in hotels and offices, but you don't see them in even the wealthiest houses in India. Something still requires that you have the floor swept and mopped in a combination of squatting and bending positions. First there is the sweeping with a *jhaadu*, then the second pass with a bucket of water and the *pochha*, the grey mopping cloth, the whole thing known as *jhaadu-pochha*, since the sweeping is incomplete without the mopping.

In these parts, someone like Phuli, who cleans my friend J's flat, would be called a '*jhaadu-pochha-waali*', 'she who does the sweeping-mopping'. Phuli is a small woman, not particularly tiny for her class, region or generation, but she disappears behind a sofa or a chair. She can't squat like she used to, so a lot of the work is done in a posture that takes an old person's spinal bend to its absurd extreme: standing, but with her head almost touching the floor.

It's difficult to tell for sure, but Phuli must be nearing seventy. Her eyesight isn't great and her hearing is going, but none of this deters her from catching a bus every day from the suburb of Trilokpuri to

Jangpura and Nizamuddin, the areas where she works in south Delhi. It's a nearly two-hour commute on good days. I imagine that even the brutal north Indian bus crowd must make space for an old woman, but that would only be a recent thing – Phuli has been taking this bus for the last thirty years. The difference, of course, is that the bus is much more crowded than when Phuli began to commute, the tripled population of Delhi squeezing her more and more with each passing day.

The pressure has increased on living space as well. Phuli is lucky that she's not of the younger generation of domestic workers who've been 'resettled', ripped out from their slums in this part of the city and packed off to areas like Bawana and Savda Ghevra at the edge of the huge continent that is now greater New Delhi. Phuli built her house early, 'when Indira Gandhi gave us land'. That would mean she moved out of this neighbourhood around 1976, when Mrs Gandhi's son carried out forced evictions across the city. Now Phuli's daughter has her own house not far from her mother and she earns good money doing the same work Phuli has done all her life.

'People don't talk to you any more,' Phuli says. 'In the old days, when I first moved here, the women would be at home, not out and working like all of them are today, and they would make you a cup of tea, give you a snack. They needed to talk as well, you know, to take a break from their own housework. Also fewer TVs then! Now they pay you well, but you don't see them for days! Both of them out! Someone gives you a key, you clean, you go, you collect your money at the end of the month. Before, the people you worked for knew the names of all your children. Now? Tchaah, forget it! No one has anything to *do* with anyone else nowadays!'

Millions of women are now working away from home, doing very different jobs – one of the fundamental changes in the country's economy. In the early 1990s, when washing machines first became freely available in India, many wealthier Delhi households held back from buying them, preferring to stick to the system of the 'maid' coming in to wash their clothes. Among the people who first ordered

the washing machines on monthly instalment plans were lower-middle-income domestic workers who no longer had the time to wash their own clothes, women who could leave their young daughters to turn the knob on the new gizmo while they rushed from house to house earning their money.

'I used to do small jobs,' Phuli continues, 'twenty to twenty-five houses a day, but just one or two things in each. Now, I only do about four to five. People doing the houses nowadays have different ideas from before. In the early days, I used to earn about ten to fifteen rupees per house, ten rupees a month, that is! Think! Now these youngsters go and charge a hundred and fifty rupees just to splash some water across a bathroom! That's *per* bathroom, so if someone has three bathrooms, you work it out.' Phuli grins, shaking her head at the sheer, thieving cheek of the young.

So the commute in the heat, people hanging from the sides of the bus, invisible employers – why does she still do it?

'If I sit down, my bones will jam up.' Then she says it again, in case I don't get it. 'If I stop working, I won't be able to move.' I can see what she's talking about. This slow momentum has built up over a lifetime of labour and without it there would be nothing to centre her body, nothing to get her out of bed in the morning. I suspect she is also unwilling to be dependent on her daughter, to be any sort of deadweight. But, yes, the bones matter too.

Until recently the first sign of money in an Indian household rising out of poverty was not a car or a fridge or a mobile phone, but the hiring of domestic help. Without this help, middle-class Indians – the IT guys, the small-suitcase entrepreneurs, the artists, the politicians, the NGO heroes – would be unable to function. Whatever may happen to Phuli when she finally stops, if the current generation of domestic workers were suddenly to decide to sit down – something impossible to imagine – I know exactly whose bones will jam up.

Shahid

The word for 'artist' in Hindi is '*kalaakaar*'. In the north of India, working-class people often take the word and turn it around to mean 'fraud' or 'con-man': 'That guy? You can't trust his weighing scales, he's a real artist!'

As I watch Shahid apply his craft, I think about this connection between art and sleight of hand, between creativity and crooked profit. One could say that what Shahid does is fraud – he camouflages damaged goods, making it possible for the shopkeeper to sell something under false pretences. However, looking at it from a different perspective, an artistic perspective, one could also say he fills a need with great and consummate skill.

The shop is one of hundreds of thousands that line India's highways and the small towns the routes bisect: tyre workshops form one part of the chief trinity of establishments you find driving across the country, the other two being truckers' eating joints – the *dhabas* – and petrol stations. Besides fuel for the stomach and the engine, the one major requirement of all the men and motors travelling these roads is the repaired puncture and, sooner or later, the new tyre.

As far as tyres go, the word 'new' is infinitely inflatable and deflatable; only as a last resort will the owner or driver of a commercial or farm vehicle actually fork out for a factory-fresh ring of rubber. Instead they will repair it as far as possible; when that no longer yields results they will send it to a re-treading factory, where the inside and outside of the main, stiff, rubber frame is scraped raw by cruel-looking instruments: expanding rings that heat and tighten, chains that lift and stretch, wheels that eviscerate with steel needles. Once the ring is clean, a new strip of rubber tread is glued on and finished off by a kind of polishing. This process is above board and supported by tyre companies providing the strips of rubber tread for a rural market they recognize as parsimonious. But even this is seen by many as a luxury, and that is where Shahid comes in.

'I started as a kid, just working for the Ustad here,' Shahid says, gesturing to his old mentor in whose shop we are meeting. 'I was just

a kid, like any other. Doing this, that and everything, but then the Ustad obviously saw something in me and he encouraged me to go further.'

Next to Shahid is an open cloth bag on which he has laid out his tools. For the next ten minutes, as he talks to me, Shahid picks up small steel scoops from the pile and sharpens them on a whetstone. Then he takes a completely bald tyre and places it between his legs. He strokes the surface, feeling for bumps and hollows. 'You can't just do this with any tyre, the piece has to have a little bit of life still left in it, otherwise this doesn't work.' He reaches for another tyre and shows me. 'Like, look at this. You see how there is a dip here? Nothing here under the surface at all. That means this tyre is really finished. Gone.'

He goes back to the piece he's gripping with his thighs and turns it, looking for the best place to start. Then, very much like an artist starting to mark a canvas or a blank piece of paper, he grabs a steel scoop and begins gouging into the ghost of the tread. It is a typical zigzag and, when I compare the path of his scoop to the still somewhat intact pattern on the sides, I can see Shahid is matching the machine-made markings exactly.

'You see, many people do this work' – Shahid now only speaks in the pauses when he turns the tyre forward, the control of breath crucial to the control of arms and hands – 'but not everyone can.' He grips the scoop, pressing down just so with his arms and shoulders. As his wrists begin to dance, a thin, squiggly vermicelli of rubber rises up from the grey-brown surface. What emerges behind his hands is a fresh, black wound of tread that eventually goes right around the tyre. Finishing one line, Shahid starts another, again using the slight give of the original trough as a guide. After fifteen minutes the job looks done to me, but Shahid is not finished.

'The main group is done' – it takes me a while to realize that he means 'groove' – 'but you see these small gouges between the main treads? Now, a lot of group-cutters would forget to do those, and that's a dead give-away – how come the big treads aren't worn while the small ones are gone? "Ah! Caught you!" But not me.' Quickly, Shahid

makes the intermediate score, not overdoing it but not forgetting even one.

'The thing is, we aren't saying to the buyer that these are new tyres. We never say that. Buyers are not stupid. What we say is, "Here is a second-hand tyre in pretty decent shape, check it out yourself before you buy it!" Now, where did this tyre come from? It could have come from many places – a totalled car where the tyres were intact, a stolen vehicle, anywhere. Not new, but in good, second-hand shape. And, in fact, there are some people who even know exactly what they are buying, a driver who has burst a tyre driving carelessly but doesn't want his car owner to find out, someone buying bulk for some company, people like that.'

Shahid switches to a tyre with a straight groove. 'Now, you see this straight group here? This is where many group-cutters take it easy, but this is where your artistry, or lack of it, really shows up! Straight can actually be more difficult than a zigzag or any other pattern.'

Surrounded by the grime and grease of the workshop, framed by hanging tubes and scattered, rusting rims, Shahid produces a dead-straight 'group'. And another. And another.

'How long did it take you to learn the trade?'

'Well, it was hard at first. The Ustad sent me to Lucknow, where this boss who taught me would throw me an occasional tyre to practise with. It was hard, the smallest mistake meant a slap on the ear, but that's how you learn! It took me five years to become a full expert, but now I can do any tyre on the market and you won't be able to tell its group is hand-cut!'

'Five years. That's how long it takes to get an engineering degree.'

'Yes, well you can call this my engineering or my craft. I call it my *kalaakaari*!'

My art.

Neym Singh's Uncle

Neym Singh's uncle is a wiry man in his late thirties, his skin toasted dark by a life spent in hard sunshine. And for someone

who sells 'country-made pistols' to the rural poor as a side profession he is polite. We are in a fertile part of Uttar Pradesh – one of northern India's largest states – but nowhere close to the so-called 'badlands' of eastern UP, famous for providing muscle and gunmen to the mafia gangs in Bombay and Delhi. The richer farmers and feudal landlords have access to far more sophisticated weapons – both licensed and unlicensed – but the hand-crafted gun, variously called a '*kattaa*' or a '*tamanchaa*' is primarily used in small local disagreements or to provide security against robberies.

'It happens like this,' he says. 'You have a dispute with someone in your village. Say, they are trying to grab some of your land. So, from shouting and yelling it moves to fighting, and one day these people come to your field, ten of them, carrying big sticks and sickles, trying to make you understand what they are saying. You are also trying to make them understand what you are saying. So, there's really nothing that you can do except...'

Neym Singh's uncle pulls a gun out of his waistband and shoots me. It's not a particularly smooth move – his left arm pistons as he pulls up his dirty untucked shirt; he jerks as he yanks the pistol from his waistband; the barrel leaps as he cocks the hammer with his thumb; and there is a jolt and a snap as he pulls the trigger. It's not greased lightning, but economical nonetheless, and fast enough to be inescapable. It's also point-blank: if the hand-piece were loaded, I'd be plugged.

'You hit one of them, just one of them, and I promise you the others will run.' He looks at me without drama. 'You have any idea the panic just one gunshot going home can create? They will run. A gun is like ten brothers.'

He doesn't make the weapons himself – he just provides the raw materials and the hidden, makeshift forge and workshop in the jungles on the other side of the fields around the village. In the jungle, he and the gunsmith are safe. They can run and hide in places that even the local police don't know about.

'The man who makes these is a poor man, an ordinary man who

lives under a straw roof. He doesn't even have concrete over his head. He makes maybe no more than fifteen hundred rupees a month because he doesn't work all the time. He travels from place to place making these for people like me who have buyers. He earns a little because he is good with his hands, he has this skill.'

The gunmaker makes maybe two guns a day, or one handmade rifle, earning 300 rupees per pistol and 500 for a rifle. Neym Singh's uncle then sells the pistols for between 1,000 and 2,500 rupees, sometimes more.

'So that's a big profit, isn't it? For something which costs you 300 rupees?'

Neym Singh's uncle gives me an appraising look.

'I pay the *man* 300 rupees for each piece. Then there are the costs of the raw material, which has to be good. For instance,' he says, picking up the gun and breaking it open, 'you see this barrel? Other people sell *tamanchaas* made out of brass or some other metal. If you shoot more than one bullet through it too quickly, the barrel just melts, or, even if it doesn't melt immediately, it gets too hot to touch so you can't reload without burning yourself. But this barrel here is from the steering rod of a Maruti car, best quality, won't melt.'

I've heard about *kukri* knives made from tyre rims in Nepal, but never this. 'You can use steering rods from other cars but Marutis have the best ones,' he continues, 'and they are widely available. That barrel also means the *tamanchaa* can be of whichever calibre you want – .303 bullets or .315 – and it will be accurate, meaning, you won't be one hundred per cent sure to hit something beyond fifteen feet but until that distance you will hit your target. Then. This spring here…this is the spring that sits at the base of a Maruti clutch plate.' Neym Singh's uncle swats away a fly and thinks for a bit before going on. 'You have to understand. I sell milk as my main profession, I'm not a car mechanic, so I make sure I don't go back to the same places for the car parts. Sometimes I need to go as far as Faridabad to get them. And then there is the sheet metal I get for the body and the sal wood for the handle and the stock of the rifles, which is the best wood. None of this

is cheap. Setting up the forge also costs money.'

He hands me the gun and reaches for his cup of tea. The weapon looks like a prop from a low-budget theatre production, but despite the rough finish of makeshift rural machines and instruments, it's beautifully made and well balanced. The metal joins are sealed with what I discover to be melted bronze, the grip of sal wood is sandpapered meticulously and varnished to prevent splinters; the spring and the hammer have their own coarse integrity.

'Does it bother you that people get killed by these guns you sell?'

He has been asked this before. The eyes flare a bit before he drops them to the *kattaa*.

'Yes, well, these don't exactly shower you with flowers.'

'Do you get into trouble if someone kills someone with one of your guns?'

'Well, that's the best thing about this *kattaa*-type gun. Say you shoot someone. Say he dies. You just dismantle the gun and throw away the different parts in different places. A licensed revolver can be traced, it leaves a sign on the bullet. This one leaves nothing, you can't trace it.' Neym Singh's uncle lowers the gun and moves his left hand over it as if erasing the weapon, as if it's already been recycled. ■

GRANTA

Hippocrates

V.V. Ganeshananthan

For the sake of propriety, although it was far too late for propriety, when I was sent away from Jaffna to Colombo, I travelled in the company of another girl. She, unlike me, had done nothing wrong, and when the train jostled us so that our sweaty wrists touched, she jerked her body away from mine, and I thought I deserved it. We had known each other since we were very young, and for many years had touched each other in the familiar way of friends and schoolmates and neighbours, but that did not matter now. When I had returned to Jaffna, no one in our village had asked me about what I had done while I was with the Tigers. They had assumed, and rightly, I thought then, that I was apart from them, and that I could not return to the life to which I had been born. No one spoke of where I had gone, or with whom I had travelled. This was not from any code of silence, but rather a sense of futility: there was no point in discussing what had already happened. We had reached a moment at which living took so much effort that no one could spare the breath to speak to me. I understood this and was not offended. Although I was not myself a Tiger, I had been with them, and I had left them. There was nothing for me in the village now, although it was still the place I knew and loved the best.

My uncle came to receive me at Colombo Fort Station. The other girl separated from me without saying goodbye, as though we had not walked down the same dusty roads to the same primary school. I watched her walk towards the rows of three-wheelers, moving, like me, into a world of strangers. Even my uncle was a stranger. I had never met him, although he lived in the same country as me and was my mother's brother. Still, I knew him immediately as I stepped off the train platform, because he held himself in the same way as my mother. He looked as though he never hurried, but nevertheless he moved quickly through the crowd. He had not brushed his hair and seemed not in the least embarrassed to be himself. His peculiarly large hands reached for my suitcase before he even said hello to me. His hands met

mine before his eyes met mine, and this, too, was like my mother: he did not wish to speak plainly.

You look like your mother, he said to me in Tamil. If he had said this to me later, perhaps now, I might have replied: So do you. But I was a girl, and I was nineteen, and he did not expect to have a conversation with me. He did not want my opinions, and I did not want to give them to him. We were to be relatives only. He wanted to exchange facts. And I did not know that this was the beginning of my exit from that life – that he was to be one of the last people I met who knew what my mother looked like.

Did you eat? he asked.

I had something on the train, I said.

Amma will have some tea for you when we reach Wellawatte, he said. You must be tired.

He did not wait for me to confirm this, but turned and pushed his way into the crowd. I followed him through the train station and out the other side, to the street. I was not slow, but I had not yet learned to navigate the crowds and foulness of a city. The people who moved for him pushed back at me, perhaps sensing my vulnerability and strangeness. By the time I caught up with him, he was waving to the driver of a big black car a few metres away.

The driver drove from Fort to Wellawatte, my uncle's neighbourhood, with the windows open. Even if they had been closed, I would have known that Colombo was not as clean as home, that it was not quiet like Jaffna. Breathing felt hard, and my ears were tired from hearing so much. I felt dirty. I blew my nose and lifted my handkerchief blackened with soot and exhaust.

My uncle did not talk to me, and so I looked out the window. Everything passed by – the lights and architecture of a city – and I did not see it. My eyes were still full of Jaffna. I wanted my brothers – my brothers, who were gone. And I wanted my mother and my father, even though they did not presently want me. This man, my uncle, looked like my family, but he did not know me, he did not want to know me, and the feeling of being surrounded by strangers made a

pocket of pain inside my chest.

The car stopped, and the driver came round and opened the door for me. I got out, and my uncle was already up the path of the house, moving deftly around a small, barking dog. A hunched, wrinkled woman at the door took the bag from him and smiled deferentially at me, holding her hand out in a gesture of welcome.

Come, she said.

My uncle vanished into the back. I stood by the door, removing my shoes with unnecessary care. I listened for and then could hear the car pulling out of the driveway.

Sit, sit, the woman said, smiling, and then she, too, disappeared down a side hallway, pulling the suitcase along.

The chair I sat in was very old, with the wooden bones of the frame pushing through the upholstery on the arms. The floor was bare and warm, its boards smoother against my toes than the concrete of my family's house in Jaffna. The walls were crowded with pictures, and I noticed, finally seeing Colombo for a moment, that some of them were of me. I was so small in some of the pictures that I did not remember being myself in them.

You look all grown up, my grandmother said, and I stood up suddenly, so fast that I almost knocked the tea tray from her hands. She steadied herself and put the tray down on a table next to the chair.

Although my uncle had referred to her, I had almost forgotten she would be here. She looked much older than when she had last visited Jaffna, five years earlier. My mother's mother was a stunningly ugly woman, with a long, skinny, black birthmark running down the left half of her face, and the milky-blue rings of her sclera showing around her eyes. I was old enough now not to be afraid of her ugliness, and to know that, later, I could be her, and that in fact the odds were in favour of that. She was the first ugly person I had ever loved, although she would not be the last. At nineteen, I was young enough to value beauty and old enough to know that certain types of it would die, while other kinds would grow stronger.

On this day I saw for the first time that I was taller than her. I was

tall for a woman anyway, and she was not short; that height ran in our family. Her face, paler now, told me how I would look when the softness had been stripped from my face. Her hands were still unwrinkled, and when she reached up to pat me on the cheek, I recalled that she coated them with oil every day to keep them that way: her sole vanity. We kissed each other twice, once on each side of the face, the way we had always greeted each other.

She talked to me while I had tea, and gave me supper. Like my uncle, she did not expect me to respond to what she said, but unlike my uncle, she loved me and I liked to listen to her. Afterwards, she put me to bed, as though I were still a small child. I let her; to be treated like a child for an hour comforted me, although even now, I am ashamed to admit that to myself.

When I woke up I could hear the bells of a temple ringing in the distance. I wondered what the temples in Colombo were like. They could not be as big as our temples in Jaffna, I thought; the gods of Colombo must be cramped and noisy, sweaty and smoky, elbow to elbow.

I could hear someone else moving around towards the back of the house, in the kitchen, the sounds of a kettle being settled on to a stove. I had already learned to count on the sounds people make, and to consider them as markings, like fingerprints for the ears. It was not the sound of the servant woman; it was my uncle's quiet, quick step. I put a housecoat on over my nightdress and went out into the corridor and back towards the kitchen, very slowly so as to not disturb his routine. Halfway there, I heard him turn the radio on. The voice of a news announcer crackled out into the morning. I heard him very clearly. I heard what he said, and then I forgot to be quiet and ran, the pounding of my feet waking up the house.

The voice on the radio said what had happened was this: a pregnant woman had gone to a government office building in Colombo. She had ridden the elevator to the top floor of this building, which was an important building that I did not know, having arrived

too recently to understand the whereabouts of importance in the city. At the top floor, she got off and asked to see a man in charge, whose office was very large and had a wooden desk. She told them that she had an appointment; the secretary checked the records and saw that this was true.

The voice on the radio did not say this, but I imagined it to be so: the woman was seated and offered tea, which she accepted, with milk and plenty of sugar. She was from Jaffna; she liked a lot of sugar in her tea. She waited for ten minutes, and then, when the secretary called her, she picked up her bag and rose from the chair to be escorted into the office. The man shook her hand and called her Madam, respectfully, although she was not very old, perhaps no older than her mid-twenties. Her pregnancy was obvious, but this did not desexualize her in his eyes; she was a very beautiful woman, wearing a large green silk tunic and trousers that brought out the fairness of her skin and the darkness of her hair. She was wearing a red *pottu* between her eyebrows, the mark of a married woman, although she was not actually married. She shook his hand back and smiled at him disarmingly.

The voice on the radio only said: She pressed a button to detonate the primary bomb she was carrying.

I suppose that was the part that mattered.

I want you to understand: I was not born to fight for a political cause. I did not feel chosen. And this woman was not born this way. She was not chosen. She was born in a village in Jaffna, and soldiers raided her house, and she was gang-raped, and she watched the men who raped her kill her four brothers. I want you to understand: this is not an excuse, or an explanation. It is a fact. She was not born to walk into an office building on an ordinary day, a day when the sun was shining and three-wheelers cluttered the streets, to try to detonate a bomb. And in fact, later, the forensics said that was what had happened. She tried to detonate a bomb. But she failed, because it had been built improperly. I want you to imagine this, as I did when I heard that: the bomb blew up, but not completely, not enough to kill them quickly as she had intended. The first small, potent blast caught her

and the man together, and with her right arm gone and his left leg severed beneath the knee, they looked like one person dancing. Her hair fell out of its pins into his open mouth. Two building security guards burst into the room after only a few moments, and she screamed, and they pointed their guns at her. She held up like a prize the other bomb, the auxiliary fuse and its detonator, and shouted in Tamil. The man reached out to wrestle with her, screaming also but in Sinhalese, and the guards aimed for her. Their training was not good enough for this. If they shot the bomb, it would blow up; if they shot the woman, she would probably manage to detonate it anyway. They aimed for the woman; they fired; they missed. They aimed again, the man shouting again, trying to push her between himself and the guards, and this time one of them hit her in the shoulder. Blood bloomed on the green silk. The other one aimed and shot her again. The bullet pierced her neck, and as she reached up to hold the wound, she let go of the other detonator.

She died and she killed other people and she did not mind, and in this she was different from me forever.

M y grandmother found me vomiting into the toilet. She came behind me and held my hair.

What is it? she asked me. Are you sick?

I wiped my mouth. I did not look up, and I did not answer. I vomited again, but there was nothing left in my stomach. I looked down at my stomach and thought of Saavi's stomach, the rounded belly of pregnancy. Some female suicide bombers use pregnancy as a disguise, not only because it is easy to conceal explosives, but also because it weakens the resolve of police officers to see a mother. Each of them, of course, has his own. A transgression against a mother is a universal transgression; when a man treats a mother kindly, he imagines that somewhere else, someone is getting up on a train to offer a seat to his own mother, or perhaps helping her to carry her groceries from the market. He is remembering what his wife looked like in her first trimester; he is thinking of his younger siblings or perhaps his own

children. He is thinking of life, and of repetition, and of things happening again, as they have happened to him. He is not thinking that anyone carrying a belly that size, that shape, would carry death.

This is why it is the best disguise. And that is why I was sick; I knew that the woman in the office building, who had ridden the elevator to the top floor, must be Saavi. Because the voice on the radio had said that: they had been able to tell that the bomber's pregnancy was not a disguise, but real. I knew how she had become pregnant; I had had to tell her that she was. And I knew the bomber had to be her. Anyone but Saavi would have faked it.

I had not seen Saavi, of course, in several months: almost exactly the amount of time it takes to train with the Black Tigers, to rehearse a scenario like the one she had executed, to grow a pregnant belly into a more-pregnant belly. I had met her when I treated her for injuries at a medical tent outside one of the rebel camps. She was not a Tiger then. She had shown up and asked for a woman quite calmly, although her nose was obviously broken and one of her ears was torn. She was about my age. She had wound her long skirt between her legs and around her waist, and gripped it tightly, as though it were all that was holding her together. I had seen some older women in the village do this; people whispered that they had had so many children that their wombs were falling out. But I knew that this was not her situation. She did not tell me what had happened to her; the sentry who had brought her in did that so that she did not have to repeat herself. He had known her from his village, from before the soldiers had come to keep peace and to rape women, and he spoke more calmly and professionally about what had happened to her than I could have managed myself, if I had already known her. One of her dead brothers had been his classmate.

She was the first rape victim I had ever treated, and so I remember it clearly, especially because now, as an emergency-room physician here, oceans away from those medical tents, I perform rape kits all the time. Back then, in Tiger territory, treating girls from the villages, I did

not have rape kits. I did not know that there was an order, a procedure, to the cataloguing of a body that has suffered this most particular trauma; I did not know that there is a script of things that are proper to say and to do. This was what our mothers had warned us about: men and their desires, men and their wills, men and their bodies encroaching on ours. Some man had taken everything inside her house that was sacred; some man had taken everything inside her that she thought sacred.

She was wrong, of course; she had not lost her value. But we were not in a world that knew that. Even I, the medic, the half-doctor, did not know enough to say that. I was too young and stunned, unrolling gauze and tapping alcohol gently on to it to clean her face. Not yet a doctor, I already knew bones: I could appreciate this face, or what this face had been until very recently. I could see in the wreckage of its topography where its lines had fallen before: the high, shattered cheekbone, the formerly slender nose, the bloodied row of teeth, the small, red tongue, which she had bitten deeply. She had long eyes with very fine lashes, eyes that stared at me almost without blinking. She was unusually fair-skinned – a coveted marker of beauty, except in this time, when coveted markers of beauty made women targets. I felt suddenly grateful for my own dark face, mannish bearing and awkward, unfeminine height.

After giving her brief history and her name, the sentry left us. The tent was big enough for only twenty patients. Although some of the people I treated were civilians, most of my patients were fighters; they were hit by bullets, or perhaps shrapnel; both civilians and fighters were sometimes captured and tortured by the army. I fixed them up and generally sent them back out. Few of them stayed with me for any extended period. Now the tent was nearly empty. I took her to the far end, where I had her lie down on a sheet on the ground. I knelt beside her.

I am sorry there is not anything better, I said.

She did not answer, but I heard her moan quietly as she lowered herself down. I gave her some painkillers. A morphine injection.

Mercifully, we had some left, and it was easy to find a vein. I cleaned her surface cuts and abrasions, but I did not bother to save and bag the evidence, as I would have done today. I left the blood under her fingernails; I untangled a long black hair from her clenched right fist and threw it away. It would not have done any good to keep it.

Then I lifted her knees so that her ankles were flat on the ground, and unwound the skirt, exposing her.

All right, I said, but this was just as much to reassure myself as her.

I had hoped that the morphine would help her go to sleep, to forget that I was retracing the path of violation, but she stared dry-eyed up at the ceiling of the tent as I examined her. The men had torn her; her raped body had ripped as though it had undergone a hellish labour. I wondered if I could stand to sew this most private wound together, and then, with a sudden rush of something that was not quite terror, I knew that I could. The knowledge was terrible, and to keep my grief for her – for us – to myself, I folded my lips together.

This is going to hurt you more, I said.

It doesn't matter now, she said.

I offered her more morphine, but she only looked away. There was nothing to wait for. I lit the match to sterilize the first needle. I wished then, as I do now, that I could have held her hand, but I needed both of mine for this.

Afterwards, I let her lie there for an hour, but I did not see her sleep. When I returned with another suture kit for her ear, and the plaster for her nose, I had her sit up. When I tilted her head away from me so I could see the ear in the waning light, she opened her mouth and started talking.

I had four brothers, she said.

I hesitated before I spoke. But then: I had four brothers, too, I said, swabbing her ear with cotton.

What did they do to yours? she asked me.

I dipped the needle in alcohol and lit a match to sterilize it.

The army killed one of my brothers, I said. The eldest. The second

one was a Tiger. They buried him at Kopay. The third has gone overseas. And the fourth one, my younger brother – he killed himself.

The army killed all four of my brothers, she said.

I know, I said. I am very sorry.

I inserted the needle. She had made no noise before, but now she hissed at the pain.

Do you want the morphine? I asked.

No, she said. I am feeling something, you know? I want to know what is happening and if the pain goes away then that might be worse.

She was right. Pain informs. Pain draws a map. Doctors resolve to relieve pain, but pain is information, and to lose it is to lose something valuable. Pain is useful, even as a distraction. If it hurts, it is there. And if your body hurts, then your mind is occupied and cannot think too deeply about what has happened to you.

I held the pieces of her ear lobe together and tried to make the stitches small. I do not know why I thought about making her scar as small as possible. It should have been obvious to me that she no longer cared about the evidence of damage. But perhaps that was part of my job: to care on her behalf.

Am I bleeding inside? she asked.

No, just outside, I said. Her bruises were beginning to colour, the dappled plums of swelling standing out on her forehead and cheeks.

It hurts when I breathe, she said.

Her ribs were probably fractured. I picked up the morphine syringe again.

I am afraid of falling asleep, she said.

Talk to me, I said.

She talked about her brothers and I did not listen to her. I thought about my own. We did not know where Dayalan was buried, but a neighbour had told us that he had been taken into a detention centre with a classmate of his, a man whose death had been confirmed. Velan's grave at Kopay was marked with the name of our village and the date of his death, but not the date of his birth. None of those stones had the dates of birth – my mother said the Tigers did not want to

remind people how young some of the rebels were. And Aran was gone, spirited out of the country by an old professor who had seen that his prize student's engineering intelligence would go to ballistics and weaponry if he stayed. Seelan had joined the Tigers, only to bite his cyanide capsule not at a moment of torture, but in a moment of loneliness. Some people told us he had died fighting, but one of his friends had come to us and told the truth.

Saavi was starting to speak slower, her voice slurring from the morphine, and I wished that I could share it, that I could lean over, exchange the syringe and pump my own arm full of sleep, that I could lie down next to her on the sheet, that we could both close our eyes and not worry. She was beautiful, and she was shorter than me, but we were not so different: two girls, from villages in Jaffna, each of us with four brothers, gone.

What about their bodies? she said. What will happen to their bodies? What will my parents do?

Go to sleep for now, I said.

She sobbed suddenly and finally – a dry, sharp sob that sounded almost like a cough. She closed her eyes, but I stayed awake by her for a long time.

I was grateful that day that I had been there to treat her. I had gone to the Tigers because of my belief that everyone deserved medicine. Still, treating them felt like wading into swampy territory. This felt different: it felt like pure medicine, medicine the way I had dreamed of it as a child. Sitting with her in the tent, at that moment, I thought that finally I had a patient whose treatment itself held no consequences, a patient who could go back to her village and lead a life – a damaged life, but a life made slightly more bearable by what I had done. I thought, truly, that some day we might both be able to return to the places where we had been born. I did not know then that I would leave. I did not know that she would go into that building, that she would ride the elevator to the top floor. ■

GRANTA

The Unnamed

Joshua Ferris

Coffee and a powdered doughnut sat on his desk, the morning offering. He might have thought to get something more substantial but he didn't care to interrupt the flow of work. Night after night, he sat at this desk just as a sphere of oil sits suspended in dark vinegar – everything blotted out but his own source of light. To save on energy costs, Troyer, Barr and Atkins LLP had installed motion sensors on the overhead lights. From six in the morning until ten at night, the lights burned continuously; after ten, the sensors took over. He worked past ten most nights, and most nights found him sufficiently absorbed in something that required only the turn of a page or the click of a mouse – too little activity for the sensors to register. The lights frequently switched off on him. He'd look up, surprised again – not just by the darkened office. By his re-entry into the physical world. Self-awareness. Himself as some task more than mind thinking. He'd have to stand, a little amused by the crude technology, and wave his arms around, jump up and down, walk over and fan the door, sometimes all three, before the lights would return.

That was happiness.

Twenty-five years ago he had decided to go to law school. It offered interesting study and good career prospects. He made it to Harvard and quickly learned how to chew up and spit out the huge green tomes on civil litigation and constitutional law. He summered at Troyer, Barr and they asked him to return after graduation. But first there was a clerkship with a judge on the Second Circuit. A year later he was married to Jane. He worked hard at Troyer. Document production for the first couple of years, boring as hell, but then junior status gave way to opportunity. He started taking depositions. He showed a gift for strategy in both civil and criminal cases, and a rare composure in the courtroom. He impressed the right people and when his seventh year came around, they voted to make him partner. He sat in the best restaurants and ordered the best wines.

But that was never the point. The point was Houston, Seattle, Pittsburgh, Orlando, Charleston, Manhattan – wherever the trial was. The trial, that was the point. The clients. The casework. The war room. He took on a few pro bono causes. And he worked in Midtown amid the electricity and the movement. And his view of Central Park was breathtaking. And he liked the people. And the money was great. And the success was addictive. And the pursuit was all-consuming. And the rightness of his place was never in doubt.

Now it was morning, and he was preparing for trial. The case involved a client named R.H. Hobbs who had been accused of stabbing his wife in a methodical way and dumping her body in a decommissioned landfill on Staten Island. The evidence against R.H. was entirely circumstantial. There was a blood-soaked bed sheet with no trace of a third party's DNA, his thin alibi of being stuck in traffic at the time of the murder, and a sizable life insurance policy. The district attorney had managed to bring charges against him only by the skin of his teeth. Grand-jury testimony revealed a case fraught with uncertainty, and the consensus among Tim and his team was that R.H., despite a loveless marriage, had not committed the crime he had been accused of. R.H.'s private equity firm generated an enormous amount of business for Troyer, Barr, and no one wanted a guilty verdict to interfere with that relationship.

Tim ate the doughnut over a napkin to catch the powdered sugar and recalled a time when he had watched what he ate. Not as a dieter, not with his daughter's sad South Beach struggle, but with a fanatic's vigilance for good health – for Dr Bagdasarian had suggested that it might be dietary. Cut out the caffeine, Bagdasarian told him, the sugar and the nicotine, and consult a naturopath. And so he did. Because nothing had shown up, repeatedly, on the MRIs, because he was on his third psychiatrist, because the specialist in Switzerland had thrown up his hands, he saw a Trinidadian in Chelsea with golden tubes and magic roots for seven days of colonics and grass-and-carrot smoothies. Jane drove and waited in the naturopath's living room among primitive wood carvings and bright tropical art. They took the highway home,

and for the first couple of days there was this breathless, anxious hopefulness. Then he walked right out of the house. Jane picked him up six hours later behind a Starbucks in New Canaan. Nothing came of the marmalade fast or the orange-juice cleansings except another possibility to cross off the list, though he could move his bowels again like a ten-year-old.

His office was calm and pleasant. The early-winter sun brightened the window behind him. Yet as every minute he remained in place moved effortlessly into the next, that new minute came with the increased anxiety that it might be his last. The wonderful warmth, his comfortable chair, the lovely rigour and stasis of practising law were growing, with time, more and more impossible to enjoy. He almost believed Naterwaul could be right, that worry alone could cause the attacks. Of course Naterwaul was also the moron who suggested that SoCal yahoo who had him re-enact his birth. Those were some dim, desperate days. He'd be goddamned if he was returning to that giant foam womb and working to cry during re-entry.

DeWiess, the environmental psychologist with the desert retreat, blamed urban air, cellphone radiation and a contaminated water table, and gave him a sheet of paper with the names of everyday toxins listed front and back.

At ten he rose to walk down to Peter's office. Standing was hard. His legs were eighty years old again. His first steps were stiff and careful, an easing back into fluid motion that stunned the cantankerous joints. He limped down the hallway.

'Knock knock,' he said at Peter's door.

'Hey hey,' said Peter.

He entered the office and sat down. Peter was the senior associate on the R.H. Hobbs case. Tim didn't think much of him.

'Maybe I'm in and out these next couple of days, Peter. Maybe, maybe not.'

Peter demonstrated the lack of curiosity required of associates when something personal appeared to be driving a partner's decision. His blank expression conveyed the theatre of total understanding.

He didn't even lean back in his chair. 'Sure, Tim.'

'We're under the gun, yeah. This thing is pressing down on us. But you don't make a move without me. Understand?'

'Tim, who–'

'Not one move.'

'Who am I?'

'You call me, understand? I don't care what it is. I'm always on my cell.'

'Of course. Of course.'

'From this point forward I'm on my cell. No Kronish. No Wodica.'

'No, no way. What for?'

'They don't know the case. You know the case better.'

'I'll call you, not a problem.'

'And you, I mean this with all due respect.'

'Yeah.'

'You're just not ready yet.'

'No,' said Peter. 'No. I'm happy to call you, Tim.'

Tim nodded and stood. Halfway down the hall, he heard his name being called. He looked back at Peter, who stood in the doorway of his office, but his body kept moving forward.

'Hobbs is due in today, right?'

'Today?'

'Just wondered if you'd be here for that.'

'He's due in today?'

He was getting further and further down the hall.

'I thought you said he was coming in.'

'I said that?'

They had to talk louder.

'Tim?'

'You call me, Peter! Understand? You don't make a move without me!'

He turned the corner and disappeared.

The first time, he woke with a start in deep night. Jane was asleep beside him. He was forced out of bed and down the stairs and into the backyard. He was disoriented by sleep and time of night and walked unevenly through the uneven yard, quiet but for the rustle of grass beneath him. Spring had barely arrived. The nights were still cold and this one was no exception. He sat down on the bench in the backyard gazebo and became tired, so tired he couldn't move. In the morning he woke up and walked back inside. Jane was in the kitchen making coffee. She stopped and turned, startled, as the glass door slid open. He walked in, pale with cold, shaking, confused. 'What were you doing out there?' she asked.

'There is no laboratory examination to confirm the presence or absence of the condition,' he was told by a doctor named Regis, 'so there is no reason to believe the disease has a defined physical cause or, I suppose, even exists at all.'

Janowitz of Johns Hopkins had concluded some compulsion was driving him to walk and suggested group therapy.

Klum dubbed it 'benign idiopathic perambulation'. He'd had to look up *idiopathic* in the dictionary. 'Adj. – of unknown causes, as a disease.' He thought the word, divorced of meaning, would have nicely suited Klum and her associates. *Idiopaths.* He also took exception to the word *benign.* Strictly medically speaking perhaps, but if his perambulation kept up, his life was ruined. How benign was that?

The internists made referrals. The specialists ordered scans. The clinics assembled teams.

He saw his first psychiatrist reluctantly, convinced as he was that his problem was not a mental one. Dr Ruefle began their session by asking about his family history. He offered what little he had. His grandparents were dead; he knew their occupations, but nothing more. His father had died of cancer when he was a boy. On the twentieth anniversary of his death, his mother had been struck by a mirror, beneath which she had been sitting in a restaurant, when it came loose from the wall, and she died of blunt trauma to the head. Dr Ruefle was never able to make sense of these facts or anything else. Tim lost the

last of his patience with her when she suggested he see a genealogical healer, on the chance that something tragic had taken place in his past – an ancestor lost in a death march or some other forced evacuation. He had no idea what 'genealogical healing' might entail and dismissed the idea as quackery.

He walked past the reception desk and through the glass doors, beyond the elevators and into the echo chamber of the emergency stairwell, where fire drills were conducted. He took the stairs with a determination never displayed during drill time, as if now there were something to flee. He kept one hand on the railing. The orange stencilled floor numbers, the fire extinguishers. The toes of his dress shoes hit one note twelve times, reached the switchback, started the note again. He avoided the vertiginous glimpse down the rabbit hole of diminishing floors.

For some people the depressing setback was a return to the hospital, it was some migraine holocaust, lower-back blowout, inconsolable weeping, arthritic flair, new shadow on the CT scan, sudden chest pain.

Hobbs was coming in today?

Twenty floors down he encountered a black man. The man sat on the landing beside the painted piping that emerged from the wall. A thick-coiled fire hose was encased in glass above him. He wore a winter coat, black but for the places where the white synthetic fibre cottoned out from tears in the shell. A collection of wrinkled shopping bags was arrayed around him. He had removed his shoes, a pair of high-tops gone brandless with grime. He was inspecting the brick-red bottoms of his feet.

'What are you doing here?'

The man looked up with a foot in hand. 'Huh? Oh. Yeah, just …'

'What?'

'Looking for cans.'

Tim walked past him and continued to descend. He was forced to turn his head in order to stay in the conversation. 'How'd you get past security?'

'It's my brother,' said the man.

'What?'

'My brother.'

'Who's your brother?' He reached the next landing and within a few stairs lost sight of the man. 'You shouldn't be here,' he cried up.

'What?'

'I said I don't think you should be sitting in our stairwell!'

His voice echoed through the upper stairs. The man no longer responded. The clop of dress shoes filled the silence. In no time he descended past the twenties and the teens and entered the lobby.

Once he ran with the goal to exhaust himself. Maybe there was no slowing down, but he could speed up. He could move his head, his limbs – hell, he could *dance* so long as he kept moving forward. Like a stutterer in song. He juked and huffed around casual city walkers until he was in New Jersey and his lungs hit a wall and he stopped. But his legs, he realized at once, had every intention of continuing, and continue they would until they were through. He couldn't believe what he had inflicted on himself, his muscles quivering with fatigue, every step like lifting out of quicksand.

He had Jane lock him inside the bedroom. The tidy circles he was forced to walk made him dizzy and half-mad.

He had Horowitz pump him full of a powerful muscle relaxant. Which worked for the time he was out. But after the medication wore off he was out walking again, this time drowsy and nauseous, his longest and most miserable walk, and he swore never to do that again.

They bolted an O-ring into a stud in the wall and tethered him with a chain and a belt made of leather. After a couple of days, that sort of containment was just too barbaric.

When the illness returned a second time, he thought of the treadmill. He'd beat his body at its own game, outwit dumb matter with his mind. But every time chance permitted him to have his body on the treadmill during an episode, he found himself stepping right off the revolving belt, into freedom. His body wouldn't be contained or

corralled. It had, it seemed to him, a mind of its own.

He told Dr Ditmar, the psychologist beloved by *New York* magazine, that he would prefer the diagnosis of a fatal disease. Ditmar bluntly stated that he was being excessive and naive. Compare his situation to someone with Lou Gehrig's, Ditmar suggested, dead within three months. Wasn't it better to be on a walk than in a grave?

'No,' he said. 'I'd rather have something I understand.' To which Ditmar replied: 'Do you think you'd understand Lou Gehrig's?'

The lobby of his building was set on a mezzanine. To access the street, one still had to ride down the escalator.

Frank Novovian looked up from his post, his eyes burdened with ripe bags, his cold-clock gaze greeting the world without humour. Yet he was deferential to the right people. 'Good morning, Mr Farnsworth,' he said.

'Frank, can I have a word?'

'Of course.'

Tim stepped on to the escalator. His feet continued to walk. He was forced to turn his head to further address the security guard. 'Will you walk with me?'

Frank got off his stool and caught up with Tim long after he had stepped off the escalator. He was halfway across the lower lobby by then. 'What can I do for you, Mr Farnsworth?'

'There's a man in our stairwell.'

'What man?'

'A homeless man.'

'In our stairwell?'

'Know what he's doing there?'

He entered the revolving doors. He gestured for Frank to follow as he fought the wind pushing against the glass.

The uprush of city life, always unexpected. A far cry from his time behind the desk. Taxis heading past, cars, supply trucks, bundled men on bicycles delivering bagged lunches. Faces were as varied as the flags

of the earth. A Hasidic Jew pushing a dolly in front of him weaved quickly between blustered walkers. The sidewalks were salt-stained; the cold swallowed him up. He walked into the wind, north, towards Central Park, a wind shaped materially by pole-whipped newspapers and fluttering scarf tails. The fabric of his suit snapped behind him angrily. His teeth were already rattling. Poor Frank, forced out in nothing but his standard-issue security man's blazer. Yet Frank followed him dutifully into the crystal heart of the season.

Could he send Frank for the pack? Frank would have to re-enter the building, wait for the elevator, walk the hallway, head back down again. By then he'd be searching for one man among eight million.

'Frank,' he said, 'R.H. Hobbs is expected later today.'

'Do you remember the floor the man's on, Mr Farnsworth?'

'Mid-thirties?'

Frank unclipped the walkie-talkie from his belt. 'Two minutes and he'll no longer be a problem.'

'Thank you, Frank.'

Frank cocked the walkie-talkie sideways at his mouth and radioed inside. A voice crackled back. He was mid-sentence when Tim reached out. 'Wait,' he said. Frank cut himself short and lowered the walkie-talkie in anticipation of further instruction, continuing to walk alongside him. 'Wait a second, Frank.'

They approached an intersection clustered by pedestrians waiting for the light to change. He turned down the side street, walking opposite the one-way traffic he was inexplicably, almost mystically spared from throwing himself in front of, and Frank followed. Some fail-safe mechanism moved him around red lights and speeding cars, moved his legs with a cat's intuition around any immediate peril. Dr Urgess had once pointed to that reprieve as proof he was in control at some conscious or at least subconscious level, although Dr Cox later claimed that the body's involuntary systems, including its sense of self-preservation, were powerful enough to override and even determine specific brain mechanisms. One located the disease in his mind, the other in his body. First he had believed the one doctor and followed his

instructions, and then he had believed the other and followed his instructions. Now he was crossing the street with Frank after the last car in line had made it through the light, and neither Urgess nor Cox had managed for all their curiosity and wisdom to bring a single thing to bear on the problem itself. Thank you for your beautiful theories, you expert professionals, thank you for your empty remedies. Frank kept peering over.

'I'd like you to leave the man alone,' said Tim. 'Let him stay where he is.'

'I thought you wanted him gone.'

'Not any more,' he said.

He was thinking of the way he'd been treated at African Hair Weaving the day before. White man walks in and asks for shelter, black women point to the folding chairs. Same white man walks past a homeless man seeking the very same shelter, has black man thrown out into the cold. Dharma guru Bindu Talati's long-ago suggestion that some karmic imbalance might have caused a material rift that provoked his walking had claimed his imagination again, but partly he was just trying to be decent. 'As a personal favour,' he said.

He looked over to drive the point home and saw that by some miracle a black wool cap had materialized on Frank's once-steaming, egg-bald head. 'There are perfectly good heat shelters in the city, Mr Farnsworth.'

'There are, that's true,' he said. 'But by a strange coincidence I know the man, Frank. We went to high school together. He's fallen on hard times. Will you do me the favour of seeing he stays put as long as he wants? And also make sure no one else harasses him?'

'I didn't know he was a friend of yours.'

'A friend of sorts. From a long time ago.'

'Consider it taken care of then, Mr Farnsworth,' said Frank, cocking the walkie-talkie at his mouth again.

'And, Frank, I have to ask another favour of you,' he said. 'Would you let me borrow your cap?'

With no hesitation Frank handed him the hat. Handed it off as if

that had been the point of bringing it outside with him, its brief respite on top of his head merely a convenient place to store it until the request was made. Tim put the hat on and tucked in his singed ears, pinning them between warm scalp and rough wool. 'Thank you, Frank,' he said.

'Is it the walking thing again, Mr Farnsworth?'

Astonishment wiped his face clean of expression. No one at the firm knew – that he had made sure of. That had been the first priority. He had elegantly explained away his two earlier leaves of absence: everyone knew about Jane's struggle with cancer. But now he wondered: did others know the real reason, and how many? Or was it simply true what they said, that Frank Novovian in security knew everything before anyone else?

'What walking thing?'

'From before,' said Frank.

'I don't know what the hell you're talking about, Frank.'

'Oh,' said the security man. 'Never mind.'

'You can go back to your post now.'

'OK, Mr Farnsworth.' But Frank kept walking beside him. 'Is there anything I can do for you, Mr Farnsworth?'

There was never anything anyone could do. Jane could handcuff him to the headboard until his wrists couldn't take another day, and Becka could feign understanding until she could flee the room again, and Bagdasarian could revisit the medical annals and run another MRI, and Hochstadt could design another pharmacological cocktail, and the Mayo Clinic could follow him with furrowed brows around the outskirts of Rochester again, and Cowley at the Cleveland Clinic could recommend psychiatric evaluation based on his patient's 'health-care-seeking behaviour', and Montreux's Dr Euler could throw up his hands again, Yari Tobolowski could prepare another concoction of bat-wing extract, Sufi Regina could smoke him with the incense promises of a spiritually guided life-force energy, his channels could be reopened and his mind–body connection yoga'd and reiki'd and panchakarma'd until he was as one, as a rock is as one – but the goddamned thing was

back. Hope and denial, the sick person's front and rear guards against the devastation of another attack, were gone.

'You can call my wife,' he replied at last, 'and tell her to expect a call from me.'

The bodhisattva had encouraged him to look deeply into his reliance upon technology. Email and PDA, cellphone and voicemail were extensions of the ruinous consuming self. They made thoughts of the self instantaneously and irrepressibly accessible. Who's calling me, who's texting me, who wants me, me, me. The ego went along on every walk and ride, replacing the vistas and skylines, scrambling the delicate meditative code. The self was cut off from the hope that the world might reassert itself over the digitized clamour and the ego turn again into the sky, the bird, the tree.

He didn't touch mouse or keyboard, keypad or scroll button all the months of his previous recurrence, and it had thrived then and now it was back, so so much for the bodhisattva.

She said his name three times into the phone, each time louder than the last. The other brokers in the open plan looked up from their preoccupations. 'You have to concentrate, Tim,' she said. She stood up and her chair rolled back to tap the desk behind her. The person sitting there exchanged a look with his colleague across the aisle. 'What's the name of the road, can you see a name?' It was impossible for anyone to ignore her. 'But what town? What town?' She seemed to regain some measure of control. She sat back down and issued careful instructions, as specific as they were mysterious. 'You have to call nine-one-one. Are you listening? If you can call me you can call nine-one-one. But if they can't locate you – Tim? If they can't locate you, you have to walk into that subdivision. I know you're tired but you don't have a choice if they don't know where to pick you up. Move away from the main road. Are you listening? Move into the neighbourhood. Go to the first house and ring the doorbell. Stay awake until somebody opens the door. If nobody opens the door, go to the next house. You tell them to call nine-

one-one. Then you can fall asleep. Somebody has to call nine-one-one before you fall asleep. I know you're tired, I know you're tired, but are you listening?' She stood again. 'Tim, are you awake?' She waited for him to reply. 'Tim, wake up!' Everyone was silent. The only sound in the office now was of telephones allowed to ring. 'Go into the subdivision! I will find you!'

He walked away from the main road to the subdivision. His body trembled with cold. It had let him know, five minutes earlier, that the walk had come to its end. He wore his suit coat backwards, the back in front, which did better against the wind, and his hands were wrapped in plastic bags. He had swooped down during the walk and picked them from the icy ground, one hand in a black plastic bag and the other in a white one.

The first house was circumscribed by a chain-link fence. He forced the latch up and stumbled to the door. He tried to think of what he might say. The right idea wasn't coming. The words behind the idea were out of reach. He was at one remove from the person who knew how to form ideas and say words.

He fell to his knees before he could ring the doorbell. He put his bagged hands on the storm door and rested his head there. The metal was cold against his cheek. He fought with angry determination for two or three seconds. If he could defy the tidal fatigue, his body wouldn't win, and he might still learn that someone had discovered him and would see him to safety.

She made calls from her desk, starting with the easternmost hospitals and moving west. She left her name and number in case he should be admitted later. She was not unfamiliar with the patient voices of the operators, their assurances that she would be contacted immediately should his name appear on the computer. Colleagues came up to ask if everything was OK. Sure, sure everything's OK. You've done this yourself, right – searched random hospitals for the one you love? Again she stared at the blank wall of explanation. She

could have asked, have you ever heard of…but there was no name. She could have said it's a condition that afflicts only…but there were no statistics. 'Everything's fine,' she assured them. She turned back to the phone and dialled another hospital.

The call came in around five, perfectly timed for rush hour. Better late than never. Better than going to identify his body at the morgue. Still, she was angry when they told her he had been admitted two hours earlier. Nothing like wasting time making fruitless calls when she could have been on her way. That was always the impulse when she finally located him: *I have to get to him*. And when she got to him: *never let him go*.

She left the office to sit in traffic and didn't reach the hospital until quarter to seven. He was in the waiting room of the ER. She moved past shell-shocked people and children playing on the floor. He sat against the far wall covered in a blanket, wearing a black wool cap. His face was windburned that distinct pink colour two shades lighter than damage done by the sun.

'Your face,' she said.

'How'd you find me?'

'I made calls.'

'You always find me,' he said.

'It's easier when you have the GPS with you.' She sat down next to him. 'Where's your pack?'

'They're worried about my toes. The blisters are bad.'

'Where's your pack, Tim?'

'I had just gone down to Peter's,' he said. 'But when I left I went in the opposite direction.'

'I asked you to always have the pack,' she said.

'Frank Novovian gave me his cap.'

She had to remember who Frank Novovian was. 'The security guy?'

'All I had to do was ask for it.'

'You promised me you would carry your pack with you wherever you went.'

'I just went down the hall,' he said.

They drove into the city to retrieve the pack and then they headed home. She drove. He sat gazing silently out the window at the nothing scenery passing them in the night. He turned to her at last and announced that he hadn't bothered to explain to the attending doctor what he was doing out in the cold for so long.

'You didn't tell the attending?' she said. 'Why wouldn't you tell the attending?'

'Those Band-Aid scientists,' he said, 'don't get to know about me any more.'

This alarmed her. They had always had faith, both of them, in the existence of the One Guy, out there somewhere, living and working with the answer. It was the One Guy they sought in Rochester, Minnesota, in San Francisco, in Switzerland, and, closer to home, in doctors' offices from Manhattan to Buffalo. Time was, he would stop anyone, interns and med students included. Time was, he would travel halfway across the world. Now he couldn't be bothered to so much as state the facts to an attending?

'One of those Band-Aid scientists may have the answer, Tim. You might be surprised some day.'

'What surprise?' he said. 'There are no more surprises. The only way they could surprise me is if they gave up the secret recipe to their crock of shit.'

They pulled off the highway, went under the overpass and down Route 22, where the stop lights and shopping centres of their life together greeted them from both sides of the four lanes. His frostbitten hands were wrapped in something like Ace bandages, intended to insulate them from the cold, a pair of taupe and layered mitts.

'I don't like the way you're talking,' she said.

'What way is that?'

'Without hope.'

They started up the hill that led into the neighbourhood, headlights illuminating clumps of days-old snow formless as manatees, dusted with black exhaust. The blacktop glowed with cold, the salted road was

white as bone.

'I must be crazy,' he said.

'Crazy?'

'I'm the only one, Jane. No one else on record. That's crazy.'

'You're not crazy,' she said. 'You're sick.'

'Yeah, sick in the head.'

He was a logical man who believed, as the good lawyer, in the power of precedent. Yet there was no precedent for what he suffered, and no proof of what qualified as a disease among the physicians and clinical investigators: a toxin, a pathogen, a genetic disorder. No evidence of any physical cause. No evidence, no precedent – and the experts could give no positive testimony. That left only the mind.

'I wish you would talk to Dr Bagdasarian,' she said.

He didn't reply, and they reached the house in silence. She took the driveway slowly as the garage door pulled up. She put the car in park and opened the door. She turned to him before stepping out. He stared straight ahead through the windshield. Tears fell down his face into his day's growth of beard.

'Oh, Banana,' she said.

She turned in her seat and placed a hand on his chest. She felt his staccato breathing, the resistance as he inhaled to letting himself go further than he already had. He didn't like to cry. He was fighting it the way a boy fights sleep, the mind pitted against the body and proving weaker. He cried so seldom that tears instinctively sprung to her eyes, too, the way they had when she was a girl and sympathy was as natural as breathing.

That night she made him an offer. She would dress according to the weather and follow him as he walked. To make it possible she was going to quit her job. How could she be at work with any peace of mind when he might be anywhere at any moment, lost in the city and scared as a child?

'I know you won't go back in the cuffs,' she said. 'So the only solution is for me to quit.'

'I don't want you to quit,' he said.

She had been able to take care of him, the last time, when he required cuffing to the bed, only because she wasn't working. Then – poof! It disappeared. Her relief was enormous. She looked back on those barren days in the bedroom with a hazy feeling of house arrest. Once or twice she drove Becka to her violin lesson after too much wine. But her efforts had been so consuming that his life, his sickness, had in many ways become her own, and until she started selling real estate, she was at sea.

'We don't need the money,' she said.

'But you enjoy your work. You've made a life for yourself these past couple of years.'

'You'll find this hard to believe,' she said, 'but you and Becka, you are my life.'

He was quiet in the dark. A peeled, flat moon cast some light through the bedroom's open windows, just enough to make their breath visible. He was on top of the bed; she huddled beneath the covers. 'Why would I find that hard to believe?'

'Because your life is your work.'

'Is that what you think?'

There was silence. 'Listen to me,' she said. 'You need someone to watch over you. You're going further away than ever before.'

She had no idea, no idea, how badly he wanted to consent. He was scared. He wanted someone to safeguard him.

'It's too much to ask,' he said. 'I don't want it to be like last time when I recover and go back to work and you get depressed.'

'I wasn't depressed,' she said. 'I just had a hard time finding my old self again.'

'It's too much to ask,' he repeated.

And she was silent then because she was relieved. ∎

Dreams in a Time of War

April 1954, Limuru

Ngũgĩ wa Thiong'o

Wallace Mwangi, 'Good Wallace'

Teachers at Manguo Primary School, 1949

I had not had lunch that day and my stomach had already forgotten the breakfast porridge gobbled before my six-mile run to Kĩnyogori Intermediate School. Now there were the same miles to cross on my way back home. I tried not to look too far ahead. My mother was good at conjuring up at least a meal a day, but when one is hungry it is better to find something, anything, to take one's mind away from thoughts of food. I did this at lunchtime when the other children took out their packed lunches and those who lived in the neighbourhood went home to eat. I would pretend that I had somewhere to go, but really it was to the shade of a tree or the cover of a bush, far from the other children, just to read a book, any book – not that there were many of them – even class notes were a welcome distraction. That day I read from an abridged version of *Oliver Twist*. There was a line drawing of Oliver, bowl in hand, looking up at a towering figure, with the caption, 'Please, sir, I want some more.' I identified with his request.

Listening to stories from the other children was a soothing distraction, especially during the walk home, a lesser ordeal than in the morning when we had to run, barefoot, all the way to school, sweat streaming down our cheeks, to avoid tardiness and the inevitable lashes on our open palms. On the way back Kenneth, my classmate, and I were good at killing time, especially as we climbed the last hill before home. Facing the sloping side, we each would kick a 'ball', usually sodom apples, backwards over our heads up the hill. The next kick would be from where the first ball had landed, and so on, competing to beat each other to the top. It was not the easiest or fastest way of getting there, but it had the virtue of making us forget the world. But now we were too big for that kind of play. Besides, no games could beat storytelling.

We would crowd around whoever was telling a tale, and those who were good became heroes of the moment. Sometimes, in competing for proximity to the narrator, one group would push him off the main path to one side; the other group would shove him back to the other side, the

entire lot zigzagging along like sheep.

This evening was no different, except for the route. From Kĩnyogori to my village, Kwangũgĩ, and its neighbourhoods, we normally took a path through a series of ridges and valleys, but when listening to a good story we hardly noticed the fields of maize, potatoes, peas and beans, each bounded by wattle trees or hedges of kei apple and grey thorny bushes. The path eventually led to Kĩhingo, past my old elementary school, Manguo, down the valley and then up a hill of grass and black wattle trees. But today we took another route, slightly longer, along the fence of the Limuru Bata Shoe factory, past its stinking dumpsite of rubber debris and rotting hides and skins, to a junction of railway tracks and roads, one of which led to the market. At the crossroads was a crowd of men and women in animated discussion. The crowd grew as workers from the shoe factory also stopped and joined in. One or two boys recognized relatives in the crowd. I followed them to listen.

'He was caught red-handed!'

'Imagine, bullets in his hands. In broad daylight.'

Everybody, even we children, knew that for an African to be caught with a bullet or an empty shell was treason; he would be dubbed a terrorist, and his hanging by the rope was the only outcome.

'We could hear gunfire,' some were saying.

'I saw them shoot at him with my own eyes.'

'But he didn't die!'

'Die? Hmm! Bullets flew back at those who were shooting.'

'No, he flew into the sky and disappeared in the clouds.'

Disagreements among the storytellers broke the crowd into smaller groups of threes, fours and fives around a narrator with his own perspective on what had taken place that afternoon. I found myself moving from one group to another, gleaning bits here and there. Gradually I pieced together strands of the story, a riveting tale about a nameless man who had been arrested near the Indian shops.

The shops were built on the ridge, rows of buildings that faced each other, forming a huge rectangular enclosure for carriages and shoppers, with entrances and exits at the corners. The ridge sloped down to a plain

where the African-owned businesses stood, built to form a similar rectangle, the enclosed space functioning as a market on Wednesdays and Saturdays. The goats and sheep for sale on market days were tethered in groups in the large sloping space between the two shopping centres. That area had apparently been the theatre of the action that now animated the group of narrators and listeners. They all agreed that after handcuffing the man, the police put him in the back of their truck.

Suddenly, the man had jumped out and run. Caught unawares, the police turned the truck around and chased him, their guns drawn. Some of them jumped out and pursued the fugitive on foot. He mingled with the crowd and then ran through a gap between two buildings into the open space between the Indian and African shops. Here, the police opened fire. The man would fall, only to rise again, resuming his flight. Time and again this had happened, ending only with him making his way through the sheep and goats, down the slope, past the African shops, across the rails to the other side, past the crowded workers' quarters of the Limuru Bata Shoe Company and up the ridge till he disappeared, apparently unharmed, into the lush green European-owned tea plantations. The chase turned the hunted, a man without a name, into an instant legend, launching numerous tales of heroism and magic among those who witnessed it and others who received the story second-hand.

I had heard similar stories about Mau Mau guerrilla fighters, Dedan Kĩmathi in particular. But until that afternoon, the magic had happened far away in Nyandarwa and Mount Kenya and the tales were never told by anybody who had been an eyewitness. Even my friend Ngandi, the most informed teller of tales, could not claim that he had actually seen any of the action he described so graphically. I love listening more than telling, but this was the one story I was eager to recount. Next time I met Ngandi, I could hold my own.

The X-shaped barriers to the railway level crossing were raised. A siren sounded, and the train passed by, a reminder to the crowd that they still had miles to go. Kenneth and I followed suit, and when no longer in the company of the other students, he spoiled the mood by contesting

the veracity of the story, or at least the manner in which it was told. Kenneth liked a clear line between fact and fiction; he didn't relish them mixed. Near his place, we parted without having agreed on the degree of exaggeration.

Home at last, to my mother, Wanjikũ, and my younger brother, Njinjũ, and my sister, Njoki. They were huddled together around the fire. I was still giddy with the story of the man without a name. Now, hunger brought me back to earth. It was past dusk, and that meant an evening meal might soon be served.

Food was ready all right, handed to me in a calabash bowl, in total silence. Even my younger brother, who liked to call out my failings, such as my coming home after dusk, was quiet. I wanted to explain why I was late, but first I had to quell the rumbling in my stomach.

I was born in 1938, under the shadow of the Second World War, to Thiong'o wa Ndũcũ and his third wife, Wanjikũ wa Ngũgĩ. I don't know where I ranked, in terms of years, among the twenty-four children of my father and his four wives, but I was the fifth child of my mother's house.

My earliest recollection of home was of a large courtyard, five huts forming a semicircle. One of these was my father's, where goats also slept at night. It was the main hut not because of its size but because it was set apart and equidistant from the other four. My father's wives, or our mothers as we called them, would take food to his hut in turns.

Each of the huts was divided into spaces with different functions: a three-stone fireplace at its centre; sleeping areas and a kind of pantry; a large section for goats and, quite often, a small enclosure, a pen for fattening sheep or goats to be slaughtered for special occasions. Each household had a granary, a small round hut on stilts, with walls made of woven twigs. After a good harvest, it would be full with corn, potatoes, beans and peas. We could tell if days of hunger were approaching by how much was in the granary. Adjoining the courtyard was a large kraal for cows, with smaller sheds for calves. Women collected the cow dung and goat droppings and deposited them at a dumpsite by the main

entrance to the yard. Over the years the dumpsite had grown into a hill so huge it seemed to me a wonder that grown-ups were able to climb up and down with such ease. Sloping down from the hill was a forested landscape. As a child just beginning to walk, I would watch my mothers and older siblings as they went past the main gate to our yard, the forest mysteriously swallowing them up in the morning and, just as mysteriously, disgorging them unharmed in the evening. It was only later, when I was able to walk further from the yard, that I saw that there were paths among the trees. I learned that down beyond the forest was Limuru Township and across the railway line white-owned plantations where my older siblings went to pick tea leaves for pay.

Then things changed. The cows and the goats were the first to go, leaving behind empty sheds. The dumpsite was no longer the depository of cow and goat dung but garbage. Its height became less threatening in time and I too could run up and down with ease. Then our mothers stopped cultivating the fields around our courtyard; they now worked in other fields far from the compound. My father's hut was abandoned and the women had to trek some distance to take food to him. The forest retreated as trees were cut down, the soil dug up and pyrethrum planted. My siblings were working seasonally in the new fields that had eaten up our forest, where before they worked only across the rails in the European-owned tea plantations.

The changes in the physical and social landscape were not occurring in any discernible order; they merged into each other, all confusing. Our compound was part of property owned by an African landlord, Reverend Stanley Kahahu, or Bwana Stanley as we called him, and we were now tenants. How did we come to be *ahoi* on our own land?

My father talked very little about his past. Our mothers, around whom our lives revolved, seemed equally reluctant to divulge details. However, bits and pieces, gleaned from whispers, hints and occasional anecdotes, gradually coalesced into a narrative of his life.

My paternal grandfather was originally a Maasai child who strayed into a Gĩkũyũ homestead somewhere in Mũrang'a, either as war

ransom, a captive, or an abandoned child. He did not speak Gĩkũyũ and the Maasai words he uttered frequently sounded to a Gĩkũyũ ear as Tũcũ or Tũcũka, so they called him Ndũcũ, meaning the child who always said tũcũ. He was given the honorific generation name Mwangi. Grandfather Ndũcũ, it is said, eventually married two wives, both named Wangeci. With one of them he had two sons: Njinjũ, or Baba Mũkũrũ as we called him, and my father, Thiong'o.

My father was born sometime between 1894 and 1896, the years that Queen Victoria took over what was then a company 'property' and called it East Africa Protectorate, which became, in 1920, Kenya Colony and Protectorate. Immediate proof of effective British ownership was the Uganda Railway from Kilindini, Mombasa – the highway of the monster that my father, as a young man, saw spitting out fire even as it roared.

I was not destined to meet my grandparents. A mysterious illness had afflicted their region and many people died. My grandfather was among the first to go, followed quickly by his two wives. Just before dying, my grandmother, believing that the family was under a fatal curse from the past or a strong bewitchment from jealous neighbours – for how could people drop dead just like that after a bout of body heat? – commanded my father and his brother to seek refuge with relatives who had already emigrated to Kabete, miles away. They were sworn never to return to Mũrang'a or divulge their exact origins so as not to tempt their descendants to go back to claim rights to family land and meet the same fate. The two boys kept their promise to their mother.

The mysterious illness that wiped out my grandparents and forced my father to take flight only made some sort of sense when years later I heard stories of communal afflictions in the Old Testament. Then I would think of my father and his brother as part of an exodus from a plague of biblical proportion in search of a promised land. I imagined them as two adventurers, armed with bows and arrows, dodging hunters, fighting off marauding lions, narrowly escaping slithery snakes, hacking their way through the wild bush of a primeval forest across valleys and ridges, till they suddenly came to a plain. There, they stood in awe and fear. Before their eyes were stone buildings of various

heights, paths crowded with carriages of different shapes and people of various colours from black to white. Some of the white people sat in carriages pulled and pushed by black men. These must be the white spirits, the Mizungu, and this the Nairobi they had heard about as having sprung from the bowels of the earth. But nothing had prepared them for the railway lines and the terrifying monster that vomited fire and occasionally made a blood-curdling cry.

Nairobi was created by that monster. Initially an assembly centre for the material for railway construction and the extensive supporting services, it had quickly mushroomed into a town of thousands of Africans, hundreds of Asians and a handful of cantankerous Europeans who dominated it.

The big houses in the plains affected the two brothers differently. After staying with their aunt at Uthiru, my uncle moved away from the hurly-burly of town to seek his fortune in the more rural parts of Ndeiya and Limuru. But my father, fascinated by the urban centre with its inhabitants, remained. My father worked as a domestic servant in a European house in Nairobi. Details of this phase of his life remain mysterious, but there are some clues. In 1914, as war broke out across Europe, it spread to the colonies. The mother country coughed and the colonial baby contracted full-blown flu. Africans were drafted as soldiers and members of the Carrier Corps – dying from combat and disease, out of all proportion to the European owners of the war. Since the Africans were being forced into a war whose origins and causes they knew nothing about, many, like my father, did whatever they could to avoid the draft. Every time he knew he was going for a medical exam, he would chew the leaves of a certain plant used in traditional medicine that raised his temperature to an alarming level. But there are other versions of the story suggesting the connivance of his white employer, who did not want to lose his domestic services.

After the war, the award of land to white ex-soldiers (some of it belonging to surviving African soldiers) accelerated dispossession and forced labour. In poor exchange for the use of land, African squatters provided cheap labour and sold their harvests to the white landlord at a

price determined by him. There was resistance in the form of Harry Thuku's East African Association, founded in 1921. Thuku captured the imagination of all working Africans, including my father. In him, an African working class, of which my father was now part, had found their voice. After the arrest of Thuku in 1921, and a mass protest outside the Central Police Station in Nairobi, which ended with the murder of 150 protesters by police and drunken settlers at the Norfolk Hotel, there was a call for all domestic workers to strike. I don't know if my father was present at the protest, but he certainly would have been affected by the subsequent call for a general strike. He fled Nairobi, avoiding the emerging political turmoil the way he had escaped the plague, the way he had evaded the draft during the First World War. He followed his brother to the rural safety of Limuru.

But Nairobi had left its mark on him. From his European employer my father had learned a few choice English words and phrases: 'bloody fool', 'nigger' and 'bugger', which he Gĩkũyũnized as *mburaribuu, kaniga gaka, mbagaĩno*, using them freely to chastise his children. He had saved enough money to buy some goats and cows that in time bred more goats and cows. By the time he fled the capital, he had a reasonable herd that his brother helped look after. Eventually he bought land in Limuru from one Njamba Kĩbũkũ, paying in goats under the traditional system of oral agreement in the presence of witnesses. Later, Njamba sold the same land to Stanley Kahahu, one of the early Christian converts and graduates of the Church of Scotland Mission at Kikuyu. This sale was under the colonial legal system, with witnesses and signed written documents. Did the religious Kahahu know that Njamba was selling the land twice, first in goats to my father and second in cash to him? Whatever his knowledge, the double transaction did not reduce the tension between the two claimants.

The hearing to determine the real owner at the Native Tribunal Court at Cura dragged on for many years but at every hearing it was a case of the legal written word against oral testimony. Orality and tradition lost to modernity and literacy. A title deed, no matter how it was obtained, trumped an oral agreement. Kahahu emerged the rightful

owner; my father retained a non-inheritable right of life occupancy of the compound where he had built the five huts. The victor immediately asserted his rights by denying my father access to grazing and cultivation on the rest of the land.

I do not know if my father ever reflected on the irony that he had lost out to a black landlord, a product of the white missionary centre at Kikuyu, under the same legal system that had created white highlands out of the African-owned lands. He had more immediate concerns than the ironies of history: how to feed his vast herd of goats and cows.

My maternal grandfather, Ngũgĩ wa Gĩkonyo, gave my father grazing and cultivation rights on the vast lands he owned, lands that stretched to the Indian shops, the African shops and beyond. My father's new hut and cattle kraal were now located between the edge of a forest of eucalyptus trees that Grandfather Ngũgĩ owned and the outskirts of the African market. My father's wives and children remained in the old homestead. So, despite the legal blow and its consequences, my father's reputation as the richest in cows and goats continued, as well as his reputation for having a disciplined home and an eye for beautiful women going all the way back to when he won his first bride.

Wangarĩ's beauty and character had been the talk across hills and valleys between Limuru and Riũki. In those days when there was no transport the two regions seemed many miles apart. Uncle Njinjũ, my father's brother, was the first to be smitten by her looks and vowed to make her his second wife. It is not known how Uncle Njinjũ first heard of her or came into contact with her family. It is not even known whether he had actually met Wangarĩ. Most likely, he had simply put in motion one of those family-to-family courtships mediated by third parties. Property, in cows and goats, and good character were more persuasive than looks and presumably the two orphans who had started with nothing but had brought themselves up to match the achievements of the young men of their age had demonstrated they did not rely on their handsome looks but on their hands and minds.

Since fleeing Mũrang'a, my father and Baba Mũkũrũ had travelled

different paths and developed different attitudes to life. My father acquired urban airs in dress and outlook. My uncle made his way through rural cultivation and herding, observing traditional values and rites. Still, the fact that Baba Mũkũrũ was now aiming for a second bride, while my father remained unmarried, was a measure of my uncle's success and validated the choice he had made to avoid the city.

Accompanied by his younger brother, Baba Mũkũrũ took a delegation that included non-family spokesmen, for one never talked on one's own behalf in such matters, and went to Wangarĩ's father, Ikĩgu. Everything went well, the drinks, the formal preliminaries, until the bride was called in to meet her suitor. They should have better prepared her because, on entering, her eyes fell on the younger of the two men, my father. Corrections afterwards regarding the identity of her suitor fell on the deaf ears of a young woman asked to choose between being the second wife of an older man or the first wife of another who exuded both youth and modernity.

By the time they returned home, the fortunes of the brothers were reversed: Wangarĩ had fallen in love with the young urbanite, my father, and eventually became his first wife. The brotherly relationship, though not broken, became strained, and remained so for life. Love had come between the two men who in their youth had depended on each other in their quest for a new life far from home.

I don't know how my father later came to marry his second wife, Gacoki. Rumour hinted that his first wife, Wangarĩ, needing extra hands to manage their growing wealth in cows and goats, had helped attract Gacoki to the home. More likely, news of the poetry of the heart and the rhythm of work between Wangarĩ and my father may have allured Gacoki, the beautiful daughter of Gĩthieya, long before my father actually proposed. The example of my own mother, the third wife, provides some evidence of my father's ways of wooing.

My mother, Wanjikũ, was of few words. But they carried the authority of the silence that preceded their utterance. Now and then, words would gush from her mouth, opening a little window into her soul. I once asked her, during one of those moments of well-being that

follows a good meal, why did you consent to polygamy? Why did you accept being the third wife of my father?

It was because of his two first wives, Wangarĩ and Gacoki, she said, the light and shadows from the fire playing on her face. They were always together, such harmony, and I often wondered how it would feel to be in their company. And your father? He was not to be denied. I don't know how he knew where I worked in my father's fields, but he would somehow appear, just smile and say a few words. What a pity if such a hard-working beauty should ever team up with a lazy man, he would tease me. Those were no small words coming from a man who had so many goats and cows, and he had acquired all that wealth by his own toil. But I didn't want him to think that I would simply fall for his words and reputation, so I challenged him. How do I know that you are not one of those who work their wives to death and then claim that the wealth comes from his hands alone? The following day he came back, a hoe over his shoulder. As if to prove that he did not include himself among the lazy, without waiting for my invitation even, he started work. It became a playful but serious competition to see who would tire first. I held my own. The only break was when I lit a fire to roast some sweet potatoes. Don't you think you and I should combine our strengths in a home? he asked. I said: Just because of one day's work on a field already broken? Another time he found me trying to clear bush to expand my farm. He joined in the clearing and by the end of day we were both exhausted but neither of us would admit to it. He went away and I thought that he would never come again. But he did, on another day, without a hoe, an enigma of a smile on his face. The crop was in bloom, the entire field covered with pea flowers of different colours. He took out a bead necklace and said: Will you wear this for me? Well, I did not say yes or no, but I took it and wore it.

My mother would not answer follow-up questions. What she had said was enough to tell me how she became the third of my father's wives, but not sufficient to tell me how she came to lose her place to Njeri, the fourth wife.

I was born into an already functioning community of wives, grown-up brothers and sisters, children about my age and a single patriarch, and into settled conventions about how we acknowledged our relation to one another. But it could be confusing and I had to grow into the system. When talking about them to a third party, the first wife was always my Elder Mother, *Maitũ Mũkũrũ*, and the other two were each my Younger Mother, *Maitũ Mũnyinyi*. Unqualified *Maitũ*, was reserved for my biological mother. Otherwise, it was always 'Yes, Mother', or 'Thank you, Mother', when addressing each woman directly. But one could also distinguish among them by referring to them as mother of any one of their own biological children. My half-siblings could call my mother Ngũgĩ's mother when talking about her to a third person.

The four women forged a strong alliance against the outside world, their husband and even their children. Any of them could rebuke and discipline any one of us children, the culprit likely to get additional punishment if he or she complained to their biological mother. They resolved tensions through discussion, one of them, usually the eldest, acting as the arbiter. There were also subtle, shifting alliances among them, but these were kept in check by their general solidarity as my father's brides. They had their own individuality. Njeri, the youngest, was strong-framed with a sharp, irreverent tongue. She brooked no nonsense from anyone. She was known to speak out on behalf of any of the other wives against an outsider, even if a man. She could openly defy my father but she also knew when and how to back off. My mother was a thinker and good listener, loved for her generosity and respected for her legendary capacity for work. Though she would not confront my father openly, she was stubborn and let her actions speak for her. Gacoki, shy and kind, disliked conflict, adopting a live-and-let-live attitude even when she was the wronged party. Wangarĩ, the eldest, was always calm, as if she had seen it all. Her power over my father was through a look, a word or gesture of disapproval, as if reminding him that she was the one who had chosen him over his brother.

One evening, my mother called me to her.

'Would you like to go to school?' she asked.

It was in 1947. I cannot recall the day or the month. I remember being speechless at first.

Most of my father's sons, including my older brother Wallace Mwangi, had gone to school, most of them dropping out after a year or two, because of the cost of tuition. The girls fared even worse, attending school for less than a year, a few of them teaching themselves at home and learning enough to be able to read the Bible. School had seemed something that involved those older than I or those who came from wealthy families. When I worked in their father's fields harvesting pyrethrum flowers, I had often interacted with the children of Reverend Kahahu, Njambi, the girl, and Njimi, the son, both about my age, but I never imagined that I could ever be of their world. I had never thought of school as a possibility and so had nursed my desire in silence.

The Kahahu estate of motor vehicles, church-going, economic power and modernity was a contrast to ours, a reservation of hard work, poverty and tradition, despite my father's wealth in cows and goats and his lip service to our ancestry. The Kahahu girls wore dresses; most of my sisters wore white cotton-cloth wraps, sometimes dyed blue, over a skirt, the long side edges held together by safety pins and a belt of knitted wool. The Kahahu boys' shirts and khaki shorts, held in place by suspenders, were a contrast to my single piece of rectangular cotton cloth, one side under my left armpit and with the two corners tied into a knot over the right shoulder. No shorts, no underwear. When my younger brother and I ran down the ridge, playing our games, the wind would transform our garments into wings trailing our naked bodies. I associated school with khaki shorts and suspenders with shoulder flaps. As my mother now dangled the prospect of school in front of me, the uniform also came unto view.

It was the offer of the impossible that deprived me of words. My mother had to ask the question again.

'Yes, yes,' I said quickly, in case she changed her mind.

'You know we are poor...'

'Yes.'

'And so you may not always get a midday meal.'

'Yes, Mother.'

'Do you promise me that you'll not bring shame to me by one day refusing to go to school because of hunger or other hardships?'

'Yes, yes!'

'And that you will always try your best?'

I would have promised anything at that moment. But when I looked at her and said yes, I knew deep inside that we had made a pact.

My father had no say in this enterprise. It was my mother's dream and doing entirely. She raised the money for tuition and uniform by selling her produce in the market. And then one day she took me to the Indian shopping centre. I had been there before but I had not seen the shops as having anything to do with me directly, except that some stocked rocks of unprocessed sugar, jaggery or *cukari wa nguru* as we called it, which we bought for a few cents a piece. But now I saw the shops advertised as Shah Emporium or Draperies in a different light: they contained what would fulfil my desire. Eventually we made our way to a store that specialized in schoolwear. My mother bought me a shirt and a pair of shorts, the plainest, without suspenders or shoulder flaps, but lack of these adornments did not diminish my joy. My only disappointment was that I would have to wait for school to start before I could wear them. And then at last!

The day I wore my khaki uniform and walked the two miles to Kamandũra, I entered a dreamland. We sat on benches without desks or tables. The three classes were held at the same time in a church of corrugated-iron walls and roof but in different spaces, without any partitions. I could hear and see everything, but, as I soon learned, woe to anyone who was distracted by what was going on outside their space. But it was hard not to look, since most of the teaching took the form of call and response, the teacher writing an alphabet on the blackboard or reading out numbers, the children repeating in singsong.

The teacher, big-eyed Isaac Kuria, started by registering new pupils. He asked me my name. Ngũgĩ wa Wanjikũ, I responded, because, at

home, I identified with my mother. I was puzzled when this was greeted with loud, mocking laughter. Then he asked me, what is your father's name? and I replied, Thiong'o. Ngũgĩ wa Thiong'o is the identity I would carry throughout this school.

Every evening, after school, my mother would ask probing questions, ending with: Is that the best you could have done? This was a question she would keep on asking in response to my schoolwork, class exercises and tests: Is that the best you could have done? Even when I told her proudly that I had scored ten out of ten, she would ask the question in different ways, until I said yes, I had tried my best. I drifted through the initial classes, not quite understanding why I had been moved from Sub B to Sub A to Primary One, all within the same quarter, a skipping of classes that continued from term to term so that within a year I was in Primary Two, and still my mother continued to ask: Is that the best you could have done?

I don't know about the best that I could have done, all I know is that one day I was able to read on my own the Kikuyu primer we used in class titled *Muthomere wa Gikuyu*. Some sentences were simple, like the one captioning a drawing of a man, an axe on the ground, his face grimacing with pain as he holds his left knee in both hands, drops of blood trickling down. The picture was more interesting than the words: *Kamau etemete. Etemete kuguru. Etemete na ithanwa!* Kamau has cut himself. He has cut his leg. He has cut himself with an axe. I tackled long passages. There was one that I read over and over again, and suddenly, one day, I started hearing music in the words:

> God has given the Agikuyu a beautiful country
> Abundant in water, food and luscious bush
> The Agikuyu should praise the Lord all the time
> For he has ever been generous to them

Even when not reading it, I could hear the music. The arrangement of the words, the cadences. I could not pick out the single thing that made it so beautiful and long-lived in the memory. I realized then that even written words could carry the music I loved in stories. It was a picture in itself and yet more than a picture or a description. It was

music. Written words could also sing. I came across a copy of the Old Testament and the moment I found that I was able to read, I read everywhere at any time of the day or night, after I had finished my chores. The characters became my companions. Some stories were terrifying, like that of Cain killing his brother, Abel. One night at Wangarĩ's their story became the subject of heated discussion. The story, as it emerged in this setting, was a little different from the one I had read, but no less terrifying. In this fireside version, Cain was condemned to wander the universe forever. He carried the mark of evil on his forehead and travelled at night, a tall figure whose head scraped the sky.

Some acts and scenes from the Bible were simply magic within magic: Jonah swallowed by a whale and then vomited out unhurt on a faraway shore; Shadrach, Meshach and Abednego, an angel among them, walking unscathed in a fiery furnace; Daniel interpreting correctly the writing on the wall – Mene, Mene, Tekel, Peres – which made me look for writings on walls so I could interpret them; and Daniel in a lion's den, emerging unhurt; or Joshua blowing the horn that brought down the walls of Jericho.

Night-time frustrated me because I read by the light of an unreliable bare kerosene lantern. Paraffin meant money and there were days when the lamp had no oil. I read by the light of the fire. Daylight was always welcome. It allowed the book of magic to tell me stories without interruption – except when I had to do my chores.

My father was known all over the region for having quality *mũratina*, a brew made of the purest of sugar-cane that he himself grew, honey and natural yeast, in gourds that were finely cut and shaped. But he had developed remarkable discipline and never drank during the workday. Those invited for a drink at his home on a weekend had to show respect for his wives and children.

In my mind, my father's patriarchy established itself in two distinct phases. I had a vague early-childhood recollection of his coming home in the evenings leading his herd into the vast kraal, a space surrounded by a fence of wood and an outer hedge of thorny bush, sometimes aided

by the older sons, or one of his wives, and then, after securing the herd inside, he would go to his hut. He was careful not to show any preference for any one of his wives' huts. When the women brought him food, he would invite us children to share.

Although it was never clear to me how the transition occurred, the second phase followed his expulsion from the fields around the homestead, because now his hut was rarely occupied and we no longer shared meals with him. The women still took food to him daily, but to the edges of my grandfather's forest, not far from the Limuru African market shops. He came home mostly on Saturdays or Sundays when he had *mũratina* to share with his friends. If he stayed for the night, he would sleep in one of the women's huts.

I had always wanted to help with the herding like some of the older boys but he never asked me. Long before I started school, I had once accompanied my half-brother Njinjũ wa Njeri to my father's new abode. Indians burned their dead among the trees of my grandfather's forest and my mother claimed that if you stood on the dumpsite at home you could see Indian ghosts walking about, holding a light. She spoke with total conviction, as if describing an encounter in the marketplace. I may not have believed her, but I was still afraid of the place – I assumed that the strange scent emanating from the trees and the undergrowth was really that of the burned flesh of the Indian dead.

The cattle and goats roamed everywhere, but mostly at the outer edges of the forest, where there were long treeless patches. After a market day, my half-brother would let the herds roam the African marketplace and sometimes let them eat the tall grass in the shops' backyards. Through the forest, near my father's new kraal, was a path that led to the station. My half-brother would stop girls passing by and chat them up, asking them to 'give it to my brother', pointing at me. The ladies would smile and walk away or call him names. I did not understand what he meant or the girls' responses. Whatever the case, it felt good just to hang around or go exploring inside the forest, not particularly worried about where the goats and cows were, except in the evening, when we led them back into the kraal and closed the gates. I

vowed that when I grew up I would ask my father to let me be his regular assistant herd boy so that I would learn how to milk the cows the way my half-brother did, and talk to the girls.

But I never got a chance. Not only had I started school, but a disaster struck our family. My father's goats and cows caught a strange illness. Their stomachs became bloated, followed by diarrhoea and death. Traditional medical expertise was no match for the disease and there were no veterinary services for African farmers. The animals died one by one. Rumours swirled that our goats and cows had once strayed to the backyard of some tea shop in the African marketplace, eating clothes drying on a line and fouling clean water held in containers. The irate owner, in vengeance, had later poisoned the grass and the water.

Whatever the explanation, the disaster that befell my father was long cited in arguments between proponents of money in banks and believers in livestock as the only real measure of wealth. One fact they would not dispute: the man who had had everything had now lost it all.

This loss of his wealth devastated my father. The proud aloof patriarch who had always left each wife to tend her house as she saw fit now tried to micro-manage the entire homestead. His interference became worse after he abandoned his hut near the empty kraal and moved into the youngest wife Njeri's, while insisting that the other wives deliver his food to him there. This upset the delicate balance of power that the women had worked out among themselves. When he tried to assuage the resulting tension, he only made it worse.

Although we all feared our father, I never once saw him beat a child. If anything, he was strict about mothers beating children, a very unusual attitude in those days. Also unusual was that he seldom beat his wives, yet he commanded their respect and his word was law. Now he engaged in domestic violence, particularly against my mother. The only woman he did not touch was Njeri. She was big-limbed, strong-bodied and it was rumoured that once, when drunk, he had tried to discipline her, but she locked the door from inside her hut and beat him, while shouting, loudly enough for all the world to hear, that he was killing her.

The proud patriarch who would never have gone to someone else's

house to drink liquor unless invited, the man who would never have drunk on a weekday, now started drinking all the time, and going to other people's houses for *mũratina*. My father hated those husbands who waylaid their wives on their way from the market for a share of the money they had made from their sales. But now he started doing just that. It was painful to see him waiting for the end of the week to demand the wages which his daughters had earned for working in the pyrethrum fields or in the tea plantations in the highlands.

He tried his hand at farming but, as he had no land of his own, he still depended on the cultivation rights from his father-in-law. Before his fall, he had grown crops – sweet potatoes, arrowroot, sugar cane and yams – on a parcel of land near the Indian shops, but more as a hobby than for subsistence. His was a model garden and he was very proud of the quality of what he produced. But now cultivation for subsistence was all, as he struggled to eke out a living from the soil, his sense of his worth as a man and his public standing were compromised.

Good as he was with his hands turning the soil, he was competing with his women, my mother particularly. His parcel of land was next to hers and it was as if the playfulness of his wooing her had now become a serious competition for power. But when it came to coaxing the land to yield, nobody was a match for my mother. Even with goats she now had an edge over my father. He had none: she had two he-goats that she fattened inside a pen in her hut. She had three others that she sometimes fed in the hut but which otherwise used to follow her wherever she went in daytime without straying.

While other people's crops seemed to wilt under the sun, hers bloomed. People sometimes stopped by the road to admire the peas, beans and maize on her various parcels of land. By the end of the season, my mother had harvested just about the best crop in the region. Corn as well. Other women offered to help her harvest and shell, filling ten sacks with peas, four with beans and her barn with corn.

My father decided that the harvest was his to dispose of, even to sell. My mother, used to the independence of her household, firmly refused. One day, he came home, picked a quarrel with her and started beating

her up, even using one of the walking sticks that my crippled half-sister, Wabia, used for support, till it broke into pieces. My brother and I were crying. Mother was screaming in pain. Despite their fear, the other women tried to restrain him, beseeching him to stop, screaming in solidarity, for all the world to hear, that their husband had gone crazy. As he turned towards them in fury, my mother managed to slip away, with only the clothes she wore, and fled to her father's house, leaving behind her goats and harvest, and her children.

For many days after, the family talked about the beating, some claiming that even her goats had screamed in protest. Nobody seemed able to explain the fury that my father had shown. But there were whispers that the cause of it was the youngest wife, Njeri, the only one who worked on the European-owned tea plantations. She was having an affair with one of the overseers. The women said that somehow my father had got it into his head that my mother was at fault. They surmised that because Njeri had once fought him, he took his anger and frustrations out on the easier target.

With the departure of our mother, the other wives, Gacoki and Wangarĩ in particular, took care of my brother and me. We waited for her to come back or for my father to go to his in-laws to plead with them for her return. That was the procedure: talks that would almost certainly end in warnings, fines and reconciliation. Everybody knew that it was simply a matter of time.

One day we were playing with our siblings in an open space between Kahahu's land and Baba Mũkũrũ's with a ball made of cloth and tied tight with a string. Even the girls had joined in. My father suddenly turned up. He stood at a distance and beckoned my brother and me to accompany him. My father had never called me to him before, let alone come all the way to a field outside our homestead to do so. We ran to him, sure that he was going to tell us news of our mother's return.

'I want you to stop playing with my children. Go, follow your mother,' he said, pointing in the direction of my grandfather's place.

We did not have a chance to say farewell to the other children and tell them that we had been banished from their company and from the

place that up to then had defined our lives. But on the way from home, I was able to dash into my mother's hut to retrieve my school material, among which was my torn copy of Old Testament stories.

The expulsion, if not from paradise, was from the only place I had known. I was baffled more than pained. My mother had always been the head of the immediate household, so home would always be wherever she was and in that sense I was headed home to Mother. But it is not a good thing to have one's own father deny you as one of his children. The move deepened my sense of myself as an outsider, a feeling I had harboured since I learned that the land on which our homestead stood was not really ours. I had been an outsider at Kamandũra School where it seemed that others belonged there more than I did. Now I was an outsider in my father's house. But there are aspects of the old homestead that would always be a part of me: the storytelling sessions; daily interaction with the other children, where alliances change from time to time; fights and tears even. Some of the scenes flitted across my mind: the songs we sang; the dances in the yard welcoming rain, for it meant blessings and made the children grow. At the sighting of raindrops we dashed into the yard, formed a circle:

Rain may you fall
I offer you a sacrifice
A young bull with bells
That sound ding-dong

Once a host of children, including my half-sisters and half-brothers, Wanja, Gacoki's daughter, Gacungwa, Wangari's daughter, and Gakuha and Wanjiru, Njeri's son and daughter, and I were playing the game of 'catch me if you can'. I was running around each of the four huts, all of them after me, when suddenly I tripped and fell. The sand scraped the skin off my left shoulder. The scar remained, a memory. Now banished from all this by my father, I was lucky to have my younger brother and book of stories for companions and the solace of reunion with my mother in her father's place, the place of her birth. ■

CONTRIBUTORS

Daniel Alarcón is the author of the novel *Lost City Radio* (Fourth Estate/HarperCollins) and two collections of stories.

Julian Barnes's essay *Nothing To Be Frightened Of* was published in 2008 (Vintage). He recently selected *The Best of Frank O'Connor* for Everyman.

Jim Crace's novels include *Being Dead* and *Quarantine*, which was shortlisted for the Booker Prize. *All That Follows* will be published in April 2010 (Picador/Nan Talese).

Joshua Ferris's *The Unnamed*, from which this extract is taken, will be published this year. His first novel *Then We Came to the End* (Viking/Little, Brown) won the PEN/Hemingway Award in 2007.

Aminatta Forna is the author of a memoir, *The Devil that Danced on the Water*, and a novel, *Ancestor Stones*. Her new novel, *The Memory of Love*, will be published this year by Bloomsbury and Grove Atlantic.

V.V. Ganeshananthan teaches creative writing at the University of Michigan. *Love Marriage*, her first

novel, appeared in 2008 (Random House).

Steven Hall was born in Greater Manchester in 1975. He won the Somerset Maugham Award in 2007 for his first novel, *The Raw Shark Texts* (Canongate).

Kent Haruf is the author of four novels: *The Tie That Binds*, *Where You Once Belonged*, *Plainsong* and *Eventide* (Picador and Knopf).

Ruchir Joshi is a writer and film-maker. His first novel, *The Last Jet Engine Laugh*, was published by Flamingo and HarperCollins in the UK and India. He recently edited a collection of subcontinental erotic fiction, *Electric Feather*.

Martin Kimani is a scholar of war and genocide. He lives in London and Washington DC and is working on a book about Catholicism and genocide in Rwanda.

Yiyun Li's most recent novel is *The Vagrants*. *Gold Boy, Emerald Girl*, her second book of stories, will be published in September 2010 (Fourth Estate and Knopf).

Colum McCann won the 2009 National Book Award for Fiction for *Let the Great World Spin* (Bloomsbury/Random House).

Ngũgĩ wa Thiong'o's latest book, *Dreams in a Time of War* (Harvill Secker/Pantheon Books) will appear in March. He is working on the second volume of his memoirs, *The Oasis in the Desert: A Memoir of Alliance*.

Donald Ray Pollock's first book *Knockemstiff* was published in 2008 (Harvill Secker/Doubleday). He is currently working on a novel.

Salman Rushdie is the author of ten novels and three volumes of non-fiction. In June 2009, he delivered part of 'On Sloth' as a lecture in Capri. His next novel, *Luka and the Fire of Life*, will be published in 2010 (Jonathan Cape/Random House/Knopf Canada).

Peter Stothard is editor of *The Times Literary Supplement. On the Spartacus Road*, from which this extract is adapted, is published this year (Harper Press/Overlook Press).

Mikhael Subotzky's prints are in the collections of the Museum of Modern Art in New York and the South African National Gallery in Cape Town. Born in Cape Town in 1981, he now lives in Johannesburg.

Derek Walcott received the Nobel Prize in Literature in 1992. 'In the Village' appears in his fourteenth collection of poems, *White Egrets*, which will be published this spring (Faber/Farrar, Straus & Giroux).

Patrick Waterhouse is an artist and designer. He is working on a new edition of Dante's *Inferno* for Mondadori. He lives in Italy.

Brad Watson teaches creative writing at the University of Wyoming, Laramie. 'Vacuum' will appear in *Aliens in the Prime of their Lives*, to be published by W.W. Norton later this year.

Contributing Editors
Diana Athill, Peter Carey, Sophie Harrison, Isabel Hilton, Blake Morrison, John Ryle, Lucretia Stewart, Edmund White

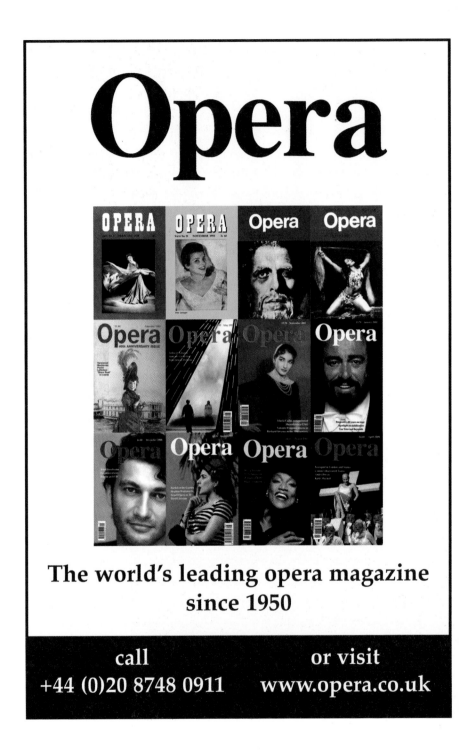

Windows panoramic grid detail

Windows panoramic grid detail

Windows panoramic grid detail

Found image (opposite) from abandoned flat (above)

Found image (opposite) from abandoned flat (above)

Found image (opposite) from abandoned flat (above)